The Family Guide to Mental Health Care

Anand Pandya, MD
Past president and current consultant to the National Alliance on Mental Illness (NAMI)
Associate Clinical Professor, Department of Psychiatry & Behavioral Neurosciences, UCLA

When someone in your family may have a serious mental illness, you will wish that you had a senior psychiatrist nearby to give advice every step of the way. The Family Guide to Mental Health Care book gives the reader this gift.

Gail Saltz, MD
Clinical Associate Professor of Psychiatry, New York-Presbyterian Hospital
NBC's *TODAY* Show mental health contributor

Many millions of people have a mental illness but most do not get the treatment and help that they need. With the knowledge to navigate the mental health care system comes the power to recover. This uniquely accessible book provides that knowledge, and is a necessary guide for patients and their families.

Linda Rosenberg, MSW
CEO, National Council for Community Behavioral Healthcare

Dr. Sederer's book recognizes the essential contributions families make, discusses every challenge they face, and provides them with clear and exceptionally well-informed advice. There is no book like it. I recommend this book to families as a highly useful guide for what is too often a confusing and frightening journey.

Connie Lieber

Past President, National Alliance for Research on Schizophrenia and Depression (NARSAD), currently the Brain and Behavior Research Foundation

In a society where the disorders of the mind and mood are too seldom understood, Dr. Sederer has provided remarkable clarity in his explanations of the illnesses for the layperson. He outlines what help is needed, where to get help, and how to manage the system for caregiving and treatment. This is a complete guide to navigating a complex and all-too-challenging world faced by anyone impacted by the challenges of mental illnesses. With outstanding clarity and sympathetic understanding he brings help to the helpers and guidance to those who can aid them.

The Family Guide
to Mental Health Care

Lloyd I. Sederer, MD

Foreword by Glenn Close

W. W. Norton & Company
New York • London

Copyright © 2013 by Lloyd I. Sederer, MD
Foreword copyright © 2013 by Glenn Close

All rights reserved
Printed in the United States of America
First Edition

For information about permission to reproduce selections from this book, write to
Permissions, W. W. Norton & Company, Inc., 500 Fifth Avenue, New York, NY 10110

For information about special discounts for bulk purchases, please contact
W. W. Norton Special Sales at specialsales@wwnorton.com or 800-233-4830

Manufacturing by Quad Fairfield Graphics
Book design by Paradigm Graphics
Production manager: Leeann Graham

Library of Congress Cataloging-in-Publication Data

Sederer, Lloyd I.
  The family guide to mental health care / Lloyd I Sederer, MD ;
foreword by Glenn Close. — First edition.
      pages cm
Includes bibliographical references and index.
ISBN 978-0-393-70794-6 (hardcover)
1. Mental health services—United States. 2. Mental illness—United States.
3. Families of the mentally ill—Counseling of. I. Title.
RA790.6.S43 2013
616.89—dc23
                        2013007244

ISBN: 978-0-393-70794-6

W. W. Norton & Company, Inc.,
500 Fifth Avenue, New York, N.Y. 10110
www.wwnorton.com

W. W. Norton & Company Ltd.,
Castle House, 75/76 Wells Street, London W1T 3QT

1 2 3 4 5 6 7 8 9 0

To families, whose love, dedication, and courage
make all the difference

Contents

Acknowledgments

I t has been said that he who travels fastest travels alone. But that road can never lead you as far or as deep as when you are accompanied by the wisdom and aid of trusted companions. I am grateful to the dear friends and colleagues who lent their able minds to the development of this book and illuminated and emboldened its journey.

The Family Guide began some years ago while I was walking the Santiago de Compostela Pilgrimage Trail in France. With hours upon hours of time every day together, Rosanne Haggerty, my extraordinary wife, asked me to tell her stories about my work. She did not want information about psychiatry or public health, but stories about the people who had turned to me as a doctor or public servant. I did as she asked and shared a series of stories and nonfiction accounts, describing the journeys, heroism, and sometimes tragedies of people with mental disorders. I realized that telling their stories might lessen the stigma that unjustly accompanies mental illness in our often too judgmental social communities.

As I began writing this book, I had the special experience of being awarded a Scholar in Residence grant at the Rockefeller Foundation's beautiful Bellagio Center. What emerged was a different book than the one I originally planned; this book became of more immediate and practical use. I will return to my earlier project of stories someday, but what struck me was the urgent need to inform and support the loved ones of those with mental illnesses. What cut through every one of my stories was the critical role of family and friends as individuals with mental disorders seek accurate diagnoses, effective treatments, and recovery.

I am deeply grateful to the Rockefeller Foundation for their confidence in my ideas and for providing the dream environment to begin this book. My agent, Jeanne Dube, believed in the importance of this project, and endured my relentless pestering. I am proud to have as my publisher W. W. Norton, where I have had the great opportunity to work with Deborah Malmud, who has edited my writing with great care and exacting standards. A big shout-out goes to Vanessa Dube who brought to the text the editorial finesse she mastered in her work with the Let's Go series as a Harvard undergraduate.

For several years, while working on this book, I learned to write for the general public, first as a regular contributor to the Huffington Post/AOL and then as their medical editor for mental health. I continue to be amazed at the HuffPost's powerful voice in the world of online journalism. It is my privilege to be a part of their team, and to work with senior editors like Alana Elias Kornfeld, whose support has been invaluable to my writing in this venue.

My friends, many of them family members of those with mental illness themselves, have made this book all the richer. Jay Neugeboren and Charlotte Fischman, in particular, have taught me about families and their kindness, dedication, pain, and struggle. My special thanks to many other family members and leaders of the National Alliance on Mental Illness who welcomed me into their meetings and their lives, and deepened my understanding of what needs to be done so that those with mental illness have every opportunity to enjoy lives of dignity, contribution, and love. I dearly hope that this book honors their efforts.

I offer my great appreciation, as well, to so many people whom I have worked with in public and private, medical and mental health services. They are the other caregivers and support staff who, though (usually) not family, still dedicate themselves to the interests and needs of people with mental illness and their families.

Yet I end these acknowledgments as I began them: with Rosanne Haggerty, my partner in so many endeavors and a woman of faith whose belief in the mission of serving our communities and in this journeyman himself ceaselessly inspires and reshapes my life and my work.

Lloyd I. Sederer, MD
New York City

Foreword
Thoughts on a Fall Day

The sky is della robbia blue. The soft, feathery seed heads of the tall grasses sway and dip in a gentle, insistent breeze coming off the water. It is fall in Maine—a changing season. I try to keep close contact with my beloved sister at this time of year because she lives with bipolar disorder and I have learned that seasonal changes can be challenging. For her, experiencing changes in the light, seeing leaves beginning to fall or flocks of birds winging south, frequently fills her, not with rapturous thoughts of the glories of nature, but with the anxious apprehension that she could easily slide into a black and crippling depression. Before she was properly diagnosed, that depression, and totally random frenetic episodes, were major recurring patterns in her life. She was always considered "the wild one"—out-of-control, moody, and undependable. We were a family ignorant of the symptoms and behavior associated with a major mental illness. We were clueless and my sister and her children suffered because of it. She is in recovery now under the supervision of a caring and vigilant doctor. She is living a full and productive life and those of us who love her have educated ourselves about the challenges she faces and the support that she needs. So I call her often and ask her how she is doing.

My nephew lives with schizoaffective disorder. When he got sick no one in our family knew what was wrong. It was difficult to know whether his strange, sometimes frightening behavior was because he was just another angry teenager or whether it was something else. It was actually a friend of my sister's who—after spending some time with my nephew, observing and listening to him—first suggested that he might have schizophrenia. As terrifying as that sounded, at least my sister's friend had enough knowledge and cared for my sister and her son enough to bravely voice her opinion. He spent two years in a psychiatric hospital. His life was saved and he is in recovery. He is a budding artist and furniture-maker, with a wonderful wife and three dogs.

I often ask myself, "How could we have been so ignorant? How could we have so disastrously misinterpreted their symptoms? How could I have been so unknowing? Why weren't we more curious . . . more compassionate?" But I also realize that my family had absolutely no vocabulary for mental illness. The words never crossed our lips: "serious depression," bipolar disorder," "schizophrenia," "borderline personality," "obsessive compulsive disorder," "posttraumatic stress," "suicidal ideation." We didn't know about any of it and it was never a topic of conversation. Mental illness was frightening, uncomfortable, and deeply stigmatized and that was that. Very strange given the fact that every generation in our family has had its own quotient of depression, alcoholism, mania, and even suicide. But we come from the tough Yankee tradition of hard work and no complaining. Get ahold of yourself! Pull up your socks! Deal with it and move on!

I sit here now and think of the pain, the stigma, the fear, and the shame that certain members of my family must have felt; how different their lives would have been if all of us had had access to a book like this and had been open to it. I respond personally to what Lloyd Sederer writes because he makes me feel like he is sitting at this very kitchen table, gently explaining to me, with great knowledge, insight, and patience, what is happening to my loved one and what my family and I can do about it. It is a human tendency to say, "It will never happen to me . . . to us," but the stunning fact is that one in four families is touched by some kind of mental illness. Mine happens to be one of them. Mental illness is part of the human condition and we must have the courage and compassion to educate ourselves about it—to have an informed vocabulary—to say the frightening words often enough so that they no longer invite the toxic fear, shame, or stigma that so many have been struggling with for so tragically long. Help is available. Recovery is possible. Mental illness is a family affair. You will find comfort in this book and it will help free you to take care of yourself and those you love.

Glenn Close
Scarborough, Maine

Introduction

John had all the makings of a high school star athlete and scholar. A freshman with solid grades, he'd earned a spot on the varsity basketball team thanks to his height. Adored by his parents and idolized by his younger brother, John also enjoyed the company of a tight-knit group of friends despite his natural inclination toward shyness. But lately he'd begun to seem different. He retreated to his room instead of spending time with his family, and he declined to go out with friends when they invited him. He slept a lot, spent endless hours alone in his room, skipped team practices, and approached homework half-heartedly. At the dinner table he picked at his plate—an odd change from the voracious appetite he was known for. Once easy-going and responsive to his parents, John was now easily irritated and critical.

Concerned, John's parents asked if anything was wrong. This produced an explosion of anger, with John snarling, "Leave me alone! I'm fine!" What had begun as an attempt to reach out to their son quickly spiraled into an argument. "You are not fine!" his father yelled. "What's going on? Are you taking drugs?" Tearfully, his mother begged him to talk to them. But John refused, storming out of the room with a slam of the door.

Millions of American families—maybe even yours—have gone through the same mix of experiences and emotions that John's parents were dealing with: confusion and misunderstanding, communication and family breakdown, tension and fear, and denial that anything is wrong. In my 35 years as a psychiatrist, I have talked with thousands of people who, like John's parents, are frightened and often at their wit's end about a loved one. I have seen how mental illness erodes an individual's potential, as it did with John, or, worse, threatens to ruin the chance for a productive, happy life. I have seen how it paralyzes families so overwhelmed by what is happening that they fail to take action. I have also seen how it compels some families to wear a sunny mask of pretense to avoid the public shame of acknowledging something is wrong, or to live half a life because caring for the family member is so consuming. The impact of mental illness doesn't stop with the person who is ill: It places great demands on families, stoking tensions and often pitting parents against each other. Sucking parents, siblings, and other family members into its maelstrom, mental illness is the visitor no one wants. But countless families find it living among them.

The good news is that there *is* help—and hope—that can be effective, and that is available to families who are able to confront and meet the challenges that mental illness presents. I say this after many years working as a psychiatrist in both the private and public sectors—including at the Boston-based McLean Hospital, a Harvard research and treatment facility for mental illness and drug dependency, where I served as medical director, and at the New York State Office of Mental Health, the largest state mental health system in the United States, where I currently serve as medical director. Time and again, I have seen patients go on to lead full lives when they receive proper diagnosis and effective treatment. And when their lives change for the better, so too do the lives of their families and friends.

My conviction that people with mental illness can recover and lead productive lives is one of the main reasons I wrote this book. I also want to demystify mental illness and its treatments—there are simply too many misconceptions and suspicions surrounding these highly common conditions and the therapies that can help.

Chief among those misconceptions is that mental illness is uncommon. Every year, 1 in 4 adults in the United States will experience a mental illness, and 1 in 10 will suffer considerable limitation of their work and family functioning as a result. One in 10 children and adolescents will have serious problems that derail their educational and social development. This means that well over 50 million adults and children in the

United States fall ill each year, with similar percentages in most other countries on the globe. Few families are spared.

Furthermore, the widespread belief that mental illnesses are more elusive and harder to treat than other serious and persistent illnesses is just plain wrong. Why that notion persists is puzzling, although I suspect it's because people have difficulty visualizing how a problem that can't be measured with blood tests or a CT scan can be fixed.

The truth is that mental illnesses are quite common and eminently treatable. In fact, people with mental illnesses can improve and build satisfying lives, just like other people with common physical illnesses such as diabetes or heart disease. With both physical and mental disorders, the earlier the treatment is received, the better.

Even serious mental illnesses—such as bipolar disorder, borderline personality disorder, eating disorders, major depression, post-traumatic stress disorder (PTSD), and schizophrenia—can respond to medications and therapy, as well as to programs that rebuild everyday skills that were diminished by or lost to illness. When medications and therapy are combined, and there is an informed, engaged, and supportive family, each element builds on the other and optimizes the chances of recovery. This is good news for the many individuals (and their families and friends) who have had to endure years of mental illness in silence for fear of losing their jobs, being shunned by colleagues and friends, or being denied the right to obtain a driver's license or health insurance. The same applies to those with conditions that may be less disabling yet still painful and dispiriting, such as generalized anxiety or panic disorders, severe phobias, and mild but recurrent depressive episodes.

The problem is that many people in the grip of mental illness are not getting the quality care they need. In fact, an astonishing 80% of Americans with treatable mental disorders do not receive proper diagnosis and effective treatment. Can you imagine patients with heart disease ever tolerating similar odds—a 20% chance of receiving what they need to get them well?

Responsibility for this appalling state of affairs belongs principally to our broken mental health care system, not to the countless dedicated professionals who try to do what is right. Yet playing the blame game isn't helpful. The veteran of the Iraq war who hasn't slept for days and is drinking compulsively because of PTSD needs real solutions, and so do the families who are watching their loved ones slip away. No one facing serious mental illness has the time to wait for the mental health establishment to repair itself.

I offer this book as a comprehensive guide to mental health care. It is your roadmap to navigating a terribly fragmented and unaccountable mental health system. In the pages ahead, I will inform and coach families of those suffering from mental illness on how to find and obtain effective treatment and recovery-oriented services. I believe that, absent a mental health care system that works, patients and their loved ones have to become powerful and unrelenting advocates for their own needs and rights.

One of the best ways for you to begin to take control of this complex and unwieldy situation is to know how the "system" works, how it doesn't work, and how to bend it to your needs. Families must become savvy about every facet of mental illness—from prevention to symptoms, from treatment to methods of recovery, from mastering the health insurance maze to working around a legal system that typically favors patients' privacy rights over families' need to know. Families that can master the unwelcome visitor of mental illness and the maze of the treatment system can see their loved one get what he or she needs to recover a life of relationships, work, and self-respect.

One great challenge that frequently accompanies mental illness and makes seeking help, not to mention recovery, so difficult is the reluctance and sometimes downright refusal of many people with mental illnesses to admit there is a problem in the first place—and, once they do enter care, to stay in treatment. A second great challenge is our country's mental health system, which is really not a system at all. Rather, it is like a puzzle: a fragmented collection of services that often fails to provide the comprehensive, continuous, collaborative care that anyone afflicted with a mental illness needs and deserves.

This book will reveal in detail the obstacles you will face as you help your family member enter and continue in treatment. I will offer concrete suggestions about how to overcome them, and what you learn will equip you for the demanding road ahead.

Fighting mental illness is not for the faint of heart. I say this because, after decades of being immersed in the provision of mental health and addiction services, I know the path to recovery can often be long and arduous. That's why I counsel family members and friends not to go it alone. You owe it to yourself and your loved one to create a support network, or at the very least to ask for the sympathetic ear of a good friend. You will understand why that is so important when the treatment and recovery process feels like a siege. But when you as a family have the information and assistance you need, you will be better able to deliver the support you want to provide to your loved one. I will help you see how you can do it.

When I started out as a young psychiatrist in the 1970s, mental illness was an unmentionable subject in most families—and certainly in society as a whole. Patients were warehoused in big institutions where they were largely forgotten; the key was literally and metaphorically thrown away. There were fewer time-tested talk therapies, and the medications to treat major mental disorders were more limited and less effective.

Today, we are fortunate to have more tools available to treat a variety of mental illnesses, and we are the beneficiaries of a greater openness about and appreciation of these disorders of the brain than ever before. We've come a long way in our social attitudes about mental illness, and we've made significant progress in its diagnosis and treatment.

But there's still more progress to be made. Too little reliable and valuable information is known about mental illness, its diagnosis and treatment, and our system of care. More research on serious illnesses like schizophrenia and schizoaffective disorders is needed if we are to produce new and different types of medication and rehabilitation for these conditions. And we have to work harder to ensure that treatments that have been proven effective are provided to patients and families who seek services. But you can still get help today in unprecedented ways if you know how to go about doing it.

I find myself answering the same questions today (in less hushed tones) that were asked of me by families decades ago. "What is happening?" "Where can we turn?" "What should we ask?" "How can we tell whether the diagnosis and treatment are right?" "Whom can we trust?"

I've written this book to answer those questions and more. I will share the knowledge I've been privileged to learn from caring for patients and their families, from my leadership of centers of excellence, and from developing psychiatric practice guidelines and policy. At the same time, I will provide you with a commonsense, straightforward guide to navigating the mental health care system and providing your loved one with the support he or she needs. This book is for the mothers and fathers, sisters and brothers, aunts and uncles, children, grandparents, friends, and coworkers of the millions of people struggling with mental illness. You deserve to know what I know as you strive to overcome the unique and daunting challenges you will face.

The Family Guide to Mental Health Care

Mental Illness:
What Families Can Do

ental illness appears in our families and homes wearing many faces, and the ways it erodes relationships, school, and work vary from person to person. There was John, described in the first few pages of this book, who stopped going to basketball team practices, skipped school, and withdrew from his close family and longtime friends. There was George, an Army Reserve soldier in his early thirties with a wife and two children in grade school, who began drinking heavily after his second tour in Iraq and was irritable, quick-tempered, and plagued by nightmares. There was Sally, a 46-year-old who, despite a life of privilege and opportunity, began turning up drunk and belligerent at parties and eventually was jailed for striking a policeman. And there was Vincent, a successful professional who, at 55, had withdrawn from work, slept all the time, and distanced himself from his family following some midcareer setbacks.

But all mental illnesses have one thing in common: Their impact extends beyond the person afflicted, affecting family, friends, coworkers, and others in the person's life. You probably know people like John, George, Sally, or Vincent. Maybe some are close relatives of yours. At the very least, you have friends, coworkers, or acquaintances who have struggled with mental illness or addiction or both. I know this because it is almost impossible in this country not to have brushed up against some kind of psychological disorder. Why? More than 50 million Americans are affected by mental illness every year, often in ways that derail their lives and threaten their safety and success.

Mental illness is an equal-opportunity thief that steals individual and family stability. It's a broad-brushed stressor of friendships, and it's a formidable opponent of productivity, vitality, happiness, and hope. Whether it is depression or bipolar disorder, anorexia or PTSD, anxiety or substance abuse, mental illness does not discriminate when it comes to the age, gender, ethnicity, race, socioeconomic status, or education of those it affects. In short, it is *everywhere*.

Yet as commonplace as mental illness is, and although much progress has been made in making the subject less taboo, we still are not where we should be in our response to and management of mental illness. Not by a long shot. Confusion and misunderstanding painfully reign among many families, and too many patients refuse to get help because of the shame and guilt they feel over being labeled "crazy." Our fragmented, all-too-unaccountable mental health care system frequently discourages people from seeking help rather than assisting them in securing and remaining in treatment. That is why only a shocking 20%—1 in 5 people—get the help they need in the form of a proper diagnosis and effective treatment to recover from mental illness.

What's more, 50% of mental illnesses come on by the age of 14, and 75% by the age of 24. You are right to be attentive to your young family members and friends, as these are the years when mental disorders surface. Many of these young people also discover that alcohol or drugs (especially marijuana) reduce their anxiety, at least at first, and the ongoing use of these substances typically worsens their condition and impairs treatment and recovery.

Partners, mothers, fathers, siblings, children, and friends arrive at my office and those of countless mental health professionals, upset and bewildered. "What happened to the person I know? What's wrong? Is it something I've done?" Above all, they want to know what to do. That is what this chapter is all about—concrete, practical, and positive steps that need to be taken toward getting correct diagnoses and effective treatments.

Many families also feel a tremendous sense of urgency. It's an urgency fed not only by fear of the unknown but also by dread that this kind of hurt, this kind of problem, won't be fixed. It's true that treating mental illness isn't as straightforward as putting a broken leg in a cast or removing a diseased gall bladder. But I'm here to tell you, as I have told thousands of people over more than three decades of practice, that mental illness can be managed and treated effectively. Those afflicted can improve and go on to build satisfying and productive lives just like people who suffer other common, chronic illnesses such as diabetes or heart disease. But this is key: *Patients and their families must be willing to take the steps needed to put them on the road to recovery.*

Family and friends must learn how to set aside their confusion, sadness, and anger—suspending any feeling of despair—about what is happening in order to get on with what needs to be done. They must learn to overcome their reluctance to the idea that someone they love is mentally ill in order to fight for what their loved one needs to get well. All too often, that battle will be with their loved one, who may not recognize that anything is wrong in the first place. Families also must become tough-minded, informed consumers and advocates for their loved one.

The following are the ideas and approaches—guideposts, if you will—that have, in my experience, helped patients and their families overcome the significant challenges and burdens of mental illness. By themselves, none are easy; each demands perseverance as well as a belief that confronting mental illness, step by step, will have incalculable value over the long run. But taken together, they can help families find a way out of the malaise and hopelessness that mental illness can produce. Your journey begins with a single step—and then another, and another.

Eight Guideposts to Navigating Mental Illness

- Analyze the behavior.
- Remember it's not your fault.
- Trust yourself.
- Don't go it alone.
- Seek help as soon as possible.
- Don't get into fights.
- Learn how to bend the mental health system to your needs.
- Settle in for the siege and never give up.

Analyze the Behavior

When families come to me for help, their stories often begin the same way. A loved one whom they thought they knew well has become a complete stranger—changing, sometimes almost overnight, right before their eyes. This is not just the moodiness of adolescence, the confusion of a career setback, or the turmoil of a troubled marriage. This is when a son like John, a father like George, or a spouse like Vincent begins to self-destruct.

But distinguishing self-destructive behavior from passing phases or momentary setbacks can sometimes be difficult. How do you decide whether to be concerned? A good litmus test is to ask this question: *Is there a pronounced, persistent change in the person's behavior toward friends and family, in moods or thought patterns, in self-care (including hygiene and habits such as eating and sleeping), in functioning, and in activity levels?* If the answer is "yes," it's a good indication that something is wrong. A general rule of thumb is that symptoms must last for 2 weeks or longer to be considered persistent—this is the time period usually needed (a criterion) for making the diagnosis of a mental illness.

Remember It's Not Your Fault

Functioning erodes in tandem with the marked changes in mood, sleep, appetite, and thinking—all of which are confusing and disturbing to families. This is when family members confide in me that they are worried—not only about the inexplicable behavior or safety of the person who is ill but also about their own safety and welfare.

As they desperately search for an explanation or a culprit to blame for mental illness, many families turn the mirror on themselves. Surely they must have done something terribly wrong for their loved one to be in such bad shape—or so they think.

The first thing I tell families—and what I want to say to you unequivocally—is that *mental illness is not your fault*. Long gone are the days of believing that mental illness is due to "icebox mothers" or "double-binding families" who inflict permanent psychological damage on their children because they haven't hugged or loved them enough.

Thankfully, we are also well past the days of blaming people with mental illnesses themselves for their predicament. Conventional thinking once held that mental illness was the result of a character flaw such as laziness or self-absorption or because someone was inherently "bad." We know now that nothing could be further from the truth.

Mental illness is *no one's* fault. People fall prey to mental illness because of the way their brains have become abnormal. We know this because imaging technologies now allow us to peer into the brains of those who have mental disorders. And what we usually see is this: Areas of the brains of people afflicted with mental illness look different than those of individuals who are not. The message could not be clearer: The brain—just like any other organ of the human body when it is diseased—is operating differently in people with mental illnesses.

It is the interplay of genetics and hardwiring within the brain, along with the effects of deeply stressful external events and relationships, that gives rise to mental illness. Some of us are indeed more vulnerable to mental disorders than others. But that is a biological vulnerability—the way in which the brain is more prone to become ill. Just as some of us are more vulnerable to diabetes and high blood pressure, others of us are at risk for mental illness because of genetics and development.

Of course, it's true that stress plays a role. It's in an already-vulnerable body where stress has its greatest power. Just as stress may contribute to mental illness in an already-vulnerable brain, so too may it contribute to the development of diabetes, hypertension, and other diseases of the vulnerable body. If a loved one developed diabetes, hypertension, asthma, Parkinson's disease, or another of many, many other conditions, you wouldn't feel that you were the cause of the problem, would you? Then why should you feel that way about a loved one with an illness of the brain? Of course, stress must be recognized, especially the overwhelming stress of traumatic situations, but families need to look to creating a different and better future, not dwell on the past for explanations.

Trust Yourself

Encountering mental illness in a loved one can be profoundly disorienting and disturbing. It can unleash a storm of raw emotions and irrational behaviors that have the potential to tear a family apart and end any semblance of "normalcy," robbing a family of stability and wellbeing. Mental illness is painful and difficult for families to face and endure, often over extended periods of time. What you are feeling is a normal reaction to an abnormal situation.

As a family member or friend caught in the midst of this storm, you may find it difficult to get your bearings. You may doubt your thoughts that a loved one has become ill. Plans to get help may be shelved again and again because of that doubt. Overwhelmed and confused, you may want to avoid seeing what is happening or despair that the troubles and pain will never end.

In my experience, the best thing to do is check your doubts at the door. In order to see clearly what is going on, you need to *trust your perceptions*. When you do, you will be able to take appropriate action on behalf of your loved one. I am not saying it is easy. But it can—and must—be done.

I caution you, though, not to get wrapped up in personally trying to diagnose a loved one's mental illness. That is work for a professional. What you *can* do is keep a written record of what you are seeing. Include how long the symptoms have gone on, at what time of day, and with what triggers if you see them.

For example, your journal might say: *On Labor Day weekend, my wife Mary almost never left our bedroom. She was buried under the covers when I woke up and she didn't join me or the kids for breakfast or lunch. Household chores went undone and she showered only once all weekend. She drank lots of coffee but hardly ate any food. We tried to get her to visit relatives or go to a movie but all she said was "go ahead without me."*

Since early August she hasn't seemed herself. She started sleeping later than usual every day, even was late for work, which is not like her at all. I thought I saw her crying in the bathroom but she covered it up. She ate very little and hardly spoke, even when friends called on the phone or visited. She had little patience with the kids, and none with me. When I asked if anything was the matter, she said no, she was fine, maybe a "little tired."

I wonder if her mother's heart attack in early July might be when she started to seem different?

This is information that will be very helpful to the health or mental health professional you turn to. Even the small act of writing things down may help you see what is going on more objectively, which in turn can help you feel less anxious.

Another way to understand what is going on *and* your reactions is to view what you're witnessing as a form of communication. Your loved one may be telling you, through his or her behaviors, attitudes, and feelings, that he or she is in trouble and needs help. *Keep your focus on what you observe and what is being communicated*—directly or indirectly—rather than on the feelings stirring inside of you. That will serve your loved one well—and you, too. This strategy can provide you perspective and, thus, help you to trust yourself. You are a good judge of what is happening, if you let yourself trust yourself.

Remember John, the high school student whom I described in the Introduction? When John's mother, Elaine, arrived in my office to discuss her son, one of the first things she said was, "He seemed to change before my very eyes into . . . well, I'm not sure who he is anymore. . . ." Elaine's confusion about what was happening to John began to cloud her otherwise clear-eyed assessment of the situation—namely, that her son was depressed. She didn't trust what she saw. Her self-doubt intensified when her husband said she was overreacting. "John's 17, this is par for the course for a teenager," he'd said. "He'll grow out of it."

Tensions within a household over whether a loved one has a mental illness are not unusual. A family's initial disbelief and bewilderment often foster painful questions about what is actually happening. Are they really seeing symptoms of mental illness? Or is something else at work? Days pass, questions go answered, nothing is resolved, and honest attempts to address what is going on are muffled.

For John's parents, as is true of so many families, the sore subject of their son's behavior was soon relegated to hushed, hopeful conversations about whether he looked better, ate more, or enjoyed a good night's sleep. They could not understand what was happening and were hoping it would pass. It also seemed like too much to face. But something was seriously the matter.

Mental illness can also push family and friends to the brink—overwhelming and even alienating them, as happened with George, the soldier whose heavy drinking, angry episodes, nightmares, and talk of suicide were clear indications of PTSD. Although he still could work as a skilled tradesman, his behavior at home had become so intolerable that his wife felt she had no choice but to leave him. After 2 years of struggling to keep it together in order to give George time to get back on his feet, his wife moved out. She needed to spare their children continued exposure to his terrible moods and despondency.

Both these families, and so many like them, became so paralyzed that they did not—could not—seek help for their loved one in a timely fashion. These situations are what keep me and my colleagues in the mental health care field up at night. The failure to take early action when help can be even more effective leaves the person with mental illness at greater risk for needless suffering and disability. It also leaves families with grievous uncertainty, where life can seem on the verge of spinning out of control.

It takes great strength to bear thinking there is something wrong with a loved one, to steel yourself against the angry denials and refusals of an ill partner, sibling, or child, and to withstand the doubt and fear when you don't know what to think or where to turn. I repeat: Trust your instincts. No one knows your loved one as well as you do, and no one will ever be as committed as you are to that person's health and wellbeing. To do the right thing, you must face the unwanted visitor of mental illness and act before it defeats the person you love—and you as well.

Don't Go It Alone

So you suspect, or have come to know, that a loved one or friend is suffering from a mental illness. Now what do you do? This is one of those moments in life where the best approach is to reach out for the support and wisdom of others: You will need company on the journey ahead.

Turning to an understanding partner at a critical moment such as this one is ideal. Siblings can also support one another, as can grandparents or other close family members. But not everyone has a partner or family member to turn to, and if they do, the relationship may not be strong enough to weather the intense emotions involved in recognizing that a family member is ill and something needs to be done. If your relationship has that type of strength, go for it. If not, move on and don't open another front of worry in your relationship when you already have so much on your plate. If you trust another family member who knows you and the person who is ill, seek that person's support. Look around, find someone.

Given that mental illnesses, including addictions, are so common, there is a good chance that other members of your family, or friends, will understand. They even may have faced similar challenges. A mother, father, sibling, cousin, or grandparent may be your best resource. Perhaps there is a colleague at work who has experienced depression, addiction, or some other mental illness and is open about it (some people are, but not many). Don't hesitate to turn to someone you feel you can trust for guidance.

Think about whom you can confide in, and then pick up the phone and connect with that person. It should be someone who cares about you—someone who wants to be helpful to you, just as you would want to help him or her were the tables turned. The person may know about mental illness, or not. But even if the person has little knowledge about mental illness, he or she still knows you. This means you'll have an excellent sounding board as you sort through the problems you are facing and the solutions you need to find for your loved one.

Mental illness is complex, and no plan of action is foolproof. Yet one thing I know for certain: There is safety and support in numbers when figuring out your next steps. Making decisions on your own about how to take action is too lonely and too demanding. *Don't go it alone.*

Seek Help As Soon As Possible

Mental illness can strike at any point in life and quite frequently when people are young. As I mentioned earlier, half of those who will develop a mental illness show signs by the time they are 14, and 75% of all people who will become mentally ill experience symptoms by the time they are 24.

Still, escaping adolescence and young adulthood without falling ill to a mental disorder does not confer immunity for life. Mood disorders, especially depression, often begin in mid to late life; even schizophrenia can show up later on, although that is not usually the case. Posttraumatic stress disorder can appear at any time following a traumatic incident such as exposure to wartime combat or to natural or manmade disasters like 9/11 or Hurricane Katrina.

How many times have you heard an uncle described as "a little crazy" or a cousin as "in his own world"? We hear of students who may be just "acting out"; spouses may mention that a husband or wife is behaving "a little reckless lately." On other occasions, a loved one's troubled behaviors or moods are explained away by statements such as "she just broke up with someone" or "he lost his job" or "he's just getting old."

These casual attitudes toward mental illness have a terrible cost. Not recognizing mental illness in a loved one, and thus not intervening early and effectively, especially when young, means the chances for recovery, for a life of functioning and relationships and contributions, are lessened. Research has repeatedly shown that an individual's chance of making the fullest recovery possible depends on receiving treatment (the right treatment) as soon as the symptoms of illness appear. We know this principle from other diseases like high blood pressure, diabetes, heart disease, and the other conditions that beset the human race.

It is no different for mental illness. For example, schizophrenia is a serious mental illness that generally comes on from mid-adolescence to the early twenties. Families will see their young family member become very preoccupied and withdrawn. He or she may neglect personal hygiene and spend unusual amounts of time alone in a bedroom. School performance suffers and friends are avoided. Although they might not tell anyone, many may be experiencing hallucinations—hearing voices or smelling unusual odors—or developing ideas about being persecuted or in touch with the heavens, which is called "delusional thinking." The young people affected are usually very secretive about these experiences, which can be regarded as both special and frightening. Their thinking can become very jumbled and hard to understand. Sometimes they will use marijuana and alcohol to lessen the intense anxiety they feel. And suddenly a 20-foot wall seems to have erupted between you and your child.

Untreated, psychotic symptoms, such as disordered thinking, hallucinations, and delusions, can be toxic to the brain—permanently damaging cells and connections within it. Over time, this further diminishes functioning in school, work, and relationships. And if the brain continues to sustain damage, the person will become cognitively impaired, with reduced concentration, attention, memory, and ability to problem solve. Untreated, these psychotic symptoms can render a person functionally disabled. Consider what that also means for the person's confidence and self-worth.

Sally's story is a sad illustration of this phenomenon. She had been ill for decades, but when her bipolar symptoms first appeared, it was at a time when not much was known about the disorder and mental illness carried a heavy stigma. Her affluent, educated family and friends missed what was going on. It wasn't until she was in her mid-forties—and alcoholic, unemployed, and serving jail time for hitting a policeman—that she was finally diagnosed.

Although Sally was popular and a good athlete in high school, she harbored a lot of frustration and anger—and sometimes erupted into wild rages. For the most part, though, she masked her inner feelings by outwardly behaving like a "character"—working as a flag girl on a road construction crew, hanging off the 75th floor of skyscrapers washing windows, driving cars that belonged to a steady stream of ne'er-do-well boyfriends. (Sally called them "hot" cars, a misnomer that led everyone to believe they were "cool" when in fact they were stolen.) That was Sally—always the life of the party, up for anything that involved an element of risk and danger. Her family and friends now shudder at memories of how they laughed at these escapades.

Many kinds of interventions and treatments were tried for Sally's alcoholism and bipolar disorder after she was diagnosed, but none worked. Today, no one is sure where or how Sally lives. Those who have seen her say it's impossible to hold a coherent conversation with her. Not long ago, she was found lying face down in a ditch on the outskirts of a small Midwestern town, suffering from exposure as a steady rain soaked her clothes. Sadly, mental health treatment did not come early enough for Sally. The result was disability that took very deep root and was resistant to change.

Although most mental disorders appear in young people, in the United States the average time between when the symptoms first appear and treatment begins is an astonishing 9 years. Doctors call that the "duration of untreated illness" (DUI), and know it is not good for the brain or for the child's normal development. What's more, youth often begin to suffer more subtle problems with mood, concentration, anxiety, and social development 2 to 4 years *before* their condition produces prominent and disturbing changes in their life.

One way to avoid such a fate for your loved one is not to attribute changes in those formative years to a phase—such as typical adolescent moodiness. It's true, of course, that typical developmental phases can produce changes in a child's behavior, but again, when these changes are severe, persistent, and intractable, it's likely that something more serious, such as a mental illness, is going on. Keep your antennae up and you will see the difference.

The same holds true for adults. Most people experience distress and feel blue at times of an important loss—such as the loss of a job or the death of a friend or relative—but they don't show the pronounced symptoms of a depression or other mental disorder. A serious depression does not go away when you distract yourself, take a vacation, or go shopping: It digs in and takes on a life of its own, featuring hopelessness, self-loathing, nagging guilt, trouble eating and sleeping, anxiety and irritability, and morbid thoughts of dying or suicide. These states of mind, these disorders of the brain, can be soul-killing and require attention, not dismissal or delay.

There are many reasons why people in a dire psychological condition do not get help. Sometimes they themselves cannot recognize they are ill; instead, they insist on being left alone or blame others for intruding. Other times, family and friends who *could* help fail to take action on a loved one's behalf because they feel helpless or don't know how to engage other family members. A family may be reluctant or outright refuse to acknowledge that someone they love needs professional help—as was initially the case with John's parents. Most people, however, don't seek help for their loved ones and friends because, like Sally's family, they are unaware that it is mental illness that is causing the problems. And even if they do, they may not know where to turn.

Again, it's important for people with mental illness to seek help as soon as possible. It may turn out that your loved one doesn't need to see a psychiatrist or other qualified mental health professional. In fact, many people do not turn to mental health clinicians first. In Chapter 3, I will discuss in detail mental health professionals and settings. Here, I list a variety of people and organizations you can turn to before going to a mental health clinician. These people and places can assist you with the problem as well as point you in the right direction for further help.

Your Family Doctor. Many families turn to their family physician first when faced with disturbing changes in a loved one, including those caused by mental illness. Some families are fortunate to have a doctor who knows them and is trustworthy—someone they can depend on with sensitive matters such as the possibility of a mental illness in a loved one. When that is the case, they can turn to their doctor and take comfort in knowing he or she will serve them well. Although the doctor may not give a definitive diagnosis, referring the family instead to a mental health specialist for that purpose, he or she can rule out other physical illnesses, such as thyroid disease, mononucleosis, lupus, or other conditions that can mimic a mental illness.

For example, suppose your teenage son or daughter is exhibiting behaviors that worry you, such as withdrawal from family and friends, loss of appetite and poor or excessive sleep, neglect of personal hygiene and dress, or intense mood swings. The pediatrician's or family doctor's office is a very good place to go. Pediatric and family practices encounter adolescent emotional problems *all* the time. Be candid with the physician, explain what you see happening, and—above all—don't accept the comment "your child will grow out of it" when you have seen time pass and the behaviors have persisted.

Clergy. If your family belongs to a church, synagogue, or mosque, and there is a member of the clergy whom you feel is thoughtful, supportive, and trustworthy, ask to privately discuss your problems with him or her. Remember, this is not the first time that a clergy person has encountered these types of family problems. Clergy cannot escape the ubiquitous troubles that mental illnesses bring. Many make it their business to know which mental health professionals, clinics, and institutions have good reputations, and they'll be able to give you information about what next steps make sense. Some clergy have degrees in pastoral counseling and therefore are familiar with mental disorders and their treatments.

School Social Worker or Psychologist. Many schools employ a social worker or psychologist to support students and their families in difficult times. These professionals can offer insight about whether a loved one's problem is situational—say, the breakup of a relationship or apprehension about college admissions—or if it is due to a mental disorder. When necessary, school psychologists may use their network of professional contacts and refer you to a specialist or a mental health center in your community. They also are in a position to work with the school and teachers to seek extra services or put accommodations in place that your child may need. Importantly, these professionals can also serve as your eyes and ears at school, actually observing your child as well as consulting with teachers to help you understand whether your child's problems with schoolwork, classroom behaviors, or friends are improving.

Employee Assistance Program. Many companies, especially larger ones, offer their employees confidential means of assessing work or family problems, as well as assistance in seeking help if it's needed. These services are called "Employee Assistance Programs," or EAPs. Generally, the process begins with a phone call to a professional clinician working for an organization that the worker's company has contracted to help its employees understand and take action with problems they face. Companies with EAPs generally make a point of letting employees know about this service because it is good not only for the employee but also for the employer—a distraught, distracted, or impaired employee is not working well and is at risk to miss work, have a work-related accident, or even go out on disability.

After a phone assessment where a problem is identified, several face-to-face meetings generally are offered, free of charge, to assist the employee in determining what is going on and how to seek help. The information gathered is confidential—it cannot be shared with the employee's supervisor or human relations office. Common problems that EAPs focus on include depression, marital discord, problems with children, and alcohol and drug use and abuse. EAPs can be valuable places to turn.

NAMI. The National Alliance on Mental Illness (NAMI) is an organization for which I have the greatest respect and that I recommend frequently. Founded to help families and friends of those suffering from mental illness, NAMI is a haven if you need support and direction. NAMI can be a place to express your feelings about what is happening, work through stress, and solve problems with others who are dealing with situations similar to yours. It offers family-to-family (F2F) meetings as well as coaching on issues such as what to ask a mental health professional and what to say to a loved one who is resisting getting help. The suggestions come from other family members who have been there—who know personally what you are struggling with as well as what can help and what might make matters worse. With a chapter in every state and a 24-hour information hotline, NAMI is the premier family go-to organization in this country for help with situations that have not changed despite your love and best efforts. So too is the Mental Health Association (MHA). These groups and others (see Appendix B) are proof, and comfort, that good support is there for the asking.

The human desire for peace and to avoid conflict—for things to feel "normal"—is powerful. It can lead families to look away rather than clearly see a loved one's mental condition. It can allow them to be talked out of their concerns that a loved one's mental state is in jeopardy. Don't let this happen to you. The personal cost is too high, the burden too great, and the regret too devastating if you don't take action on behalf of family and friends who have a mental illness—as early as possible when they are young, as soon as possible when they are older.

Don't Get Into Fights

By the time that Vincent's spouse and adult children spoke with me, they were fed up. Begging and pleading with him to see their family doctor for what was a deep depression had fallen on deaf ears. They told me that Vincent had been passed over at work for a senior management position. He had dedicated himself to his work and had been a loyal employee for over 10 years in a midsized professional firm. He often was the last to leave at night and prided himself on beating deadlines and anticipating what would yield success for whatever project he was working on. Not getting the promotion sent him into a tailspin. Feeling worthless about himself and pessimistic about the future incapacitated him. He stayed in bed for days at a time and missed work. Yet Vincent resisted his family's entreaties to get help; he said repeatedly that he was useless, that "it" was over. Sometimes the arguments even turned ugly, with Vincent saying he felt persecuted by his wife and children.

Like so many others, this family was bursting with conflict about Vincent's unwillingness to seek help. The acrimony only made a bad situation worse. "Stop fighting," I pleaded gently. "Take a deep breath and we can figure out how to succeed with Vincent. But that will mean also learning to control what you say and do, at least for a while. Fighting is making matters worse."

That piece of advice may be the hardest to follow for families when a member has a mental illness and won't get needed help. Like Vincent, your loved one may be spending more time fighting you than getting better. Having overcome your *own* resistance, fear, confusion, and guilt, you want to take action—*now*—so that a family member can get better. Your love and worry are moving you to push harder, to insist that your loved one *do* something!

Unfortunately, what many families learn the hard way is that the more they push, the more they are likely to be defied. Their arguments, pleas, and tears continue to be met by what feels like a concrete wall of resistance—the immovable force of a loved one who refuses to seek help and is sinking even deeper into illness. Family strife is now a fellow unwelcome traveler to an illness that itself is more than anyone wants. It is a sad irony of mental conditions that often the biggest obstacle to getting desperately needed help can be the person with the illness.

Families that have been in this situation can tell you that fighting just doesn't work. What you *can* do for your loved one is describe, calmly and clearly, what you see going on. For example: *David, you've spent the past 5 days in bed, and when you do get up you go right to the couch. Your clothes are hanging off you because you've lost so much weight, and even when your favorite roast beef sits in front of you, you pick at it, leaving it almost totally uneaten. . . . When was the last time you shaved or showered? I also worry about some of the things you say, like how "hopeless" it all is, how you can't possibly go to work to finish a report you need to do.* Be specific, telling the person what you see day after day. At the same time, be sure to say, *I have not lost confidence in you. I love you and I believe in you. I know that this is not who you are, the person I've known for so long. . . . It's my love for you that has me insist we find help. I won't stop until we do.* You can also try saying, *Often there are two different parts in all of us—the part that wants to stay the same and the part that wants to change. I am on the side that wants to change and get better. What I take from all the ways you are behaving, whether you say so or not, is that you are calling out for help.*

Most important, look your loved one in the eye and resolutely say, *I will always be there to support whatever you do to take care of yourself and improve whatever is going on.*

Although the exact words you choose will depend on the specifics of your situation, the example here applies widely, often with little change. The key is to be specific, nonjudgmental, loving, and persistent!

If a depressed wife, for example, says that she is useless, you can say that you know better—that that may be how she feels now but it's not who you know her to be. To a brother who has developed schizophrenia, you can explain that your taking him to a hospital was done out of concern for his safety, out of fear that he might be injured or even die when he wandered the cold city streets at night. If your loved one is a teenager, I suggest saying, in a sympathetic voice, that you understand that one part of her wants and needs to be left alone, but that as a parent you also know that another part needs to be protected, and that you are a parent who cannot risk not protecting your child. You don't want a fight—what you want is to see an end to her suffering.

The universal message you want to convey to your loved one, no matter what his or her age, is this: *I don't want to take over your life—I want you to have your own life, for you to take care of yourself and have the life you want to live. But I love you and will step in if needed. I'll also gladly step aside when that is no longer the case.*

It's also extremely important for families to *try to find out what the loved one may be thinking and feeling*. I believe that all behavior has a *purpose*. Sometimes, however, we don't know what the purpose is—or it may be very different from what we think it is. Avoidance of people or work may be an attempt to escape shame or terrible anxiety. Anger may be due to a person's belief—accurate or not—that you are trying to control or harm him or her. Restrictive eating in a person with anorexia may be the best way to manage the overwhelming anxiety or panic that eating brings on.

You can try to ask questions in order to understand how a loved one's behavior may be serving inner needs that you don't yet comprehend. Over time, you may discover that your spouse calls in sick and sleeps all day to forget how unable he is to focus and contribute at work. Or that your sibling feels overwhelming anxiety when trying to leave the house. Or that your son is convinced that enemies lurk outside the window and aim to destroy him or others in the family. Or, and perhaps even more painful to hear, that your daughter believes that *you* are the problem and are destroying her life.

Once you have the attention of your loved one—by describing behaviors, conveying your love, being persistent, and using what leverage you have—the next step is to try to convince the person to seek help. If your loved one is doubtful that there's a problem or is fearful of getting help, it may take many conversations, over the course of time, to convince him or her. It's rare for someone to immediately agree to begin treatment. Again, be gently persistent. The following are some useful guidelines for what you need to accomplish in the talks.

- Focus on your loved one's behavior. Avoid labels like anorexia or clinical depression. Instead, mention specifics: You might tell them, "Your clothes have become three sizes too big for you," or, "You spent the whole weekend in bed."
- Mention others who support your viewpoint:
  - "Your brother called to say he was very concerned about your not going to work."
  - "Your hockey coach says you are almost always late for practice and don't seem to care like you did before."
  - "Your best friend came to visit and stayed only minutes, saying you didn't want to see her."
- Speak to your loved one's strengths (as a problem solver, caretaker, hard worker, loyal friend, etc.):
  - "You may think you have been like this forever, but I know you as the guy who never would quit."
  - "Where is the mom who made sure that everyone got what they wanted for breakfast even when she had a work deadline?"
  - "Your friends at the town meeting say they need your help."
- Be open to reluctance and listen carefully to it—the reluctance is the clue to future action:
  - "Maybe you're not ready today, but let's set a date for you to see our family doctor."
  - "I sense that if you were more confident that you could do your work, you'd be there in a heartbeat."
- Identify a trusted person who might continue the conversation—a sibling, a friend, a doctor, a colleague:
  - Perhaps the sister of a 17-year-old with anorexia can find a time to speak with her about what she sees happening
  - A coworker who's been open about her husband's mental illness might offer to speak with your brother

- o Your family doctor might agree to call your spouse to ask why he missed his annual checkup and to urge him to visit
- Extract an agreement for a small, specific, and immediate step in the right direction. What can you and your loved one agree to today? Tomorrow? The next day? Take it step by step.
- Leverage your support—give generously for what is helpful and be determined about not supporting continued harmful behaviors:
  - o "I can't give you money to spend unless I know what you are using it for."
  - o "I was thinking of getting you that smartphone but not until I see how you plan to get out of what seems to me to be isolation in your room."
  - o "I want to invite the kids and grandchildren over for dinner on Sunday, but not if you are going to be in bed."
- Use guilt reasonably:
  - o "It's not just me who is worried, but also our son."
  - o "Your coworkers can't keep up with the demands without you."
- End the conversations on a hopeful, positive note:
  - o "We can find a way out of this together."
  - o "We are a family, whatever we face."

So how would these goals play out in an actual conversation? Take a look at the following example. Imagine a husband and wife are sitting at the breakfast table on a Saturday morning, when the weekday's demands are not crashing at the door. Their son, Sam, is still asleep in his room, so they have some quiet time to talk.

WIFE: Last night before you got home, Sam asked me, "What's the matter with Dad?" I asked him what he meant. He said, "Dad is so hard to be around . . . he seems to snap at anything. I feel like I have to walk on eggshells when we are together."

HUSBAND: What else did he say?

W: Not much, but I kind of feel the same way, honey. I can see how hard it is for you to get your work done, for you to show interest in anything new or being with our friends. Your sleep is really restless. Did you know that?

H: Yeah, I'm not sleeping well.

W: That's not good. We do so much—a good night's sleep is no small thing. But have you also noticed that you seem to have lost interest in a lot of things you once loved to do? Even little things have become difficult for you to cope with.

H: What's the use in talking about this?

W: Because this is not you—you are not you anymore. Sam and I . . . we need you back.

H: I'll get over it. Don't worry. Besides, I don't see there is much that I can do about how I feel.

W: Well, I thought you'd just "get over it" too, but that was months ago. I can't sit by, watch you suffer, and see how hard it is for you to function. After Sam spoke to me, I said to myself that I have to speak with you, even if you get mad at me.

H: I've had times like this before.

W: Not for a long time, and this seems different—it seems worse. Don't you think so?

H: I suppose. But nothing can be done anyway.

W: I don't buy that. That's what people say when they are discouraged, down. That's not the problem-solving, determined man I know.

H: What do you have in mind?

W: You trust our family doctor. Why don't you go speak with him? Or remember Bill, who you used to work with? He had a time where he seemed to be really down. Then he rebounded. What about asking him what he did?

H: Maybe.

W: Before we both leave this table, before Sam wakes up, tell me one thing you will do between today and tomorrow that is a step toward you feeling better—getting past whatever it is that is bothering you.

These may be among the hardest conversations a family has. But they're also the most important. Every time they happen, they strengthen a family, as they will strengthen yours.

Learn How to Bend the Mental Health System to Your Needs

The health care system in the United States is a mess. It is broken, far too unaccountable, and more apt to both under-treat and over-treat than to effectively prevent, intervene early, and ensure effective diagnosis and ongoing evidence-based services. And its first cousin, the mental health system, isn't any better off.

If the mental health care system were not so broken, if it served patients and their families as it should (and can), I might not have had to write this book. Understanding what you can about the system will equip you to make it work better for your family. Think of this book as a primer on the subject, and me as your coach. You *should expect* to take up the cudgel on behalf of your loved one in order to secure proper diagnosis and treatment of mental illness—as well as to ensure the provision of recovery-oriented and hope-restoring services that need to follow.

In other words, you will have to become something of a mini-expert on everything including what good treatment looks like, how to pay for care, the dizzying array (and quality) of private and public programs, and the laws governing mental health care, particularly patients' rights. Medications, therapies, clinics, insurance coverage, mental health and addiction laws, the role of school and work in recovery, and much more are about to become your subjects of study. You might have preferred learning about gardening, or sports, or film. It's not fair. But it is necessary.

Settle in for the Siege and Never Give Up

Few chronic illnesses, mental or physical, arrive with the sun and are gone, "cured," by day's end. Most persist for years, sometimes decades— think of hypertension, heart disease, and diabetes. But patients (and families) adjust, learn to live with illness, and discover how to effectively manage their conditions. When they do, they can recover a lost quality of life and hope for a life worth living.

Patience will be an elusive virtue because you want to see a rapid end to suffering and functional limitations in your loved one. But patience needs to become your ally—and that of your loved one. Especially with more serious illnesses such as bipolar disorder, obsessive-compulsive disorder, PTSD, anorexia nervosa, and schizophrenia, families and patients want to take big leaps ahead and become frustrated when progress doesn't meet those expectations. But frustration will only slow your progress.

It's also important to remember that although you cannot tell your loved one what pace he or she should set, you *can* support his or her careful, step-by-step plans. For example:

- "One course may be fine, you can take two next semester."
- "What about working part-time before going full-time?"
- "What about reducing medications slowly so you can understand what each medication and dose are doing?"

Recovering from a mental illness, like from most persistent conditions, takes time. There is a healing process that must go on. One person's response to treatment may not be the same as another's, or feel fast enough for all concerned. It may take time to figure out the right combination of medication and therapy, or to find the right therapist or treatment program. And through it all, your loved one may kick and scream, complain and resist, and not want to do many things you believe are necessary to get better. Your determination will be tested and your morale put at risk; you may wonder if the Old Testament story of Job wasn't written with you in mind. I have one piece of advice for you: *Never, ever, give up.*

I recommend reading a few different wonderful books that will help you understand how important it is to stay the course when it comes to helping a loved one recover from mental illness: Elyn Saks's *The Center Cannot Hold: My Journey Through Madness*, Andrew Solomon's *The Noonday Demon*, and *Henry's Demons*, co-written by a father and son. I'd like to end the chapter with an excerpt from Saks's beautifully written book:

I don't wish to be seen as regretting that I missed the life I could have had if I'd not been ill. Nor am I asking anyone for pity. What I rather wish to say is that the humanity we all share is more important than the mental illness we may not. With proper treatment, someone who is mentally ill can lead a full and rich life. What makes life wonderful—good friends, a satisfying job, loving relationships—is just as valuable for those of us who struggle with schizophrenia as for anyone else. . . . If you are a person with mental illness, the challenge is to find the life that's right for you. But in truth, isn't that the challenge for all of us, mentally ill or not? My good fortune lies in having found my life. (p. 336)

The Facts About Diagnosis and Treatment

People often use words or terms that are meant to more rigorously identify an actual psychiatric diagnosis: "I'm so *depressed* that vacation is ending." "My boss is such a *narcissist*." "My girlfriend's been calling me *obsessively*." It's true that certain feelings or behaviors may be reminiscent of mental illness symptoms, but actual mental illness is something quite different. As I mentioned in Chapter 1, people suffering from it need to be diagnosed and treated as soon as possible.

It's important not to try to diagnose your loved one yourself. That's a job for a professional. But it *is* important to trust your instincts and observations when you sense that something is wrong, and to communicate those to the person suffering and to the professional whose help you seek.

This chapter is about diagnosis and treatment. I'll start by going over some guidelines about how to recognize the presence of a mental illness in a loved one. I'll then consider the following questions about diagnosis and treatment:

- What do I need to know as my loved one seeks a clear diagnosis for a new or existing condition?
- How are diagnoses made and how are treatment plans formulated from that diagnosis?
- How can I avoid unnecessary, confusing, and expensive tests?

- When treatment begins, how can I best advocate for my loved one, ensuring that he or she receives the best that science has to offer, with a comprehensive care plan that is continuously reviewed to optimize success?

Recognizing Mental Illness in a Loved One

Families and friends often ask, "How can I tell if my family member or friend is going through a mental illness rather than some temporary problem or phase?" They need to know that what they are seeing is serious and warrants the kind of effort that surely will follow. They don't want to get into unnecessary arguments or alienate a loved one if what is going on will pass with time and patience.

If you haven't gone to medical school or taken graduate studies in psychology, social work, or nursing, you can't expect to be able to make a clinical diagnosis of a mental condition. Although some disorders, like a clinical depression, are more evident to an observer, they can be due to a variety of causes both physical and psychiatric. Also, disorders often co-occur with other conditions, like depression with PTSD or alcohol abuse. On top of that, mental illnesses can appear very differently in adolescents, adults, and seniors. Making a valid diagnosis is the job of the professionals to whom you will turn.

Your job as a family member or friend is to figure out when a professional diagnosis may be needed and help your loved one to get it. I suggest the three following simple criteria to use in determining whether there is a mental problem that warrants seeking a diagnosis.

The person has shown significant changes in behavior, mood, and thinking that impair functioning.

These changes have persisted for at least 2 weeks (they are not limited to hours or days).

These changes have occurred without an evident cause (like a serious physical illness) or a major traumatic life event (like the loss of a loved one, a natural disaster, or a significant job or school problem).

More specific criteria that you can observe are changes in:

- **Basic habits like eating and sleeping**
  - Eating may be diminished or increased, or there may be new eating habits such as unusual choices of foods, secretive eating, or not wanting to eat with others. With changes in eating there is frequently weight gain or loss that you can notice, but not always.
  - Sleep may be decreased or increased, or its pattern changes significantly. There may be significant difficulty falling asleep, staying asleep, or waking early and being unable to return to sleep. There may be noticeable daytime sleeping or staying in bed during the day for long periods of time.
- **Hygiene and self-care**
  - Showering or bathing may become infrequent, with a person not only looking dirty but smelling poorly also.
  - Dress may become unkempt, including wearing the same clothes for days or the clothes appearing dirty or disheveled.
  - A person's hair may go unwashed, unbrushed, and look matted or ragged.
  - A person's room may reflect the same inattention to hygiene, self-care, and tidiness (to the extent it existed before).
- **Activity**
  - There may be a significant reduction in a person's movements, making him or her look leaden or slow. Or there may be an ongoing increase in movement, including pacing or what looks like frantic activity.
  - Work activities, chores, interests and hobbies, studies—any way the person usually spent time—may be markedly reduced. Or there may be a rather sudden, almost explosive, increase in activities, usually with few if any being completed.
- **Behavior** (these changes can be of many different sorts—what you want to pay attention to is behavior that is significantly different from what you have seen *in the past*). Also look for:
  - Isolation at home or in one's room.
  - Appearing highly preoccupied, as if something compelling is going on inside the person that he or she is not talking about.

- o Talking to oneself, or when alone talking aloud as if someone else were there.
- o Strange new behaviors, like locking doors, sealing windows, abruptly turning off a TV or radio (or responding oddly to something said on a program), wearing odd combinations of clothing or multiple layers of clothing when the weather does not call for it.

- **Socializing or other activities with people**
  - o Not wanting to spend time with family. Avoiding family meals and outings.
  - o Not wanting to spend time with friends.
  - o Not answering calls or text messages that before were always attended to.
  - o Not going out on what were regular nights with friends or not attending team events or practices with no reasons given.

- **Mood**
  - o Mood may become blue, sad, or tearful. A person may talk of having lost interest or pleasure, or that life is not worth living. Pessimism prevails.
  - o There may be periods of intense worry, fear, or anxiety.
  - o A person may become highly irritable or quick to get into arguments.
  - o Excitement may be prominent, without clear reasons. Everything seems overly important, for a brief moment, and then another matter takes over.

- **Thinking**
  - o Thinking may be sped up, or slowed down, resulting in an increase in talking or a marked reduction.
  - o Indecision can prevail and a person is unable to decide even on simple matters.
  - o Guilty feelings may be out of proportion to any event.
  - o A person may express odd thoughts, different from what you have come to expect. He or she may interpret what is going on in strange ways, including thinking that the world has suddenly changed or that there are forces we don't know about or that are dangerous.

- ○ Thoughts expressed may not make sense, or may seem disjointed or confused.
- ○ The person may respond to what he or she believes is a voice when there is no one speaking, or react to other nonexistent things (like wrinkling the nose at a nonexistent odor or training the gaze on a corner of the room with nothing in it).
- ○ The person may act in response to what appear to be highly developed and threatening concerns from within.
- • **Smoking and alcohol or drug use**
  - ○ Smoking more or chain smoking.
  - ○ Drinking more, drinking in order to fall asleep, or drinking alone or secretively.
  - ○ Heavy use of marijuana or other street drugs.

> If you see significant changes in a loved one's behavior, mood, or thinking that impair functioning, and these changes last for weeks, seek professional help as soon as possible.

Let's now consider the process by which mental health clinicians arrive at a diagnosis. Understanding this process will help you appreciate why certain information is sought, why history is gathered, and why tests may be ordered. It may also assist you in explaining to your loved one (or other family members) what is happening. Finally, it may be a way by which you can judge if the clinician is doing the right thing.

Getting the Right Diagnosis*

Although brain-imaging technologies *have* shown us that mentally ill brains function differently from healthy ones, at this time there are few scientifically verifiable laboratory or imaging tests that can identify specific mental illnesses. We are used to these types of tests for physical illnesses like diabetes, hypertension, and pneumonia. Unfortunately, there is no MRI for schizophrenia, no blood test to confirm bipolar disorder.

* Portions of this section were published on *TheAtlantic.com* on July 18, 2012 (www.theatlantic.com/health/archive/2012/07/how-thoughts-become-a-psychiatric-diagnosis/260012).]

I have seen families bewildered by this time and time again. After I spoke at a public forum, a mother lingered to ask if her 23-year-old son, suffering from serious depression and anxiety problems since adolescence, should have a brain MRI. At a neighborhood dinner, another mother asked me about getting psychological testing for her adolescent daughter, who was struggling with anxiety and eating problems. At work, a worried father asked if gene testing could help clinicians to understand his daughter's newly erupted mental illness. My answers were all pretty much the same: These tests are not apt to provide any clinically useful information for diagnosis (or treatment). In fact, some test findings can raise additional unanswerable and therefore confounding questions, especially when what has been found may have no clinical importance or bearing on treatment.

Fortunately, the psychiatric diagnostic process *does* have a very reliable framework, which is built on observation, patient history, and talking with families. But diagnosing disorders of the mind is still a difficult business. And although there are notable advances in functional brain imaging, genetic analysis, and cognitive neuroscience, these have yet to add much to our understanding of how the brain's malfunctions produce its myriad mental pathologies.

Ironically, this knowledge gap exists alongside effective treatments. The field of psychiatry knows *what* works—just not exactly *why* it works. Indeed, psychiatric medicine has learned which biological and psychological interventions improve which symptoms and conditions, even if the "how" and "why" continue to elude scientific comprehension. And it's exactly this knowledge that may help us to, in the future, better understand the "how" and the "why." In fact, this seemingly backward process has led to important medical advances in the past. For example, the discovery of germs happened only after a 19th-century physician observed that when doctors washed their hands before delivering babies, the babies had a much lower mortality rate. Once that doctor realized *what* worked to lower the mortality rate, he was able to figure out *why* it worked.

HOW PSYCHIATRIC DIAGNOSIS WORKS

Any illness is a complex of *symptoms* (what a person experiences, such as fatigue, nausea, or nervousness), *signs* (what can be observed or measured, such as increased blood pressure, shortness of breath, weight loss, or pacing), and *data* (objective measures of an illness, such as thyroid hormone levels, masses on an MRI, or the presence of abnormal cells on a slide).

Because blood tests, tissue examinations, and imaging technologies can't be used to diagnose common and even disabling psychiatric illnesses, we instead arrive at a diagnosis mostly by listening, observing, and asking the patient—as well as others who have witnessed the patient's symptoms—to describe what has happened. The diagnostic process uses an old-fashioned approach: The doctor takes a careful history, asking how the patient feels and observing how he or she looks, acts, and thinks. Often a clinician's intuitions about a patient can be useful, if sometimes imprecise.

Patients are routinely asked: "Tell me what brings you here. When did your problems start, and then what happened?" Further inquiry typically delves into what makes the condition better or worse, which can be very helpful for a clinician in determining what may be causing the problems. Sometimes the information obtained through this history reveals a pretty clear picture. For example, reports of an unrelenting blue mood, guilty feelings, trouble sleeping, loss of appetite, reduced libido, hopelessness, and a wish to no longer live, all of which persist for weeks or longer despite environmental changes and everyday efforts to "snap out of it," fit the profile of a major depression.

Other times, answers to the history taking are too vague to provide a clear clinical profile. Symptoms like loss of energy, isolation from friends, and trouble concentrating are worrisome and interfere with functioning, but they do not sufficiently or specifically portray a particular illness.

However, whatever the initial history provides, clear or not yet clear, the diagnostic process remains the same: keen observation, active listening, identifying clusters of symptoms, and recognizing the course of the condition over time.

During a history taking, the clinician is trying to formulate what's called a "differential diagnosis"—the systematic process of telling two (or more) conditions apart. As I mentioned earlier, a symptom that is typical of a mental illness may actually come from a different problem. For example, fatigue can be the result of thyroid disease or mononucleosis, while weight loss can result from an undiagnosed tumor. Your doctor may communicate this process of differential diagnosis by saying something like: "While you may have depression, it's possible there is a problem with your thyroid." Or, "Your heart medicine may have unwelcome side effects that cause low mood and energy . . . we need to find out more." In other words, just because a patient presents with serious emotional symptoms, it does not mean that the causation is mental, especially if the problems have developed without a clear psychological stressor. Physical causes need to be ruled out before a psychiatric diagnosis is conclusively made.

In addition, many clinicians (and families) have discovered that psychiatric symptoms that persist despite treatment efforts, and that continue to impair a person's functioning, mood, or thinking, were the result of the use or abuse of alcohol, non-prescribed medications, or street drugs (like Spice or K2 or Ecstasy), or marijuana, that adversely affect the nervous system. Alcohol abuse can cause depressed feelings, as well as lower inhibitions, which sometimes results in dangerous or troublesome behaviors. Amphetamines of all types, especially methedrine, first stimulate and then deplete the brain of essential neurotransmitters and can produce excitement or psychosis. Ecstasy is neurotoxic for its users. Taken abusively, narcotic analgesic pills like Oxycontin and Vicodin produce withdrawal and serious mood problems. The various psychiatric complications of substance use and abuse are called "organic mood disorders," sometimes also referred to as "organic cognitive disorders" or "organic psychotic disorders."

Information from trusted people who know (and have observed) the patient may be needed to detect substance-abuse disorders that could cause psychiatric symptoms or aggravate other mental disorders. Blood and urine tests can often detect these substances. Simple questionnaires are quite effective in identifying alcohol and drug use disorders. Thankfully, these questionnaires are becoming standard screening tools in primary care and mental health centers as a first step in unearthing common drug-induced conditions.

It may seem backwards, but in psychiatric diagnosis, sometimes doctors can use the results of treatment to infer the cause of the symptoms. In other words, a diagnosis may be revealed over time as a patient responds to a treatment. For example, response to a mood stabilizer like lithium or valproate acid supports the diagnosis of bipolar disorder. Abstinence from alcohol or non-prescribed drugs that results in improved thinking and mood tells everyone that these substances were instrumental to the problems a person was having. In this way, the logic of the diagnostic process is a bit of deductive reasoning. It may seem old-fashioned, but it works.

Infrequently, special brain scans (magnetic resonance imaging, or MRI) or psychological tests can be necessary or helpful to the diagnostic process. Neuroimaging—radiological tests of the brain or spinal nervous system (like MRI, CT, and PET scans)—has the potential to identify a physical illness producing the psychiatric symptoms. A brain scan can examine anatomy or investigate brain functioning by measuring blood flow and even actual brain physiological activity (for example, how much energy a section of the brain is using during a task). Brain scans are commonly used to detect tumors, blood vessel or bleeding abnormalities, skull fractures, or loss of brain tissue (as seen in Alzheimer's disease). But imaging has yet to be helpful in the diagnosis of schizophrenia or bipolar disease, even though symptoms can be so prominent.

Psychological testing has come a long way from the days of the inkblots in a Rorschach test. Intelligence tests and other tests of cognitive functioning, administered by an expert psychologist, can help to identify problems with mental attention, focus, and decision making. Tests that help with workplace dynamics, the best known being the Myers-Briggs, which profiles how people think and feel, can be useful in understanding and getting along with coworkers and supervisors. Additionally, there are psychological tests to track the progression of dementia. But again, these tests cannot be used to diagnose specific mental illnesses.

Since 1990, scientists have been detailing the human genome and trying to target treatments based on the response (or lack of response) of an individual gene to a specific treatment. Patients, families, and practitioners have been hopeful that genetic evaluation will influence clinical decisions in the future. Dr. Harold Varmus, former head of the National Institutes of Health, said: "The human genome is good for science but not for medicine." His candor is refreshing. Your family member or friend may want to participate in rigorous and safe psychiatric genetic research, but patients and families shouldn't waste time, money, and precious hope on genetic research (or imaging studies) that someone says will change the course of treatment or recovery from common mental disorders.

We're just not at that point yet. It's more important to focus on getting the right diagnosis from a careful clinical evaluation, followed by proper evidence-based treatments.

Treatment Decisions

Given that psychiatric diagnosis lacks biological and radiological testing and instead relies on clinical information and judgment, how can you know if a proposed treatment is right for a given diagnosis? I want to offer you a set of questions that you or your loved one can ask the treating doctor or mental health professional. These questions will help you determine the quality of the care provided to your loved one.

Is the treatment supported by scientific studies? Treatments that have been scientifically validated are called "**evidence-based practices**." Although not every mental (or physical) condition has treatments that meet this standard, many do. Whenever it's possible for clinicians to use evidence-based practices, patients should be treated at that standard of quality. You and your loved one can learn from reliable sources of medical information (see Appendix B) if there are evidence-based practices for the condition your family member has. If an evidence-based treatment does exist, you and your loved one should insist that it is the standard of care that is delivered.

What specific symptoms or functioning is the treatment meant to target? This question is important. Treatments are there to improve symptoms and functioning, not eradicate the disease. For example, a patient may always have a diagnosis of schizophrenia, but through proper treatment may be able to mitigate or substantially control its symptoms. Ask the doctor what symptoms or daily functional capabilities the prescribed medication will help. This is how you will know if your loved one is responding to treatment. Will sleep improve? Will concentration or memory become sharper? Will productivity at school or work get better? Will anxiety or agitation lessen? Will there be improvements in mood? Will sexual interest rebound?

Treatment based on specific and quantifiable goals is called "**measurement-based care**." Urge your family member or friend to take the time to write down what he or she wants to improve so you all can be clear and specific about what to watch and measure. In doing this you will have the information needed to determine if the treatment is working.

What happens if symptoms and functioning do not improve? You want to know if there is a plan to regularly review the treatment, and change it if needed. The process of reviewing and reconsidering a treatment is called "**stepped care.**" If the patient is not getting better, then there should be a review of the treatment, consultation with another mental health professional (if needed), and changes made to optimize the likelihood of a response.

Is the treatment comprehensive? Effective resolution of symptoms often— but not always—includes a combination of medication and psycho- therapy or skill-building techniques. If medication is being prescribed, ask whether it is being done in combination with psychotherapy or skill- building techniques, and if psychotherapy or skill-building techniques are prescribed, ask whether medication might further the effectiveness of therapy or rehabilitation. Good illness management today (for serious and persistent physical *and* mental disorders) is based on the additive effects of medications, therapy, and health and wellness techniques. Comprehensive treatment involves more work, but it's worth it. (See Chapter 3 for a more in-depth discussion of comprehensive treatment.)

Will the treatment be continuous? Inconsistent treatment may allow an underlying condition to reassert itself by a relapse or a recurrence. *Relapse* is when a patient falls ill during the course of an episode of illness; *recur- rence* is when the same illness comes back after it has abated.

Ask the mental health professional about what the patient needs to do to prevent relapse and recurrence. Ask what role you, as a key support person, can have in preventing further suffering and loss of function for your loved one. Also ask how your loved one might best organize his or her life to optimize recovery and prevent further episodes of illness.

All patients, whether they have a physical or mental disorder, should receive **evidence-based, comprehensive, continuous treatment.** Their attention, as well, to **wellness and effective self-management** techniques will maximize their chances of recovery and of staying healthy.

Are caregivers making the patient a full partner in treatment? Both the patient and the clinician should be responsible for making decisions about the treatments chosen. This is called "**shared decision making**" (see Chapter 11 and www.samhsa.gov/consumersurvivor/sdm/StartHere.html). Treatment decisions, certainly those beyond very acute care, are best when the clinician and patient become a team, when there is a partnership and mutual trust. And when family and friends are enlisted to support the conditions needed for effective treatment, recovery becomes even more possible. Building a partnership between the clinician and patient can be hard work, but over time the results of treatment will be far better when a patient actively participates in all treatment decisions.

Does a spirit of hope prevail in the caregivers? Do they focus on people, not diseases, and believe that people with mental illness can live a full life—even with the illness? Listen carefully to the way your clinician talks about your loved one's mental illness—this will give you a sense of whether the clinician believes that recovery is possible for people with mental illness. It may seem hard to believe, but some clinicians still think that mental disorders mean a life of compromise and marginalization. Don't waste your time with those caregivers. If you can't get a sense of the clinician's beliefs from just listening to the way he or she talks, ask the person directly: "How hopeful are you that my loved one will be able to live a full life, even with this mental illness, if it's treated?" Hope is critical to living with and managing any serious, persistent condition. And it needs to reside in the caregivers as well as in patients, families, and friends. People with diabetes don't need to view themselves as fated to live at the end of an insulin syringe—instead, they can see themselves having a good life, with illness. The same applies for people with mental illness.

Similarly, people with mental illness should not be reduced to the label of their diagnosis. A person with schizophrenia, for example, isn't *just* a schizophrenic. He or she is a whole person, and schizophrenia is a condition that person has. Patients, family members, and friends should remember this. And so should those entrusted to treat them.

Taking Care of What Needs to Be Done, Now

As scientific research pursues better explanations for mental illnesses, too many people continue to be ill, impaired, and at risk of taking their lives. Even if an illness eludes our current understanding about causation, you and your loved one want to be prudent shoppers of treatment, not desperate ones. Be wary of diagnostic tests that are not an essential part of an evaluation or differential diagnosis. Ask what the test will offer in terms of clarifying the diagnosis or informing how treatment will proceed. Wait for an answer clear and meaningful enough to convince you to lend your support to what may be suggested.

Principles of Good Care

Mental illnesses are treatable: More than two thirds of people who receive effective treatment (delivered early and consistently followed) see sustained improvement or even remission. Even with persistent illness, the vast majority of people can recover functional lives through treatment when specific principles for mental health care are followed.

But mental health care can be confusing and overwhelming. Anyone watching even just several minutes of television commercials can become overwhelmed by how many prescription drugs claim to treat myriad conditions. How do you and your loved one know how to choose a medication? How can you know if the therapy prescribed is apt to be effective? Or that the rehabilitation program your family member has joined employs the right approaches for returning to school or work?

Although you may never be able to research every medication or therapy, you *can* understand the core principles of mental health care. By insisting that *core principles* be adhered to, you can help your family member or friend recover and build a productive and meaningful life.

As a family member or close friend of a person with an illness, you will need to advocate for these principles of care, as far too often they are not followed. When that happens, the consequences include interrupted and ineffective treatments that can usher in suffering, disability, and economic and family burden. Health care in general—not just mental health care—demands that we all become knowledgeable, vocal advocates for getting treatment right. It may not seem fair, but it's necessary.

This chapter examines the following principles of mental health care:

Treatment should be safe.

Treatment should be evidence-based or evidence-informed (effective)—and measurement-based.

Treatment should be comprehensive and continuous.

Treatment should be collaborative ("shared decision making").

Treatment should meet linguistic and cultural needs.

Treatment should be recovery-oriented.

It will conclude with a discussion of *prevention*, another principle of care that can guide your efforts.

Treatment Should Be Safe

The medical principle regarding safe therapies is captured by the ancient medical oath *primum non nocere*—"first do no harm." To do no harm, a treatment must be safe.

During the 14th century, surgeons abandoned what had been the established treatment for gunshot wounds. Instead of removing debris, washing gently with water, and covering the wound to protect and encourage natural healing—a medical practice that started with the Egyptians—they began pouring boiling oil into battle wounds. That disastrous practice continued for over 200 years until a French army surgeon rediscovered gentle cleansing and protection of wounds when he ran out of oil on the battlefield. Psychological wounds also need gentle care, protection, and the opportunity for healing, not boiling oil.

However promising the potential benefits of a treatment may be, that treatment must, above all, be safe. We tend to focus on safety when it comes to medications. But safety is a principle that should apply to every form of psychiatric treatment, including psychotherapy and other psychosocial treatments.

As a family member, you want to ask about the risks attached to any form of intervention. Standard medical practice requires that any prescription of medications be done with *informed consent*. A doctor needs to tell the patient why he or she is suggesting a specific medication, as well as explain its potential benefits and risks, its common side effects, and what alternatives exist. Many good doctors will also speak with their patients about potential risks of *no* treatment. As a family member or friend, you may not be privy to this conversation, but it is a concern you can talk to your loved one about or raise yourself if you join some portion of the treatment meetings.

No medication, psychiatric or otherwise, is without risks and side effects. A doctor should engage patients (and family members, when possible) in a genuine discussion of the benefits, risks, and side effects of medications, as well as the alternatives to any medication. This should be a real discussion, not a rapid-fire burst of information that sounds like the end of a television drug advertisement. After the pros and cons are discussed, the doctor should ask the patient for consent to proceed with medication treatment. The patient either signs a piece of paper or verbally agrees to proceed with the treatment. The consent form or a doctor's notation of the verbal agreement becomes a part of the patient's medical record.

When considering the safety of treatments, it is important to remember that some treatments will be fine for some people yet too risky for others. For example, emotionally intensive psychotherapy carries risks, especially for people whose mental illness causes problems in thinking (as occurs in schizophrenia and other psychotic illnesses) and for patients who are despondent, traumatized, or highly anxious and frightened. In my view, a psychotherapy that explores the underlying causes of emotional trauma before an individual has created a stable and functioning life is premature and often not safe for that individual; it runs the risk of further destabilizing that person's mental condition or prompting impulsive or self-destructive behavior.

Psychotherapy that is emotionally confrontational for people with psychotic illness (and many other conditions) carries great risk. As does a family-therapy approach that demonizes families, which is not only ineffective but also cruel. Families with a loved one with mental illness face many problems, but *they* are *not* the problem. In fact, families are generally an ill person's major source of ongoing support; they often are essential in helping that person engage, and remain, in treatment.

There is no need to bite that hand that feeds: It is unsafe to blame and alienate families.

Of course, any treatment or contact with a therapist that exploits the patient (sexually, financially, or otherwise) is both unsafe and wholly unethical. Fortunately, unethical practices are uncommon—but it's important to remember that they sometimes occur. Usually, unethical doctors or therapists avoid consultation, because it threatens to expose their behavior. If you or your loved one has reason to believe that unethical behavior is going on, insist on a consultation. Opening a window that may expose misconduct is usually the best first step in ending it. State agencies have procedures by which you can bring allegations against the professionals they license, if that becomes necessary.

Medication, talking therapy, family education and support, and skill building are among the most essential—and proven—services for people with serious and persistent mental illness. But, as I mentioned, each treatment carries risks (which means safety is at stake), not just benefits. As the principal support system for your loved one, you want to know all you can to help your family member make informed decisions about treatment and recovery. Don't be shy. Ask the clinician about the risks and consider them carefully. You may need to be the most vocal advocate for your loved one's care.

Treatment Should Be Evidence-Based or Evidence-Informed (Effective)—and Measurement-Based

Mental health clinicians, like clinicians in all the helping professions, should be knowledgeable about—and use—the best evidence available in choosing treatments. And prudent consumers (patients, family members, supportive friends) should expect clinicians to explain why they are recommending the treatments they are.

A number of terms are used synonymously with "evidence-based treatment"—"evidence-based medicine," "scientifically proven treatments," and "practice guidelines" (rigorously developed medical information provided by professional associations and scientific experts). All of these terms refer to treatments—in all branches of medicine—that have been scientifically studied and whose results demonstrate that they are more effective than no treatment or than a placebo.

From 2000 to 2002, I worked for the American Psychiatric Association (APA), the national medical specialty association for psychiatrists. One of my responsibilities there was to direct the office that produced the APA practice guidelines (PGs). These PGs were derived from peer-reviewed scientific studies on how to best care for a great many psychiatric diseases. The PGs were then organized according to how strong the evidence base, or *clinical confidence*, was for specific treatments of specific disorders. Treatments were ranked along a continuum from a low level of confidence to substantial clinical confidence. At the low end is "may be recommended on the basis of individual circumstances," which means that expert clinicians are using the treatment in everyday practice but the treatment hasn't been around long enough to be thoroughly studied yet. (Published papers about a treatment can appear years after practices are adopted.) Because of the lack of research, clinical confidence remains low. (This doesn't mean the treatment doesn't work, of course—it just means it hasn't been adequately studied yet.) Moderate to high levels of confidence are based on mounting evidence, especially by randomized controlled studies that are replicated, that a treatment works. You can access the APA practice guidelines online anytime at: www.psychiatry-online.com/pracGuide/pracGuideTopic_11.aspx.

During my work on the PGs, I discovered how limited the evidence base is for psychiatry. Whereas a fair number of medication studies exist, there is far too little research about psychotherapy, rehabilitation, or community-based support services, all of which are essential components in the comprehensive care of serious mental disorders.

Why? Because clinical studies cost money. Funding for a clinical trial comes from a few limited sources. As you might imagine, the greatest investments come from pharmaceutical companies who studied their product during its development. Medications researched by well-financed clinical trials can have a very significant evidence base; in fact, this evidence is typically needed to shepherd a new drug through the safety and effectiveness requirements of the Food and Drug Administration (FDA), whose approval is needed to go to market with a medication. This is why there is more evidence on medications than on other forms of treatment.

The APA and other organizations who publish practice guidelines need to have evidence to arrive at their assessment of a treatment. Thus, they have principally focused, especially in the United States, on medications because that is where the scientific evidence is most developed and available. Other important sources of evidence do exist, however, such as the Patient Outcomes Research Team (PORT) in the United States, the National Institute for Health and Clinical Excellence (NICE) in the United Kingdom, and Cochrane Reviews. The PORT and NICE are referenced in Appendix B.

As I mentioned earlier, just because a treatment hasn't been rigorously studied doesn't mean it doesn't work, and practice guidelines take this into consideration by including what they call "evidence-informed practices." An evidence-informed treatment is one that's backed up by expert opinion, even if it hasn't been thoroughly studied.

There is a wonderfully ironic editorial about evidence-based medicine that appeared some years ago in the distinguished *British Medical Journal* (2003). The editorial reported on how we should not expect to see randomized control trials on parachutes because getting control subjects to agree not to use the "anti-gravity device" (the parachute) had proven too difficult. Thus, proof of the effectiveness of parachutes was scientifically limited because rigorous evidence (which requires control subjects) was lacking. What this tale means is that there are some treatments you will want your loved one to use even if they haven't met the standards of proof required by medical journals and professional associations.

What's more, some treatments will probably never have a scientific base because no one will pay to research them. For the longest time, psychotherapy—especially what's called "dynamically oriented psychotherapy"—was in this category. Some limited results on this form of treatment have emerged as part of a campaign to prove its effectiveness. Very limited evidence exists for psychoanalysis. Do these therapies work? The answer is yes, but accompanied by many qualifiers: yes, for some people, selectively, at certain times in the course of a person's life, and when done by capable practitioners. However, a great deal of high-confidence evidence has developed for cognitive-behavioral therapy and interpersonal therapy (see Chapter 8).

My advice to you is to learn what there is to know, and to understand what can work for your family member's condition. Go online to trustworthy sites (see Appendix B), attend NAMI educational sessions, speak with other families that have been through what you are experiencing, read reliable books written for a lay audience, and question caregivers. Compare what you come to know to what you see your family member or friend receiving, and talk with your loved one and his or her clinician if a gap exists between what has been demonstrated to work and what treatments are being delivered.

In other chapters of this book, I discuss specific treatments and evidence-based practices for conditions like depression, bipolar disorder, eating disorders, PTSD, anxiety disorders, schizophrenia, and other mental illnesses. In addition, the National Institute of Mental Health (NIMH), the National Alliance on Mental Illness (NAMI), and the Substance Abuse Mental Health Services Administration (SAMHSA) websites can provide you and your loved one with reliable information about effective treatments.

MEASUREMENT-BASED CARE: HOW TO TELL IF A TREATMENT IS WORKING

At some point, every patient and loved one wants to know: *How can I tell if my treatment is working?* At first glance, the answer might seem obvious: An antidepressant is working if the patient regains a sense of pleasure in life, is not crippled by sadness, resumes normal sleep and eating habits, thinks more clearly, and sees hope in the future. Or a course of cognitive-behavioral therapy for obsessive-compulsive disorder is working if the patient can leave the house without dashing back a dozen times to check that the stove is not on. These changes are called "symptom-based improvements"—they can be understood and measured. And the good news is that they can often be achieved in weeks or months with proven treatments that are consistently provided and adhered to by the patient.

But, in many situations, the answer may be less clear-cut. For example, for patients with schizophrenia, bipolar disorder, or alcohol and drug use disorders, the road to recovery may not be as prompt or straightforward as all would wish. Treating trauma-induced conditions (from abuse, neglect, or torture) is often more complex. Although patients with these conditions have a good chance of recovery *over time*, the horizon for improvement tends to be farther off. Early in the course of treatment, they may suffer repeat episodes of illness, relapses, or recurrences, which can require repeat emergency-room visits or hospital stays before treatment takes hold and recovery begins.

A simple, practical approach to being able to answer the question of whether a treatment is working is to identify, from the start, what the patient (and family) are seeking from treatment. I like to ask my patients and their families not only *Why are you here?* but also *What do you want to accomplish?* This helps us all know, in the future, whether the patient is getting what he or she came for. Does the patient want to be able to sleep better and feel hopeful? Be less angry and get along with other family members? Return to work or do better in school? Have a date or feel more comfortable in social situations? When goals are clearly stated at the outset of treatment, it's easier to assess whether the treatment is working later on down the road.

Some doctors, clinics, and treatment programs use measurement tools, like depression-severity self-reports, PTSD scores, or quality-of-life rating scales (see Appendix C) to measure where a person is at the beginning of care and to regularly assess a person's response to treatment. Don't hesitate to fill out these forms—or to have a conversation about specific goals. They are meant to keep the focus of the care on the patient. If your family member or friend is not asked about goals, be a vocal advocate and ask "why not?" Ask how you and your loved one can clearly express why you've come for treatment and what you want to achieve.

> Clarify your goals at the outset of treatment. Write them down, communicate them to the clinician, and come back to them on a regular basis to determine if what everyone has agreed to pursue is happening.

Treatment Should Be Comprehensive and Continuous

Treatment that is *comprehensive* combines different and complementary approaches that seek to address symptoms and functioning. Often this means combining medication and therapy. Treatment that is *continuous* is provided regularly, beginning with diagnosis. Continuous is not the same thing as forever—but it does mean not stopping and needing to restart. Some treatments can last months, some years—not unlike the treatments for a variety of physical conditions. But all medical disorders benefit from patients sticking with the treatment for as long as it is needed.

COMPREHENSIVE TREATMENT

Care that is comprehensive is far more likely to reduce episodes of illness and enhance the chances of recovery. For example, critically important research on 1-year relapse rates for schizophrenia teaches us that relapse can be reduced by about 50% when patients take an antipsychotic medication *and* receive case management (see Chapters 7 and 8 for discussions of case management). If family psychoeducation is added, the risk of 1-year relapse goes down *another* 50%. And by adding problem-solving therapy and social-skills training, the risk goes down about *another* 50%! These compelling statistics demonstrate that a comprehensive care approach for a person with schizophrenia is likely to reduce the risk of relapse to 1 in 8, a mighty difference from no treatment at all or medication alone.

The same applies to depression. A treatment plan that utilizes medications and psychotherapy (cognitive-behavioral or interpersonal therapy, for example) improves a person's likelihood of responding to treatment. One intervention can complement or augment the other. So, too, for bipolar disorder, for which medications are necessary, but in themselves not sufficient, for your family member.

I have seen patients and doctors pursue the "perfect medication" approach to treatment. Frankly, that leaves me cold. I am all for choosing the best medication (and sometimes a combination of medicines) as an essential aspect of treatment for many mental disorders. But endless efforts that singularly focus on medication are generally short-sighted and not likely to be helpful enough for your loved one.

For conditions like personality disorders or eating disorders, the utility of medications is limited, and other treatment approaches are necessary. You should question the validity of the treatment plan if all your clinician recommends is medication. Similarly, if only therapy is being offered, ask whether medication might be added to enhance the treatment. It may be that medication or therapy alone will sufficiently treat your loved one's illness—particularly if the condition is mild to moderate in severity. In these cases, comprehensive treatment may be *good* but not *necessary*. For moderate to severe non-psychotic illnesses (such as major depression and debilitating anxiety disorders), however, both medication and therapy are generally the best option. For psychotic conditions, treatment that includes medication, therapy, and rehabilitation, combined with family education and sometimes case management, shows the best outcomes. (I'll discuss all these illnesses, as well as medications and therapy, in later chapters.) Whatever mental illness your family member or friend is battling, a good clinician will consider combining treatment approaches to produce the best chance of response and recovery. He or she should *also* explain the reasoning behind the suggested treatment approach.

CONTINUOUS TREATMENT

The course of many a serious mental illness is one where the condition comes on in adolescence or early adulthood and persists, with periods of worsening, if not treated early, effectively, and continuously. During this roller-coaster experience, every effort needs to be made to make treatment continuous in order to reduce relapse and disability.

For example, psychosis, if not consistently and effectively treated, is neurotoxic, or damaging to the brain. Indeed, schizophrenia is associated with damage to brain cells and circuits when left untreated. This neurotoxicity helps explain the functional disability that psychosis can produce over time. Some people worry that antipsychotic medications are toxic to the brain. Although medications certainly do affect the brain and can cause many side effects, there can be greater harm in allowing an untreated psychotic illness to damage it.

When mood disorders go untreated, or treatment is insufficient (either incomplete or prematurely ended), similar problems can occur. For example, we know that with each episode of depression (or mania), a patient's risk for another episode increases. After a few episodes, the likelihood of another episode increases exponentially. This phenomenon of increasing risk of relapse or recurrence in mood disorders has been called *kindling*. This brain phenomenon is also seen in some seizure disorders. In simple terms, every time you get sick, you are at greater risk to be sick again in the future. Good treatment is continuous and aims to prevent kindling.

Treatment Should Be Collaborative ("Shared Decision Making")

When we were developing measurement-based care at McLean Hospital (a Harvard teaching hospital where I was medical director), we used a patient self-report called the BASIS-32. The BASIS-32 was a wonderful tool because we had a chance to ask our patients what *they* thought about their symptoms and functioning. We used the BASIS-32 upon hospital admission, during treatment, upon discharge from the hospital, and subsequently in outpatient programs. It allowed our clinical staff to determine if the patient *him-* or *herself* thought the treatment was working.

When presenting our work at conferences, I was often challenged about the "validity" of these self-reports. Colleagues would assume, for example, that people with acute psychotic illness tend not to report problems with hallucinations or delusions. Or that people with personality disorders, like borderline personality, report minimal problems with other people. Or that individuals admitted into alcohol and drug treatment programs would not report high levels of difficulty with substance abuse. While that was often the case, each group of individuals *did* report significant problems—with mood, ability to function, troubled relationships, and, sometimes, with the law—just not necessarily the ones that clinicians tended to focus on.

The BASIS-32 was very good at telling clinicians about how individuals experienced *their* difficulties. By eliciting **the patient's perspective**, we were able to better understand what a person wanted to achieve. For example, patients who reported wanting to improve specific relationship problems were telling us that relationships were a concern and goal for them, even if they didn't check off concerns about delusional thinking or share our opinion about their diagnosis. The BASIS-32 met the person where he or she was, which often was different from what the doctor was thinking. I've therefore come to view self-reports as highly valid of patients' perceptions of their conditions and the effects of being ill on their lives. If we are to succeed as clinicians, we need to know our patients' concerns and goals, and we need to respect and partner with them about what they want to achieve. This is called **shared decision making**.

Similarly, in considering and offering treatment, we need to ask and respect a person's preferences. For mild to moderate depression, we know that both psychotherapy and medications are apt to be helpful, and that they can complement each other. But what does the patient want? One person may be reluctant to take medication while another prefers medication to therapy. Clinicians should listen to patient preferences and take them into account, if at all possible. That said, not all clinicians *do* practice shared decision making. What should you do if you find yourself in this situation?

There are some questions you as a family member or friend can ask a mental health clinician:

- "I've heard about the importance of patient preference in medical care. Do you and your staff take patient preference into consideration when making treatment decisions?"
- "What do you believe can be gained from asking us about our treatment preferences?"
- "What happens if our loved one thinks your treatment approach does not fit with how he thinks treatment should go?"
- "What do you do if what you suggest for treatment is not what our family member wants?"

This is *not* to say that mental health professionals should meet a person's preference if he or she happens to prefer a treatment like wearing an amulet around the neck or engaging in primal-scream therapy for psychosis. A clinician has a professional standard to uphold. But unless a clinician understands and works with a person's preferences, the likelihood of alliance, engagement, and retention in treatment is in peril. A good mental health professional, or team of clinicians, will ask for or respond to a patient's preference during discussions about medication and other treatments.

SHARED DECISION MAKING

Let me introduce the critical concept of **shared decision making** by telling you a story about a colleague, Dr. Pat Deegan.

For many years, I had heard Pat Deegan's name mentioned with admiration, even a bit of awe. When I was asked to give comments on a talk she would deliver at the 2003 NAMI NYC conference, I was glad to meet her at last. When Pat stood up, the crowd seemed to go very still, paying special attention.

Dr. Pat Deegan was not always a PhD. She'd had three psychiatric hospital admissions as a teenager, the first when she was 17. During the second admission, Pat was told that she had chronic schizophrenia and that her dreams of life as an athlete or joining the Peace Corps were over. She described the experience of receiving the diagnosis like this:

> I was beginning to undergo that radically dehumanizing and devaluing transformation from being a person to being an illness; from being Pat Deegan to being "a schizophrenic." As I look back on those days, I am struck by how all alone I was. This profound sense of being all alone only served to compound my sense of feeling worthless and of having no value. No one came to me and said, "Hey, I know you're going through hell right now. I know you feel totally lost in some nightmare. I know you can't see a way out right now. But I've been where you are today. I got labeled with schizophrenia and a whole bunch of other things too. And I'm here to tell you that there is a way out and that your life doesn't have to be about being in mental institutions."

After her diagnosis, Pat spent numbing months smoking, sitting, staring, and sleeping. She was losing her spirit and her wish to live, feeling deadness and wondering what there was to live for. Her hopes had been dashed and there was no one to tell her that there could be help, and even hope. But Pat refused to let that lonely, empty life be her fate. She told the NAMI crowd that day how she had rebuilt a life *with* the illness. Her personal and professional example has greatly advanced the field of mental health and has inspired many other people and their families.

Dr. Deegan is acutely aware of how difficult it is for other people to spend time with those who have a mental illness and are in great psychological distress. She likens the strain of being with someone in psychic pain or desperation to that of being with someone who has lost a loved one. She points out that mental health professionals sometimes manage their *own* intolerance of these feelings by "being busy doing things *to* you, rather than being *with* you." She wants patients to know that while they may *have* an illness, they *are* not an illness. She is open about how she hears voices that degrade her—about how, at times, her thoughts are in disarray and it is hard for her to be her usual highly articulate self. Sometimes her illness makes it difficult for her to work.

But her illness also allows her to have a special vantage point in the mental health field. She spoke about why many people with mental illnesses are angry: For one thing, they often are denied the right to take risks and have failures like the rest of us because when they do, it is immediately attributed to their illness. That is where *shared decision making* comes in. During her presentation, Dr. Deegan showed the group a clinical tool she had developed to promote shared decision making. Her elegantly simple questionnaire helped patients (or "consumers," as she calls those with mental illness) turn their psychiatric appointments into occasions for shared decision making. I knew then why she had earned such trust and respect among her peers.

A critical understanding that Dr. Deegan has, and that she urges others to consider, is that being in recovery is not being cured. Pat knows that her illness has not gone away. The recovery she describes is hard work, *and* she expects to be an equal partner in her care. Who better to make major decisions in her life than she?

Shared decision making means respecting a patient's role in making choices about his or her own life. It is the opposite of "doctor knows best." Although shared decision making can be a tough adjustment for doctors used to the medical model, those who can adjust discover that their patients *prefer* to join in decisions about themselves (don't we all?)—often for the better, and, yes, sometimes for the worse. When patients are involved in decision making about themselves, they also are far more likely to follow up on their chosen treatments.

When considering shared decision making, it is important to distinguish *acute* conditions from *chronic* conditions—be they mental health problems or physical ones. If the condition is acute, it is the *doctor* who may need to make the immediate treatment decisions. For example, a person with blood pressure of 190/135, on the verge of a stroke, is experiencing an acute medical state that carries great risk of irreversible damage to the body and brain. Under these emergency circumstances, a doctor needs to take control of the treatment plan—especially since the patient's capacity to think clearly is compromised by the acute medical condition. But when it comes to managing *chronic* high blood pressure, for example, patients need to be equal partners, sharing in decision making about their health and treatment.

Mental disorders are no different. When people with bipolar disorder are acutely manic, their judgment usually goes out the window. People experiencing mania are at risk of engaging in highly damaging behaviors like reckless spending or sexual escapades that endanger their health and family relations. Acute mania is the mental health equivalent of being on the verge of a stroke. (As is suicidal depression or an episode of intense paranoid psychosis.) At these times, shared decision making has its limits. But once the mania has subsided, shared decision making needs to come back into play.

Treatment Should Meet Cultural and Linguistic Needs

Patient preferences are integrally tied to a person's cultural identity and beliefs. How does a person's culture affect how he or she thinks of the illness, or what the acceptable approaches to treatment are? What does mental illness mean in one cultural group and how is it different from another? What supports are culturally acceptable and what stigma does mental illness confer upon the person affected and the family?

These are complex questions that need to be incorporated into the work of mental health services. In many mental health programs, though not all, cultural assessments of patients are standard practice. Staff training includes learning about a patient's background and culture in order to develop a treatment plan that responds to the person's cultural beliefs and needs.

When you seek treatment for your loved one, try to find clinicians and programs that recognize the importance of understanding different cultural beliefs and values. Local NAMI, MHA, and Network of Care referral agencies can often be helpful in learning about which agencies can meet your needs. Similarly, patient and family linguistic needs must be met. In New York City there are 181 languages spoken, and about a third of people residing in the city have English as a second language. Countless other large cities are also wonderful melting pots where the primary language spoken can change every few blocks. But the more diverse the community, the more responsive and thorough the clinic needs to be in attending to its patients' needs.

In screening for depression, for example, there is a patient questionnaire that has been translated into nine languages (see the PHQ-9 in Appendix C). This allows medical and psychiatric practices to identify and manage depression where it would otherwise not be possible because of the limitations of language. But a great workforce challenge in mental health is the availability of clinicians who can speak the primary language of their patient and family. When possible, this is the most desirable scenario. When it is not possible, using other family members and trusted friends is essential to ensure that what is said by patients, families, and clinicians is understood by all involved.

Treatment Should Be Recovery-Oriented

There have been two U.S. Presidential Commissions on Mental Health. The first, in 1979 during the Carter administration, was led by First Lady Rosalyn Carter. Almost 25 years later, in 2003, President George W. Bush called for a second Mental Health Commission, which was led by Michael F. Hogan, PhD, then the Ohio Commissioner of Mental Health.

Among the very first people that Dr. Hogan asked to testify before the President's New Freedom Commission was Mrs. Carter. When asked how she thought mental health had changed since her commission, Mrs. Carter did not say that treatments were more advanced, or that greater civil liberties were assured for people with mental illness, or that stigma had been reduced. Instead, the former First Lady said that the biggest change was that the concept of *recovery* was transforming the field of mental health.

I think of recovery as rooted in *hope*. A fundamental tenet of recovery is that people with mental and addictive disorders can have (or rebuild) satisfying lives for themselves. Patients in recovery, as well as their families and other supports, must believe that they can achieve what we all want: meaningful relationships, purposeful work, and pride in the lives we lead.

Before recovery became a de rigueur goal in the mental health field, far too many people with mental illness were told what Dr. Deegan was told: to bury their hopes for a satisfying life and reconcile themselves to a marginal life as a mental patient. Not much hope there. Instead, recovery-oriented treatment says it is possible to have a *life with illness*. Recovery does not pretend that a person is not ill; rather, it recognizes that illness calls for *adaptations*. Just as people with diabetes or arthritis will have to manage physical symptoms and functional challenges, so too will individuals with mental illnesses have to manage their symptoms and their daily lives.

Doctors who practice a recovery orientation discover how much their patients can motivate themselves and achieve their goals. And that's a pleasure for patient, family, and doctor alike!

So what does recovery-oriented treatment mean in practice? It means that clinicians believe the following:

- *Recovery is optimistic*. It means helping the patient and family identify and accent the person's strengths, so that life is not singularly focused on illness and disability.
- *Recovery is about accountability*. It is helping patients set their own goals and take responsibility for themselves.
- *Recovery is about being a good manager*. It is about a person learning how to best manage his or her illness, which includes learning about triggers that induce symptoms or relapse and how to cope with them, how to use medication effectively, how to build supportive communities of friends, and how to regain a life in the world of school or work.

Don't be shy about encouraging your loved one to ask the mental health professional about his or her orientation. (You can also ask, if you have the chance.) I encourage questions like:

- "Have you heard about recovery in mental health? What does it mean to you?"
- "Can people with mental illness, including persistent conditions, work or have satisfying relationships?"
- "Have your patients been able to return to school? Work? Marry?"
- "What do you think gives people with illness the strength to rebuild their lives?"
- "If I were to ask another of your patients, or their family, to describe you, what might they say? Especially about your belief in patients getting better?"

I will return to how recovery works in Chapter 11.

Three Terms: *Prevention, Course,* and *Prognosis*

Before moving on to discuss how and where you can obtain mental health services, let's take a short look at a few basic terms you may hear as you travel through the world of healthcare. Although these terms may seem a bit technical, they'll help you better understand the thinking and practices that you will encounter in clinical care and the delivery of mental health services.

PREVENTION

Most people think of *prevention* literally: doing something that prevents something unwanted from happening. In medicine, mental health, and public health, *prevention* is a complex and layered concept. It is defined as: all actions taken to (1) reduce the onset of a disease, *or* (2) decrease disease severity or duration, *or* (3) decrease the likelihood of a disease becoming fatal. Descriptions of the different types of prevention—*primary, secondary,* and *tertiary*—can help you understand this concept as it is used by mental and public health professionals.

Primary Prevention. This is what we customarily think of when considering prevention. It refers to the actions we take to *prevent the development* of a disease in the first place.

Primary prevention in general medicine would be good nutrition and exercise to avoid heart disease or limiting the use of sugar and salt to help prevent diabetes and high blood pressure. It is washing your hands frequently during flu season. It is using a condom during sex with an unknown partner. It is not smoking.

In mental health, primary prevention is avoiding drugs and alcohol as an adolescent and young adult if your family has a history of mental illness. It is about helping mothers and fathers effectively parent. It is about rooting out domestic violence and maintaining supportive and non-abusive relationships.

Secondary Prevention. This is *early detection of a disease and then early intervention*. Examples of secondary prevention are: screening for high blood pressure, mammograms for women, colonoscopies for adults over 50, and screening for PTSD, depression, and substance abuse in veterans. Secondary prevention also includes identifying depression or drug abuse in youth and helping them receive effective treatments. It is taking a family member to a family doctor, therapist, or clinic if you notice serious changes in mood or behavior that last more than a couple of weeks.

When a condition is detected, secondary prevention also involves initiating treatment as soon as possible, and delivering proven treatments as consistently as possible over the course of illness. Doing so increases the likelihood that a person will suffer a less severe illness with a shorter duration.

Tertiary Prevention. This is *disease management*. Tertiary prevention enables a person who already has an illness to achieve maximum functioning with minimal pain and suffering, including minimizing any relapses and halting the progression of a disease. Tertiary prevention includes delivering evidence-based treatments coupled with self-management and wellness efforts (see Chapters 8 and 11). For people with bipolar disorder, for example, tertiary prevention means taking mood-stabilizing medication, recognizing and managing interpersonal and work stresses, getting proper sleep, eating well, and monitoring and limiting alcohol consumption. For people with schizophrenia, tertiary prevention means taking antipsychotic medications, strengthening interpersonal and work skills, staying in school or in a job, having supportive, informed families, and living in communities that are not stigmatizing.

For people with alcohol and drug dependencies, tertiary prevention is learning relapse-prevention techniques and using trustworthy people, medications, and alternative-medicine practices (like nutritional supplements, yoga, and acupuncture) to assist in staying clean and sober.

COURSE AND PROGNOSIS

Diseases have a path they take over time. Most mental disorders, like other medical disorders, do not go away in days or weeks—they persist over time. The severity of the symptoms, and how those symptoms affect daily life, will vary, as with any persistent illness. How long a disease lasts and its pattern over time is what's known as *the course of an illness*. As you can imagine, the course can vary significantly from patient to patient, but each patient's course of illness can be quite responsive to effective treatments and health-oriented self-management.

Prognosis refers to where the path of illness will take someone. Its roots lie in the Greek *pro* (before) and *gnosis* (knowing). Prognosis literally means knowing ahead of time—or at least having an educated guess. Even a best guess or informed prediction of a disease's outcome in terms of *morbidity* (which means severity of symptoms and degree of functional loss) and *mortality* (the likelihood of death) is just that: a guess. There is enormous variation in prognosis for any illness, including mental illness. I have seen people with what might be regarded as minor anxiety disorders do poorly over time, and people with serious mental disorders, like schizophrenia and bipolar disorder, build lives of purpose, quality, and contribution.

Don't let any doctor or mental health professional tell your loved one that he or she is fated for a life not worth living—or, alternately, that there is nothing to worry about. There are just too many variables that affect the course and prognosis of a mental illness for any clinician to give these kinds of absolute—and dismissive—messages. What you and your loved one should hear is that recovery is possible, and that there is every reason to be hopeful—but only if we all work together using all that we know and all that we can learn and do.

Getting Help:
The Referral, the Doctor, the Meeting

L et's recap. You have a strong sense that a loved one or friend is suffering from mental illness, and you know you need to trust your judgment. You believe that person—partner, brother, sister, mother, father, son, daughter, or friend—needs to be seen by a doctor or mental health professional who can make a diagnosis, develop and initiate a treatment plan, and, in the process, help begin to settle your fears.

Moreover, hopefully your loved one has admitted that something is wrong (perhaps the suggestions given in Chapter 1 helped)—or, at least, has agreed to see someone, whether it's the family doctor, a mental health professional, or someone else you trust.

You are off to a good start. You have overcome one of the biggest hurdles for families facing a mental health problem: persuading a reluctant person that he or she has a problem and needs help. That is a big, critical step. But *now* what happens?

That's what this chapter is all about. I will describe the various options available for those about to take the crucial next step of finding help for their loved one—not just any help, mind you, but help from someone who is humane, experienced, and competent in diagnosing and treating mental illness and assisting in the demanding path of recovery. You want to find the right professional because a strong, trusting relationship between patient and clinician is an essential ingredient for recovery.

For too long, most Americans—4 out of 5—with a treatable mental disorder have not received appropriate mental health care to start them on the road to recovery. Many culprits are responsible for this abysmal statistic: confusion about where and to whom to turn for help, misdiagnosis, inattention to evidence-based (proven) treatments, poor follow-up once treatment has started, and demoralization along the way—to name a few.

This does not have to be your story. With sound information about how to find, access, and sustain quality mental health treatment, your family's course can be better. I want you and other families to be prepared when you walk in the door of a clinic or a psychiatrist's office and be able to judge whether what you hear feels right for your loved one.

In other words, "forewarned is forearmed." When you know what to look for as well as what to avoid—and go into appointments with a list of clear, thought-out questions that deserve to be answered—you will be far more able to assess and obtain the quality of mental health professional or program that your loved one needs. That maxim holds true whether you live in a large city replete with mental health services or in a rural region where the nearest help may be 75 miles away.

Finding Help

As I mentioned earlier, many people who suspect a loved one may be mentally ill first go to other professionals or organizations—a family doctor or pediatrician, school social workers or psychologists, the clergy, EAPs, or NAMI. All of these sources can provide referrals to specialists if needed. However, some people will be in a position to seek services directly from a mental health professional. There are a number of ways this can be done.

One of the best ways to find a mental health professional is to ask friends or relatives, people whom you trust, for a referral. Many people find a good mental health professional by word of mouth. Those with experiences with services in the world of mental health, whether they are other families, friends, or patients themselves, usually know more about doctors and mental health professionals than anyone else. If you know a family or someone who has a mental illness for which he or she is being treated, do not hesitate to ask that person.

There are generally two other ways by which families find local services. One is through resource phone numbers or websites in your own community. (National information and referral programs can also identify the services in your area.) The other is by turning to local brick-and-mortar professionals or programs.

Hotlines or Help Lines. These are phone-based programs, run by local or national organizations, which you can call for information and a mental health referral. Check your city or town's website to see what is available. Another excellent resource is the Network of Care website (www.networkofcare.org), which lists community-based mental health services available to both children and adults across the country. The site includes information on everything from outpatient and inpatient psychiatric facilities for mental health assessments to clinics that offer counseling to individuals and families. Network of Care also features an extensive digital library that offers practical articles on medications and therapies.

Private Practitioners and Clinics. In the next section I will review the major types of mental health professionals. Private practitioners may work solo or in small groups. They set their own fees, and many take insurance payments. Some practice in multidisciplinary groups where a psychiatrist teams with other mental health professionals or has working affiliations with other mental health professionals.

Local Hospitals and Mental Health Clinics. There are a great many nonprofit organizations, including hospitals and mental health or addiction clinics, across the country that provide services. These group practices generally take all forms of third-party insurance and some are able to discount their fees.

Who's Who in the World of Mental Health?

After you have obtained the names of one or more mental health professionals, you may see an alphabet soup of letters next to these names— MD, LCMSW, MSW, PhD, PsyD, RN—and feel bewildered. That's to be expected—which is what I told Melissa when she came to my office some time ago. Close friends and a minister had given her my name, along with two others, because she was experiencing debilitating anxiety in the midst of a separation from her husband of 9 years. Melissa selected me because she thought she should see a psychiatrist (which generally is a matter more of preference, especially for people not in crisis or with serious mental illness); the other names on her list included a social worker and a clinical psychologist.

"What do you do and how is it different from these other professionals?" she asked. "Do I really need to see a psychiatrist or can someone else help me? What is your fee and how does it compare to what these other professionals might charge?" You too may have the same ques-

> **Mental Health Professionals**
>
> Therapist or psychotherapist
>
> Social worker (MSW, LCSW, and LMSW)
>
> Psychiatric/mental health nurse practitioner (PNP)
>
> Psychologist (MS, MA, PhD, PsyD and EdD)
>
> Psychoanalyst
>
> Psychiatrist (MD and DO)
>
> Psychopharmacologist (MD and DO)

tions. Here are some answers.

Therapist or Psychotherapist. These terms generally refer more to the type of work a clinician does than to his or her credentials. Theoretically, anyone—trained or not—who offers counseling can call him- or herself a therapist, so you will want to know if the person has licensed credentials in your state that qualify him or her to provide you with professional care. Of course, having a license does not always equate with someone doing good, or bad, work. It does mean, however, that the clinician has completed a recognized training program and passed standardized professional examinations. There are excellent non-licensed therapists, but if you decide to use their services, make sure you check their reputation first.

Social Worker. Social workers are trained professionals who may offer counseling, psychotherapy, or assistance with managing the complexities of the mental health system. Someone who is a master of social work (MSW), a licensed clinical social worker (LCSW), or a licensed master social worker (LMSW) is trained in psychiatric diagnosis and treatment but cannot prescribe medication, although many work in a group practice or affiliate with a psychiatrist or physician who can. Typically, a social worker's fee is less than that of a doctoral-level clinical psychologist or psychiatrist.

Some social workers work in private practice; others work in mental health and medical clinics, schools, or hospitals, where they provide evaluation, therapy, and support services to people in need. They work with individuals and at times with families. Some especially focus on knowing and linking people to a range of social services (like entitlement programs such as Medicaid or Medicare, community clinics and rehabilitation programs, and housing). This often is considered "case management" and reflects the profession's roots in community services.

Psychiatric/Mental Health Nurse Practitioner. These highly trained and licensed nurses can evaluate, diagnose, and treat individuals with mental health disorders. They provide counseling and therapy services in a variety of settings. Some prescribe medication under the supervision of or in collaboration with a psychiatrist. Their role in prescribing medication has become increasingly common, as physician time is so limited, especially in high-need and rural areas.

Psychologist. A psychologist has a master's (MS, MA) or doctoral degree (PhD, PsyD, or EdD) in clinical, educational, experimental, developmental, or social psychology. Many people think psychologists all have doctoral degrees; many do, but not all. What may be most important for you is their experience in caring for patients and families, not just their degree or whether they have research experience.

Some states allow psychologists to prescribe medication if they've been trained to do so, but even in those states it's generally rare for psychologists to undergo that training. Very few psychologists prescribe medication. They often, however, work with psychiatrists (or primary-care or family doctors) who do.

Psychologists take formal graduate training after college and are licensed by the state they practice in. Some practice on their own and some in groups with other mental health or medical practitioners. Some psychologists devote their lives to teaching and research. Those who work with patients are known as *clinical psychologists*. Psychologists may specialize in certain treatment approaches such as cognitive-behavioral therapy, interpersonal therapy, or psychodynamic therapy; I'll talk about these types of therapy in subsequent chapters.

Psychoanalyst. A psychoanalyst is a highly specialized mental health professional who has taken years of specialty training in the technique of psychoanalysis—the intensive, lie-down-on-the-couch approach about which the media has produced its share of cartoons. Psychoanalysts can be psychiatrists, psychologists, or social workers, and there are some lay (nonprofessional) analysts as well. Cartoons notwithstanding, there are not many psychoanalysts in practice, and they concentrate in large cities. Very few people are good candidates for the exceptionally demanding work of psychoanalysis. The analytic technique calls for years of treatment and 2 to 5 sessions per week, often lying on a couch, with a focus on exploring the inner workings of the mind, relationships, and dream interpretation. I know of no insurance today that pays for psychoanalysis.

Psychiatrists. Psychiatrists are physicians—medical doctors (MDs) or doctors of osteopathy (DOs)—who graduated from medical or osteopathy school and then completed a 4-year psychiatric residency. A psychiatrist can prescribe medication and has a state medical license. Many, but not all, have a board certification in psychiatry, which means they passed written tests and are examined in interviewing, diagnosing, and treatment for patients. Fewer and fewer psychiatrists today provide therapy (in addition to medication); instead, many tend to concentrate on diagnosis and prescribing medication. Some are treatment-team leaders or administrators in hospitals and clinics. **Psychopharmacologists** are psychiatrists who specialize in psychiatric medications and their management.

FEES

The fees for professional treatment vary enormously. Some fees are set by insurers (like Blue Cross/Blue Shield, Aetna, or United Health Care) or by government payment programs (like Medicaid and Medicare). I discuss insurance in more detail in Chapter 9. Some clinics and hospitals have their own fee schedules (which are available to you); these fees may be different from what has been either set or agreed to by your insurance plan. The same applies to private practitioners. This means that you may be responsible for the difference between what your insurance pays and the fee charged by the mental health professional or practice. Social workers, advanced-practice nurses, and master's degree psychologists tend to be at the lower end of the fees charged, with doctoral-level psychologists and psychiatrists tending to be at the higher end. However, some practitioners of any discipline (even lay therapists) may have fees that instead reflect their experience and how much they are in demand.

Qualities of a Good Mental Health Clinician

Regardless of the degree the mental health care provider has, you want someone who *listens, explains, and tries to develop a set of common goals with the patient*. You also will want to know if the clinician believes in combining medication with therapy and treatment techniques that build skills for school, work, or family life. Not all treatment has to involve both medication and therapy or skill building, but the combination *should* be considered, and psychiatrists who assert treatment only with medication or clinicians who insist only on therapy should be considered cautiously. It's also important to ask if the clinician appreciates the importance of family and friends, of school and community, of hope for recovery and having a life one can be proud of.

If choosing a psychiatrist, try to find one who is board certified. If you know you may need specialized services—such as for a child or adolescent, or a senior, or for treatment of recurrent depression, bipolar disorder,eating disorders, trauma, substance abuse, and so on—then seek those services from the start, if available and possible. Such a degree of specialization may more easily be found in cities and some academic centers but may not be possible in other geographic areas or clinical practices.

I cannot emphasize enough how important it is that you and your loved one become highly educated consumers of mental health services and the professionals who provide them. You *don't* need to go to psychology or medical school, take exams, or get a state license to practice. But you *do* need to come to understand who has the skills to provide therapy, medications, and other services your loved one may need. By asking the right questions you can gain information that helps you judge whether your family member is getting the right care.

What to Ask (and Know)

As a family member or friend you may be involved, first hand, with the treatment your loved one receives. Or you may be on the sidelines assisting and supporting. The questions I offer here are meant to be asked by whoever can ask them. That might be you, or it might be the person seeking treatment. In either case, you can try to inform your loved one and help sort out whether he or she is in good hands.

In first meeting with a mental health professional—even in the midst of an urgent situation or crisis—you want to know that person's training, experience, and skills. If you can, search online for the clinician your family member will see or encourage your loved one to ask, when meeting, about the clinician's training and work experiences. Of course, a young clinician with less than a PhD may still be able to provide good service, but knowing that person's credentials beforehand will better equip you to make a decision about whether the treatment provided is of good quality.

You also want to ask questions about the clinician's approach to diagnosis and treatment. What types of clinical settings has the clinician worked in, and what kinds of mental health or addictive problems does he or she have experience with? Patients seeking surgical services, for example, have learned to ask how many surgeries a doctor has done, and at what hospitals, because for operations, "practice makes perfect."

Even if practice doesn't make perfect, it's usually a lot better than no practice at all. A clinician's training, experience, and understanding of illnesses and their treatments can also help in matching your loved one's needs and preferences with the "right" professional. At the end of this chapter, I offer specific suggestions about how to prepare for the appointment and what else to look for.

A word about clinicians-in-training. These include social-work interns, psychologists in practicums (training sites), and psychiatric residents (fully trained physicians during their 4-year post-medical-school specialty training), among others. These trainees are supervised by senior clinicians where they work, though supervision can vary tremendously. In my opinion, talented, dedicated, and highly responsible trainees, in good programs with good supervision, can offer very capable and helpful services. The problem, sometimes, is that they move on to other training sites or complete their programs—so don't be shy about asking how long a trainee will be at the program or hospital you turn to.

Other Factors that Affect Where to Turn for Help

There are many other factors that shape the selection of a mental health professional. One is where your loved one lives. Geography can be destiny when it comes to mental health care in the United States. If you live in a rural area, there are far fewer mental health care specialists available than there are in more urban settings.

In many rural areas, in fact, the family doctor may be the person your loved one turns to, because finding a psychiatrist—especially one who has practice time available—may be very difficult. If assessment by a family doctor or a local social worker reveals a serious mental disorder in a family member, you may need to seek additional help in a nearby big town or city. Even if you do pursue treatment in a larger city, be sure to maintain contact with your local doctor or clinician, as many family doctors can call psychiatric colleagues if they need immediate assistance in making decisions about your loved one's treatment.

Your family member's health insurance coverage will often play a very great role—often more than what seems right or fair—regarding which professionals and what treatments will be covered. Some insurance companies have their own network of clinics and clinicians and require the insured person to seek care within that network in order to obtain insurance payment. Others contract with private practitioners (psychiatrists, psychologists, social workers, nurses, and others) and will provide the insured person a list of professionals whom they identify for you to call for an appointment. I have heard, as have others, countless stories of people who call clinicians on these lists only to be told there are no appointments available, or that the next appointment isn't available for weeks, or that the doctor isn't accepting new patients, and so on. This state of affairs, sadly, is a reflection of the anger that many clinicians have developed with insurance companies, whom the professionals believe overly manage yet underpay them. Some clinicians stay on lists as "insurance," if you will, in case their practice dries up, but avoid taking referrals if they can.

Insurance companies, especially commercial payers (not Medicaid or Medicare), typically cap the number of visits (or money paid for services) a patient can have. In 2008, a federal law was passed on what is called "parity" mental health coverage; it requires that mental health and addiction coverage be no different from medical/surgical coverage. This is a great legal breakthrough that has yet to fully translate into practice. Some insurance companies also require that subscribers obtain "preauthorization"—that is, approval—for a service on the phone before an appointment will be granted or paid.

If your loved one is covered by Medicaid, the state insurance for people living in poverty as well as for many children, this will require going to a local mental health clinic or hospital, as virtually no psychiatrist (and very few mental health professionals) in private practice will take Medicaid because the fee paid is less than what it costs to fill the gas tank of a small car. But keep in mind that many clinics have good teams of mental health professionals that include a psychiatrist; many provide the comprehensive psychiatric and therapeutic care that a serious mental illness requires.

If your family member is covered by Medicare, the federal insurance for seniors and the disabled, the chances of getting an appointment with a psychiatrist are usually better, because fees are a little higher and because there are fewer hassles with managed care or payment.

Even though insurance may be the last thing you or your loved one wants to deal with, deal with it you must. (See Chapter 9 for more on paying for mental health services.) Make it a priority—for your loved one or another family member—to call the insurance carrier even if you're busy making appointments or trying to manage distress at home or work. You will want to know what professional and program choices are available, and everyone involved will want to avoid surprises (also known as "denials of care"). Being unable to pay for treatment will add grievously to your loved one's or family's troubles. As I discuss later in the book, some people wisely seek services in the public mental health sector in order not to be left with bills that will add crushing financial misfortune to their problems.

Dealing with insurance companies may seem overwhelming, but, as I will say again and again in this book, mental health problems (including addictions), are among the most common medical problems that exist, and they cause serious suffering and interfere with functioning at home and work. These conditions can be reliably diagnosed—and there are treatments that work. But those affected need to get care, as soon as possible, and stick with it. Your family has good reason to seek help and be hopeful.

A Word About Patient Preference

All medical care, mental health and addiction treatments included, understands the power of what is called *patient preference*. We all have preferences—in what we eat, drink, wear, and will seek (and stay with) as a treatment. Skilled doctors pay attention to what patients and their loved ones want, especially when there are several effective options available for treatment. A treatment that a patient prefers is far more likely to be followed (and believed in) than one the patient has doubts about. A good doctor knows how important it is to recognize patient preferences and use them to improve adherence to treatment, and thus outcome.

Take mild to moderate depression, for example. Scientific studies indicate that medication alone or psychotherapy alone can be effective. A crucial question then becomes not which treatment is "right," but which the patient *prefers*. The same holds true for physical illnesses. For example, some patients with serious heart conditions prefer surgery, whereas others prefer diligent management with medications and lifestyle changes. Similarly, if someone suffering from depression is reluctant to take even the occasional aspirin for a headache or muscle soreness, that person may not be too keen on taking an antidepressant, preferring changes in diet, exercise, and therapy instead.

Decisions about combining treatments also may be heavily influenced by patient preference. Siding with a patient's preference for one over the other, instead of insisting on both, may be better than going against a patient's preference, where the result could be that neither treatment is followed. If the patient's choice works, case closed. If not, a doctor can then advise again about combining treatments to optimize results.

It's important to remember that you don't want to waste time—yours, your loved one's, or the doctor's—by making promises you won't keep.

Whenever possible, have your loved one talk through treatment options and decisions with the mental health professionals involved in the person's care. Together, clinicians, patients, and families want to select treatments that work *and* consider patient preferences, including culture, beliefs, and lifestyle.

Prepare for the Appointment

Take the time to prepare for the meeting with the doctor or mental health professional. The initial meeting is crucial for helping the clinician understand your loved one's concerns—and for helping *you* understand what the clinician thinks about those concerns. It's when initial ideas about the treatment plan will be developed, and it's your chance to learn about what that treatment will entail. You have a limited amount of time to cover a lot of ground in the initial meeting, so preparing for it ahead of time is critical.

MAKE A LIST OF CONCERNS

Create a list of what concerns your loved one (and your family) has. You want to be clear and concise about what you will say when you go to the appointment. Get someone you trust to help you. Ask your loved one to summarize what has happened, over time, that has led to the troubles that have emerged. Be honest. Don't leave things out because of guilt or shame. Everything will come out in time, so the sooner everything is disclosed, the sooner you'll be able to get help for it. Summarize this information on a single side of a piece of paper that your loved one (or you) can refer to during the meeting with the clinician.

For example, your concerns might include:

- I haven't been able to sleep more than a few hours at a time for 3 months.
- When I try to work, my mind wanders, I feel very nervous, and I want to run away from whatever I need to do.
- My family is worried that my weight loss and eating habits will

cause a heart attack.

- My mother is on my case all the time about my staying in my room and listening to music and playing video games.
- I've lost all desire for sex.
- Not a day passes when I don't wish that my life will end.
- Everything seems hopeless. I'm hopeless, and I have no future.
- My parents don't understand that there are microphones in our house listening to everything we say.
- Since I got back from deployment, I have to drink myself to sleep.

MAKE A SHORT LIST OF QUESTIONS

I can't tell you how many people leave initial appointments disappointed, discouraged, or angry because a few basic, critical questions they had were not answered. The clinician can't read your mind. Don't assume that what you feel you need to know will be addressed. At the *beginning* of the appointment, tell the clinician that you have a few critical questions to ask and that you need to leave time for those questions before the appointment is over.

For example:

- What is the explanation for the feelings or behaviors I (or my family member) have had?
- Is there a name for these types of problems?
- Do others have these problems? If so, what helps?
- Are there specific treatments for this problem? If so, what are they? How do they work? How long do they take to work?
- Will I (or my family member) ever get over this problem? What are the chances for improvement?
- I wonder if I (or my family member) is drinking too much, or if other drug use is affecting my (or his or her) thinking.
- Is my loved one safe from him- or herself? Is our family in any danger? Are others in danger? If so, what do we need to do to protect ourselves and others?
- Did our family do anything wrong to cause these problems?
- How can our family help our loved one?
- Are there any support groups or programs that our family can turn to?

There are many other questions your loved one or family may want to consider or ask about. The important thing is that you as a family take the time to prepare. Use these examples to help you make a list that is specific to *your* family and situation.

MANAGE TIME WISELY

If you see that the clinician may not have time to answer your questions (for whatever reason), you and your loved one need to try to manage the time. Remind the clinician 10 minutes before the end of the meeting that you want to turn to your questions. That is when your family member, or you, needs to focus on what you need to know, even if there is too little time for the questions to be fully answered. Remember, try to select a few critical questions, as time will not allow for many (at first), and have them written down. Don't surprise your loved one with any unexpected questions during the meeting. For example, if you plan to ask the clinician about your loved one's drinking or drug use, make sure your loved one knows ahead of time that you plan to ask about that subject.

Is the Clinician a Good Fit?

How can you tell if the clinician is right for your loved one? When your family member (or you) meets the clinician, see if the clinician listens and accurately reflects back what you are saying—and does so in a respectful manner. If you sense a gap between what you are saying and what the clinician seems to understand, then say so; you want to know sooner rather than later if any communication gap that may exist can be closed or if differences can be worked out.

If the clinician talks more than listens or has a plan that doesn't seem to have much to do with why your loved one is there or with what your loved one wants to accomplish, you will need to think of where else to turn to succeed. Patients who feel that they have been heard and respected, and whose goals have been considered, are the ones who stay in treatment. Nothing good comes from dropping out of needed treatment. Mental health professionals are getting better at practicing shared decision making, but not all clinicians have adopted this technique, so some may need your help in arriving at a true collaborative approach to treatment.

Finally, in meeting with a psychiatrist or other clinician, keep in mind that he or she is human, just like you. Mental health professionals are not gods; they don't know everything—no one does. Good doctors and clinicians are modest about themselves and the art of clinical care. They put the patient's interests first and offer realistic hope. They consider and respect your loved one and the family, just as you would consider and respect them.

In all cases, remember to trust your feelings and listen to your heart. If you have prepared for the meeting and are clear and honest about your situation, you will have a very good sense early on if you have found someone who can help you in the hard work of recovery from a mental illness. Once you've found the right doctor or therapist, the important work of diagnosis and treatment can begin—with a focus on what needs to be done rather than on wondering if you are in the right person's office.

5

The Places You May Go

When your loved one is suffering from a mental illness, you may find yourself in places you never imagined you would visit. An ER or psychiatric inpatient unit, even a mental health clinic, can be a bewildering place if you don't know what to expect—or how to leverage what you know to make your experience as painless, drama-free, and productive as possible.

By describing some of the settings you may find yourself in, and taking you through what may happen while you're there, I hope to reduce some of the surprise, confusion, and distress you may feel. This will help you obtain the best care possible for your loved one, whether it's in a clinic, an ER, or a psychiatric ward. See Appendix A for a few detailed portraits of specialized mental health settings to which some families may also turn.

Outpatient Clinics

Let's start with the outpatient mental health clinic. A clinic is often the point of entry to the public mental health system or to a hospital outpatient department. It is a service site commonly recommended by doctors, school clinicians, and other professionals, especially when referral to a private therapist or doctor is not possible. The initial clinic appointment is very much like a first appointment in a private mental health professional's office; by understanding what attending a clinic appointment is like, you'll also be able to imagine many office-based mental health experiences.

People who are seeking an evaluation and not experiencing a *true* emergency (a life-or-death situation where someone is at risk of self-harm or harming others, or is showing highly abnormal behavior or thinking) will sooner or later be in a mental health professional's office. Let's look at what happens in this setting.

At the end of Chapter 4, I talked about how to prepare for your appointment with a private physician or mental health professional. You should prepare the same way for your visit to an outpatient clinic:

By way of recap:
- Make a list of concerns you and your loved one have.
- Make a short list of questions you hope to have answered at the end of the appointment. At the beginning of the appointment, tell the clinician that you want to set aside time at the end to have these questions answered.
- Don't surprise other family members or your loved one with new information or unexpected questions. There should be no surprises to anyone who attends the meeting.

If you are informed and vocal, you improve the likelihood your loved one will receive the care he or she needs. The following is the story of one family's experience, which resulted in their son receiving exemplary care.

Tony had always been shy and awkward. He had few friends, and, although he never behaved badly at school, he often had trouble doing schoolwork. He moved on from grade to grade, sort of lost in the crowd. Born to immigrants from southern Europe, he and his younger brother were cherished by their parents, who themselves were uneducated but hardworking people. They attended church regularly, grateful for the life that God had given them in the United States.

When Tony was 17, his behavior began to change quite profoundly. Worried and scared, Tony's parents reached out for help. Tony's mother, Anna, made an appointment for him at a neighborhood health clinic. Although Tony resisted the appointment, he reluctantly went with his mother for an evaluation.

When they entered the reception area, Anna began to worry that one of her neighbors or friends would see them registering in the mental health section of the clinic. This kind of embarrassment about a family member's condition is very common and can prevent families from seeking care. Thankfully, Anna was able to manage her feelings in order to respond to her son's problems. Tony and Anna filled out insurance paperwork and HIPAA forms to ensure that Tony's mental health history would be shared only with those designated to know. (HIPAA is the Health Insurance Portability and Accountability Act, a federal law described in Chapter 10 that requires privacy protections for patients.)

Mr. August, a social worker, introduced himself to Tony and his mother. He suggested that the meeting start with both of them and then continue just with Tony. Anna didn't understand why they weren't seeing a medical doctor, but she was too timid to ask. But Mr. August explained that he was part of a team of mental health professionals (including a psychiatrist) who worked together to care for patients. He said his job was to help Tony and his mother understand what was happening and what could be done to help.

Mr. August then asked Tony if he wanted to start by explaining what had brought him to the clinic. "I came to get her off my back," Tony said, adding, "I believe in Jesus and he will show me the way." Tony then fell silent and averted his eyes from Mr. August and his mother. After failed attempts to reengage Tony, Mr. August turned to Anna. Anxious and ashamed, she said: "We are a Christian family. We go to church and we work hard and care for our children. But Tony is changing—he's so hard to talk to now, he wants to be alone, and he doesn't even spend time with his brother. The school says he is missing days and not paying attention. And a few nights ago, he woke us all up screaming. When I went into his room, it looked like a storm had hit it."

In response to Mr. August's questions, Anna provided some family history and details about Tony, but there was not much of note: No members of the family had suffered a mental illness, had alcohol or drug problems, been to jail, or attempted or completed suicide, and there were no weapons in the house. Mr. August followed up by asking Anna about Tony's development as a child, as well as about his school performance and social history with friends and dating.

Throughout these questions, Tony sat immobile, staring at the wall and clenching his fists. Eventually, Anna left so that Mr. August could continue the interview just with Tony.

Mr. August understood that he would need to begin talking, not just ask questions. He began speaking about other young men and women who had come to this clinic when they were having a hard time or knew that they could do better at school or with friends. He tried to ask questions about what kind of music Tony listened to, or sports he liked to watch or play, and how he liked to spend his time; he got mostly one-word answers.

However, Tony came alive when asked about his religious beliefs. He said, "I have a special relationship with God. . . . That was what caused the devil to target me for destruction. The devil has been hiding in my room, but when I search I can't find him. I was yelling the other night, like my mom said, but that was to show him who was the boss."

Mr. August recognized Tony's outburst as characteristic of a psychotic illness, where imagined ideas take on the full force of fact. He could recognize that what Tony was describing was different from a deep religious belief and was, instead, the disordered thinking, delusional ideas, and likely hallucinations that are signs of serious mental illness. Mr. August's next step was to consider what might be causing Tony's psychosis. In medicine, separating out one causal condition from another is known as "differential diagnosis," a technique glorified in the television program House. The technique is also used in the diagnosis of mental illness. Mr. August wondered (to himself) about a drug-induced psychosis (for example, from high doses of marijuana, powerful synthetic drugs like K2 or Spice, or Ecstasy) as well as about potential physical causes, such as an infection or brain tumor. (Non-medical mental health professionals should consider these physical causes in diagnosis and turn to physicians if there is good reason to suspect such a cause.)

Mr. August completed his meeting with Tony by asking if there were any goals Tony wanted to achieve. Tony did not respond, having retreated into himself once again. Mr. August told Tony he would ask his mother to return. When she did, Mr. August briefly described what he and Tony had spoken about, and he described which of Tony's behaviors supported his initial diagnostic impression. Mr. August told them that he thought Tony was having difficulty with his thinking: that his troubled thinking was affecting his ability to be the son and student they both knew and wanted to see again. Mr. August did not yet use the word "psychosis," although he wrote it in his clinical notes.

Instead, Mr. August told them that Tony should meet with the clinic psychiatrist, Dr. Smith. He explained that although Dr. Smith was not a child and adolescent psychiatrist by training, she often worked with young people like Tony. Mr. August ended the meeting by telling them that, although Tony's behavior was distressing, he could be helped through treatment. Mr. August thought that Tony was not an immediate danger to himself or others, and he gave Tony and Anna appointment cards for further evaluation with Dr. Smith. He also gave them his personal office number, to call in case any questions or concerns arose before their next appointment.

SIGNS OF A GOOD CLINICIAN

Mr. August demonstrated all the signs of a good clinician who is prepared to give quality care.

- He spoke with both Anna and Tony, engaging them both in the evaluation in order to obtain information.
- He took a family history and social history.
- He used differential diagnosis in assessing Tony's condition and developing his initial impression.
- He did not offer a diagnostic impression that went beyond what he could support—or that was more than the family could bear to hear.
- He involved Tony in the evaluation and treatment process by asking about his individual goals (even though Tony declined to state those goals).
- He assessed that Tony would be safe until his next appointment.
- He made himself available before the next appointment, if needed.

Why didn't Mr. August tell Tony and Anna that he thought Tony was experiencing a psychotic illness? There are at least two reasons:

- He didn't want to scare them away by using a term they might find unfamiliar and frightening.
- He wanted to confirm his impression with another mental health professional and through more meetings with Tony.

If consultation with another mental health professional and future meetings with Tony supported Mr. August's diagnostic impression, he would then share more information with the patient and the family, encouraging them to ask questions as they began to understand Tony's illness.

SIGNS OF GOOD DECISION MAKING BY A FAMILY MEMBER

Tony's mother was resourceful, and she did the right thing by bringing Tony to her neighborhood health clinic. If she'd let her embarrassment or fear stop her from seeking care so early, Tony's psychosis might have escalated, and they may have found themselves in a crisis situation.

Anna was fortunate in that she was able to convince Tony to go to the clinic, and their situation had not yet worsened to a state that threatened Tony's safety or the safety of those around him. But what if you aren't as fortunate as Anna? What should you do if your attempts to engage your loved one in outpatient treatment are failing, and you believe that he or she may not be safe? Going to an emergency room is one option, but there are other places to seek help before you take that more extreme, if sometimes necessary, measure.

Crisis Services

Some communities have what are called *crisis services*. These services are operated by community mental health agencies and staffed by professionals who respond to crises in the community. Generally, two clinical staff members come to a patient's home to evaluate the person and the situation and suggest what can be done. As a rule, no treatment is begun (including no medication) at that time. Crisis-service response time varies, from hours to days. If you can safely wait a few days for the evaluation, then do so. If you can't, skip ahead to my discussion of emergency services.

A national hotline can help you find crisis services: Call the National Suicide Prevention Lifeline (1-800-273-TALK). Although their name indicates suicide prevention, the Lifeline is a great resource for all mental health crises, as well as non-crisis situations.

Safety must always be your number one priority—the safety of your loved one *and* the safety of your family and community. It is not dramatic to classify a family member as having a "mental health emergency" if you fear for that person's safety or your own—in these cases you need to go to where emergencies are the daily fare: a hospital emergency room. Just as you would go to an ER if a loved one were having an urgent physical problem, you should also visit the ER if your loved one is having extremely disturbed thinking or behavior, especially if it's threatening anyone's safety.

The Emergency Room

Few places are as unnerving as an ER. It's better to evaluate a patient in an outpatient office than to go through the stress of the emergency room, but in some cases that's not always possible.

WHEN TO USE AN EMERGENCY ROOM

There is a reason these places are called *emergency* rooms. They're there for crisis situations that demand immediate attention. The following situations are examples of when to go to the ER:

- After a suicide attempt
- If you discover someone in the process of attempting suicide
- If you are assaulted or threatened with assault by a person with a mental illness, or if you have reason to believe that person may hurt someone else
- If a person appears overwhelmed with hearing voices or feeling persecuted (or other seriously distressing disturbances of thought)
- If a person's thinking is seriously and suddenly confused—confused about where the person is, what day or month it is, or if the person has trouble recognizing familiar people or places

There may be other situations in which a visit to the ER is called for, although they're less common. For example, a family member described how she had tried countless times to take her father, who had become reclusive and deeply depressed, to a doctor for evaluation. He refused every time. Then one day, out of the blue, he said, *"I will go now."* Now meant now. Not tomorrow, but right then and there. Worried, his daughter took him to an emergency room for evaluation.

I've also seen many families go to an ER after becoming discouraged with other mental health care services—usually after being told they'll have to wait 6 weeks (or more) for an appointment with a psychiatrist in order to obtain needed medications. These situations are not emergencies—they are a desperate response to the failure of our mental health system. As such, they are understandable but, unfortunately, not very effective.

Emergency rooms are hectic places. To begin with, you are surrounded by the anxiety and stress of emergencies: You are *in* an emergency *and* in an emergency *setting*. You have come to the ER (or ED, emergency department) because someone you love or are responsible for requires urgent attention. He or she may have attempted suicide or become threatening or violent, or your efforts to secure other mental health services have failed and you believe the risk of something terrible happening can no longer be endured.

WHEN NOT TO GO TO AN EMERGENCY ROOM

Don't go to an emergency room for:

- A medication refill
- To find a psychiatrist or arrange an outpatient appointment
- To apply for Medicaid or some sort of social welfare benefit

Using an ER for these kinds of services is not only unproductive for you but also requires the staff to put aside actual urgent cases in order to spend time on your request.

GETTING THROUGH AN EMERGENCY ROOM VISIT

Throughout your emergency room visit, you need to remember that your loved one often does not want to be there. Not knowing how your loved one will react adds to the stress and unpredictability of the moment. In order to best serve your loved one, try to think about your visit in terms of what he or she may be thinking or feeling.

Calling upon another family member or friend to come with you can be very helpful. A family member or friend who is less emotionally involved may be better able to help sort out what is going on as well as understand what is happening with your loved one.

It's also important to remember that your loved one's mental illness is impairing his or her thinking and judgment. Those with a psychotic illness like schizophrenia or mania may be adamant that there is "nothing the matter" with them—except for the problems or persecution that you or someone else is raining down upon them. If the person is severely depressed or has had a profound loss or disappointment, you may be there because he or she wants to die or has already attempted suicide. Shepherding your loved one through a mental health emergency is not like bringing a grateful patient with a broken arm or chest pain to the

ER. This is a battle that you have been pressed into with someone who is far from grateful; in fact, your loved one may resent you for bringing him or her to get help.

If your loved one *does* acknowledge that there is a problem, he or she may be terrified about it. As scary as it is for you as a family member to realize that your loved one is in danger, it can be even more frightening for the patient him- or herself. And the seeming chaos of the emergency room setting may only amplify that fear. These are moments to stick together, to support one another, and to stress that you will find the help that is needed, together. This brings us again to your own personal situation. You are not exactly in a great state of mind. You are frightened by what is going on with your family member. You may have tried other ways to get help but not succeeded. You're probably not a doctor or mental health professional and therefore don't know what to expect from emergency services, let alone psychiatric emergency services. To make matters worse, when you realized there was a crisis, you probably tried to contact the clinicians who normally treat your loved one, only to be told that they "can't speak to you" because of "privacy laws"—or perhaps the emergency happened after the clinic had closed for the day and the voicemail message told you to go to an emergency room. By the time you're in the ER, you're anxious, you may be alone, and you're in an environment you may never have experienced, television notwithstanding.

Although taking a loved one in a mental health crisis to the ER can be overwhelming, it's important to remember that you are doing the right thing. An unchecked mental health crisis can lead to a person being violent—against him- or herself or someone else. And without your intervention, your loved one could spiral deeper into crisis. With your help, your loved one can find the help he or she needs, even in an urgent crisis situation.

THE EMERGENCY ROOM INTAKE PROCESS

Part of the reason the ER can be so anxiety-producing is because it is a strange place filled with doctors and nurses who seem to have their own language. In this section, I'll try to demystify what typically happens so that you can feel knowledgeable and prepared.

Registering. This part of the process involves filling out paperwork and answering often repetitive questions, especially about insurance.

Triage. This is a rapid assessment, generally by a registered nurse, which aims to quickly determine if there is risk of death or irreversible harm. In psychiatric ERs, the triage nurse also tries to separate physical illnesses from mental disorders. A triage nurse is responsible for judging what type of problem a person has and how behaviorally troubled (or dangerous) the person is. What this generally means is that people who are extremely agitated will be seen before someone who is quiet and despondent, just as someone with acute chest pain will be seen before someone with muscle aches.

Clinical evaluation. During the clinical evaluation, a brief history is taken and a psychiatric examination is performed, usually by a doctor (a resident in psychiatry or a psychiatrist; sometimes by a medical doctor) but sometimes by an advanced-practice nurse or physician's assistant. After this clinical evaluation, what's called a "working diagnosis" will be made, and a plan of action to help your loved one will be developed, for both the immediate situation and for ongoing services.

Treatment. Actually, little psychiatric treatment goes on in an ER, even in a psychiatric ER. Only highly specialized psychiatric emergency rooms (called "comprehensive psychiatric emergency programs," or CPEPs), which can keep patients for up to 3 days, will start what will be ongoing treatment. Generally, only large urban areas have a CPEP. The care you can anticipate in a regular ER will probably be one or a combination of the following: tranquilizing medications, brief crisis counseling, a clear explanation of what is happening, referral for further treatment, and, hopefully, information about where you can find support (like through NAMI).

Disposition (discharge). A crucial service of any psychiatric ER is directing you about where to go next. People who are deemed a "danger to self or others" (the standard legal criterion for involuntary hospitalization) will be offered admission to an inpatient unit (described later in the chapter), either in the same hospital as the ER or at another hospital with available beds that insurance will cover. People who refuse admission and are judged dangerous can be committed to a psychiatric inpatient unit for up to 3 days (for more on commitment, see Chapter 10). Most people in a mental health crisis are not hospitalized, so they will return home or to wherever they were living.

AN IMPORTANT NOTE ABOUT THE DISPOSITION PROCESS

One of the most important decisions made during disposition is evaluating a patient's "danger to self or others." Too often, family members seeking inpatient treatment find that the ER doctor will not admit their loved one to a hospital.

For example, you may have been struggling for months to get your son, daughter, parent, sibling, or partner to the emergency room. Your family member's symptoms have been worsening: He or she has become more despondent and has talked about suicide, or has become paranoid and is barricading the door and windows, or is reluctant to leave home and have visitors, or is eating poorly, not bathing, and pacing incessantly. Your loved one has repeatedly refused to go to an outpatient appointment and his or her condition is worsening before your eyes.

Finally, for reasons you can't explain, your loved one agrees to go to the local hospital emergency room. You get there as fast as you can, knowing that the moment's willingness can change on a dime. You may think, *Finally, here's a chance to get him into the hospital so treatment can begin and maybe take hold.* You arrive at the hospital and rush to the intake desk, where you're given paperwork to fill out and told to wait for the next available clinician. The minutes waiting can turn into hours, and your family member grows restless; still, you manage to keep him there. Finally, the doctor sees him. Afterward, you try to speak with the doctor.

The doctor emerges and tells you that she is discharging your loved one. Although she clearly finds problems of a mental illness, the doctor has concluded that there is no "immediate danger to self or others." She explains that she offered your loved one admission on a voluntary basis, but he refused it. He cannot be committed, she says, because there is no immediate danger. The doctor gives you the phone number of a clinic to call for an appointment. Your heart sinks: You don't know what your loved one may have said to the doctor, but you know it's unlikely that he will seek any follow-up care.

Your loved one probably managed to pull himself together for the doctor, however briefly, and promised to get help (a promise you know is not likely to be kept). All you can think is: *What awful event has to happen before he will be admitted to a hospital? And will that be too late?*

Thankfully, there are things you can do to prevent feeling helpless and hopeless at this moment. When you know the danger is there, consider using the following script before the doctor meets with your loved one:

Doctor, my son [or daughter, brother, parent, etc.] is going to put on a good face with you. But you need to know that he threatened to kill himself today [or whatever the scenario specific to your loved one is].

After the doctor has met with your loved one, say:

Doctor, whatever my son told you, you need to know that I am very fearful that he will attempt suicide [or whatever you are fearful about]. I understand that what you can say is limited, but I also know there is no prohibition against your listening to what I have to say, and I can't stress enough how fearful I am about what he may do [fill in details that show why you are fearful]. What's more, even if he told you he would go to an outpatient appointment, we have tried for months to get him to go, and he never does. Your referral will not work. We will be back, maybe with the situation having worsened.

Doctor, I am afraid. If you let him leave the emergency room there will surely be a terrible event. That will be a tragedy for our family, and I am afraid your name will be attached to it. Neither of us wants that to happen.

That should work. You may have a lot of explaining to do to your loved one later on. But given the choice of discharge to a dangerous situation or taking a stand, you should do what your gut tells you is right for your loved one.

Because so little treatment is done during a mental health emergency—no bones are set or wounds sewn up—the goal of a trip to the ER is to ensure your family member's safety and to engage the patient in follow-up treatment in the community. However, finding treatment that your loved one will actually go to and stay with can be difficult. In fact, one of the biggest problems in the mental health system is that so few people who go to ERs are provided with timely outpatient appointments, and even if they are, they often do not go to the appointment. Hospital ERs infrequently contact community services after discharging a patient, clinic appointments are often not possible for days or weeks after the emergency, and a visit with a psychiatrist for medications can sometimes take 6 weeks. What person who is seriously ill can remember an appointment 6 weeks out, let alone have the motivation to attend it?

As your loved one's support system, one of the most important things you can do is to try to ensure that your family member completes all of the steps related to recommended care after an emergency visit (including calling the clinic to confirm the appointment, picking up and taking any prescribed medication, or refraining from drinking or taking unprescribed or street drugs). If these interim steps are followed, the chance that your loved one (and you) will have to go through the ER experience again will be reduced.

Psychiatric Inpatient Units

Perhaps your loved one agreed to admission (or required commitment) to a psychiatric inpatient unit from the ER, or his or her private physician arranged for hospitalization. Although you may balk at the prospect of placing a family member into the "psych ward" or mental hospital, you need to remember that the professional or team that evaluated your loved one did not arrive at the decision to admit lightly. Reluctance to hospitalize a loved one may be, in part, because many families do not know how different psychiatric inpatient units are from their unfortunate (and dated) depiction in films, books, or television. Remember that everyone's goal is to get the patient the right care at the right time. Hospitalization during a crisis may indeed be the right, and necessary, decision.

Gone are the days of warehousing patients in psychiatric hospitals. Civil rights laws and better treatments have allowed almost all people with mental illness to live their lives in the community, not in long-term mental hospitals. But many mental illnesses—including depression, mania, obsessive-compulsive disorder, schizophrenia, schizoaffective disorder, and PTSD—flare up, just like diabetes, heart disease, and asthma. At these times of *acute illness*, an inpatient stay may be needed to understand what destabilized a chronic condition. The careful observations, tests, and clinical interviews done on an inpatient unit can help physicians and other mental health professionals understand what has happened. The goal of an inpatient team is to determine what can be done (usually with medication, therapy, and social supports) to enable your loved one to return to an active life at home and in the community.

Most acute psychiatric care is provided on a specialized psychiatric ward in a general medical hospital. There are also hospitals that specialize in psychiatric treatment of people with mental and addictive disorders. Time spent on an acute psychiatric unit usually ranges from 5 to 14 days, although some people stay for weeks and a very few for longer. Although an inpatient stay gives hospital teams more time to diagnose and treat your loved one than an ER does, the team is still under pressure from the patient, insurance, or managed care company to discharge as quickly as possible. But before discharge, the inpatient staff must ensure that their patient will have access to quality care in the community.

Some patients cannot recover their safety or functioning in the very short period of time that characterizes acute inpatient units. A very small percentage of people may need hospitalization for as long as several months. Some states have psychiatric hospitals that provide what is called *intermediate length of stay hospital care*. A typical intermediate length of stay can range from 2 to 6 months, sometimes even longer. Intermediate lengths of stay allow some patients the time they need to respond to treatment and to rebuild the daily living skills they need to function in the community.

For example, New York State has preserved many of its hospitals for treating people with mental illness who need intermediate lengths of stay. These hospitals, called Psychiatric Centers, specialize in children and adolescents, in adults, and in people with forensic problems (a combination of mental illness and criminal behavior). New York State's Psychiatric Centers aim to be centers of expertise, where a small number of people who do not respond to short-term care in acute hospitals can be admitted for however long they need to recover. These hospitals are nationally accredited in the same way as your local general medical or teaching hospital, and their mission is to provide active programming, medications, and preparation for community living.

The goal of a stay (short- or longer-term) in a psychiatric unit should always be to enable your family member or friend to leave the hospital and have a successful reentry back into the community, as soon as that is safe and possible. With your support and love, effective treatments, and solid post-hospital services, your loved one can function in the community and pursue a life of purpose.

VISITING A PSYCHIATRIC INPATIENT UNIT

As you walk down the corridor toward the psychiatric inpatient unit, whether in a general or a psychiatric hospital, the first thing you will encounter is a locked door. Locked doors keep patients in and (some) visitors out; they require a staff member to monitor your entrance and exit. Although they may seem scary, locked doors are actually a sign that safety and privacy are paramount to the workings of the unit.

As I mentioned, the door is locked to keep some patients from leaving. Many people admitted to a psychiatric unit are there on an "involuntary status," which means that they are in the acute phase of a mental illness and were committed against their will. Inpatients often lack insight into their illness and can be dangerous to themselves or others, so if given the chance to leave, they are apt to do so. The other reason the door is locked is to keep out visitors whom the patient does not want to see or shouldn't see, such as people who have been emotionally or physically harmful to the patient, "friends" who may bring in contraband like pills, cigarettes, alcohol, or drugs, or people who may bring in dangerous objects like razor blades or scissors that a person could use in a suicide attempt at the hospital.

After you ring the bell or pick up the phone outside the unit, a staff member will meet you at the door. You will be asked to identify yourself and whom you want to see. This is a good thing. Privacy is fundamental to the practice of psychiatry and it should start at the front door. If you are there to meet with a member of the clinical staff, let the staff person at the door know who.

Depending on what time of day you enter, the ward corridor may be empty or may have patients milling about. Psychiatric units are often terribly boring places, so patients tend to pace the halls or hang around the door to see if anyone interesting shows up. You may be as much a curiosity to the patients on the unit as they are to you. Even to this day, despite having spent a good deal of my adult life working on psychiatric inpatient units, I still can feel uneasy being stared at by patients or seeing them try to use my entry or exit to escape. Thankfully, once inside, you can find your loved one and a comfortable place to visit, whether in a community space (a day room, lounge, or kitchen area), a family area, or in his or her room.

Inpatient units are communities of routine. Wake up and "lights out" are at specific times every day. Meals are on invariable schedules. Medications are dispensed in an even more regimented manner. Doctors usually round at particular times. "Rounds" is the term for when doctors come onto a medical floor to review their patients—literally it used to mean when doctors walked from room to room to see patients. Today "rounds" often means reviewing cases with ward staff and reading (and writing in) medical charts in the nursing station, just as is done on general medicine wards. Patient meetings with the doctor vary from individual sessions in offices to seeing people briefly in their room on rounds on the unit after rounds in the nursing station. Diagnostic testing is scheduled and can include labs (blood tests), cardiograms, and tests of brain functioning (an EEG, CT scan, or MRI of the brain). Treatment has its routines as well: Meetings with therapists, psychiatrists, and groups and discharge planning meetings are scheduled throughout the day. If your visit comes during one of these routine moments, be prepared to accede to the rhythm of the community.

As visitors to an inpatient unit, we need to be alert to how our assumptions may have been influenced by films or television programs that demonize mental patients or their caregivers. Psychiatric inpatient units are no longer like the place portrayed in *One Flew Over the Cuckoo's Nest*. Caring clinicians are working to assist people with acute mental illnesses with treatments that have been modernized over recent decades. What's more, no patient can receive treatment over his or her objection without a specific court order. Shared decision making and humane treatment are what work, and are now the standard of good hospital care. The goal of an inpatient stay is to clearly understand what could be causing a person such dysfunction or despair. Ideally, hospital admission allows a mental health team to intervene with medications, therapy, family work, and social services so that a person can return to his or her community to continue the process of recovery. Human suffering comes in many forms, from broken bones to broken hearts. We need hospitals for both.

These are but a few of the places you may go on your journey to find your loved one the right care. Appendix A elaborates on other places you may go, taking you on a virtual visit to a large urban ER, a peer-run recovery program, and a supportive housing setting. Now that I have prepared you for where to turn, whom you might meet, and the places you may go, we will turn to examining the illnesses themselves in an attempt to understand the disorders that compel individuals and their families to find help.

A World of Hurt:
The Faces of Mental Illness

The term "mentally ill" has replaced many worse terms—"lunatic," "madman,""neurasthenic,""hysteric,"and"psychopathically inferior," to name a few. The stigma associated with mental illness is far from gone yet, but times have certainly improved.

To help a loved one whom you think is showing signs of mental illness, you first need to understand what mental illness is and what its diagnosis might mean for your loved one. For mental health clinicians, the diagnostic bible in the field is a manual called the *Diagnostic and Statistical Manual for Mental Disorders*, or *DSM* for short. The *DSM* has information about the signs and symptoms of every major and minor mental illness. Over the years, the *DSM* has undergone several revisions to keep up with new developments in our understanding of mental illnesses. The *DSM-5* (the fifth edition) will be the most current version as of its planned publication in May 2013.

President George W. Bush's 2003 Freedom Commission on Mental Health defined a serious mental illness in an adult as follows:

> Adults with a serious mental illness are persons age 18 and over, who currently or at any time during the past year, have had a diagnosable mental, behavioral, or emotional disorder of sufficient duration to meet diagnostic criteria specified within DSM-III-R (*Diagnostic and Statistical Manual for Mental Disorders*), that has resulted in functional impairment which substantially interferes with or limits one or more major life activities.

The last lengthy clause is crucial: "functional impairment which substantially interferes with or limits one or more major life activities." What this means is that to have a serious mental illness in the eyes of clinicians using the *DSM* (as well as government policy makers and insurance companies), a person must meet specific criteria for illness *and* experience limitations in work, school, or social relations. How mental illness is defined matters: Definition determines diagnosis, which in turn shapes treatment, insurance benefits, insurance payment, and potential entitlement supports.

It can be helpful to consider mental illnesses as fitting into one of two main categories: *non-psychotic* illness and *psychotic* illness. The distinction has to do with the patient's *view of reality*. In a psychotic illness, a patient is unable to distinguish the real from the imagined; in a non-psychotic illness, reality is maintained. Both types of illness, however, are serious if left untreated, and both can cause great suffering to those afflicted.

Mental Illness Is a Disease

There is a distinct difference between meeting *DSM* criteria for an illness and having a bad day, a bad mood, or transient distress. People with serious mental disorders are not faking it, complaining, or just wallowing in a bad mood: They have a *disease*. You would never blame a person with heart disease for his chest pain or shortness of breath, and you wouldn't tell that person to "get over it." Mental illnesses are no different.

Mental disorders also often co-occur (such as depression and anxiety, or PTSD and alcohol dependence), just like physical illnesses co-occur (such as hypertension and diabetes). Moreover, mental disorders also commonly co-occur with *physical* health conditions like diabetes, heart disease, asthma, Parkinson's disease, and cancer.

Mental illnesses are real. You need to understand, and to help others understand, that your loved one has a condition that is affecting how he or she feels, thinks, or acts. People who struggle with mental disorders deserve the same considerations as individuals with any medical condition deserve. And people with mental illness who recognize that they are ill and take responsibility for their recovery, with the support of others, do far better than those who do not.

It is *not* my aim in this chapter to give you a quick reference tool for diagnosis or to try to simplify the complex process by which a clinician makes a diagnosis. The official manual of the American Psychiatric Association details the diagnostic criteria for mental illnesses, and you may want to turn to it as a supplementary resource. What I want to do here is look at the various conditions you may observe and want to understand as a family member or friend. These are the disorders that produce the world of hurt that is mental illness.

This chapter is divided into three sections. In the first two sections, I'll look at non-psychotic states of mental illness: Section I will cover depression and the anxiety disorders, including acute stress disorder and PTSD, obsessive-compulsive disorder, panic disorder, and generalized anxiety disorder. Section II will cover personality disorders, including borderline personality disorder and narcissistic personality disorder, as well as eating disorders, including anorexia nervosa and bulimia. In Section III, I'll look at psychoses, including schizophrenia, schizoaffective disorder, acute psychotic disorder, and bipolar disorder.

For each of these disorders, I'll talk about the behaviors and other clues you as a family member or friend might see in your loved one, and explain how a mental health professional makes the actual diagnosis. In some cases, I'll discuss theories about the cause of the illness or other important issues surrounding it. Finally, I'll go over the common treatments for the illness, including what are called *biological treatments* (primarily medications, but also other treatments, such as nutritional rehabilitation or brain stimulation, that target the physical functioning of the body and brain) and *psychosocial* treatments (therapies and other treatments that involve talking, assistance with daily life, and skill building). Because I discuss different treatments in detail later in the book, I won't describe them in this chapter, except to mention which ones are considered most effective for the particular illness.

There are, of course, many other mental disorders that are not discussed in this chapter. I've chosen to focus on the ones here because of their prevalence and burden. You'll also notice that I have not included alcohol- or other substance-use disorders. This is not due to any lack of awareness of their great prevalence and burden, but rather because the subject of these disorders and their treatment is so vast that it warrants a book of its own.

SECTION I:
Depression, Acute Stress Disorder and PTSD, Obsessive-Compulsive Disorder, Panic Disorder, and Generalized Anxiety Disorder

This section examines the non-psychotic mental disorders of depression and anxiety. Depression has been troubling families and perplexing doctors for centuries. Legendary Greek physician Hippocrates had a theory of body "humors" (vital body fluids) and suggested that an excess of "black bile," one of the humors, was the explanation for melancholy. Modern science has moved us well beyond Hippocrates's theories; we now have more insight into how depression works and there is a great deal that can be done to help people recover from it.

There are many kinds of anxiety disorders, but the ones I discuss in this chapter are: acute stress disorder and PTSD, obsessive-compulsive disorder, panic disorder, and generalized anxiety disorder. Too often, anxiety is dismissed as some sort of Woody Allen self-absorbed form of indulgence. The fact that people with anxiety disorders are aware of the irrationality of their symptoms can also lead people to assume that they can simply "get over it." Not so. Anxiety disorders are real, very common, and often persistent. And they can terribly limit the quality and pleasure of a person's life, as well as strain a family and drain their resources.

Stigma in the form of minimizing or mocking a person's anxiety symptoms can present a great challenge for people with these disorders. The tragedy of this stigma is that it interferes with people being properly diagnosed and treated. But anxiety disorders are highly treatable, and those affected deserve a proper diagnosis and effective remedies.

Depression

In her essay "A Journey Through Darkness," published in the *New York Times Magazine* (May 6, 2009), Daphne Merkin wrote of her own experience with depression:

> Depression—the thick black paste of it, the muck of bleakness—was nothing new to me. I had done battle with it in some way or other

since childhood. It is an affliction that often starts young and goes unheeded—younger than would seem possible, as if in exiting the womb I was enveloped in a gray and itchy wool blanket instead of a soft, pastel-colored bunting. Perhaps I am overstating the case; I don't think I actually began as a melancholy baby, if I am to go by photos of me, in which I seem impish, with sparkly eyes and a full smile. All the same, who knows but that I was already adopting the mask of all-rightness that every depressed person learns to wear in order to navigate the world?

Depression, in its many forms, is one of the most prevalent of all non-psychotic disorders. In any given year, about 7% of adults—or 21 million Americans—will suffer from a major depression. And 21%—1 in 5—of Americans will suffer from a depression at some point in their lifetime. According to the World Health Organization, depression is the leading cause of disability globally. In addition, this potentially highly disabling illness co-occurs with many physical illnesses, like diabetes, heart disease, and cancer. Perhaps most frightening is the fact that depression can be fatal: 500,000 people in the United States between the ages of 18 and 54 attempt suicide annually; in 2012, over 35,000 people took their own lives. Most of these people suffered from depression.

But the effects of depression echo far beyond the person diagnosed— for family and friends, it can be a painful monster that seems to envelop their loved one. Thankfully, with the right kind of treatment, depression can be a manageable condition.

WHAT MIGHT DEPRESSION LOOK LIKE TO YOU?

Unfortunately, "depression" has become an umbrella term for much of what ails (or even just upsets) us. People throw around the term "depressed" as if it has no clinical meaning at all: They are "depressed" after seeing a sad movie or "depressed" because the dry cleaner closed before they could get there. But depression is different from a bad day, or disappointment, or grief. Major depression is a disease, with hallmark symptoms, a clinical course, and dangers; it should not be confused with everyday distress, or minimized in its gravity and the pain it produces.

What might you as a family member or friend observe if your loved one is depressed? Most people with depression will show changes in their appetite and sleep—both usually become diminished, although there are exceptions (see the discussion on atypical depression, later in this section). But even more prominent than the loss of interest in food (and frequent weight loss) is a general loss of interest and pleasure: The person no longer seems to enjoy what he or she did before. It's as if pleasure has been drained out of the person—his or her expression loses its vitality, movements are slowed down, and responses to most everything are colorless. Many people, especially older people, complain of a variety of physical problems, including back pain, gastrointestinal troubles like constipation and heartburn, and headache; often these are a worsening of what was before a mild and manageable condition.

Some people appear sad and cry easily, but that is less likely with adolescents and older people; depression without sadness is not uncommon. But depression typically induces the feeling that one is a burden, and the person will avoid being around other people and will become unable to take care of everyday responsibilities. People with depression feel hopeless about the future, and when approached about getting help they are apt to say, "Why bother?" They may make passing references to life's being not worth living, or even frank statements about being better off dead.

When you observe these problems in your loved one, and they persist for weeks on end, it is time to help that person find help.

DIAGNOSING DEPRESSION

Although there is no blood test for depression, no cuff to put around your arm that measures how depressed you are, there is a highly sensitive and specific screening test—available in nine languages and equally reliable among Caucasians, Asians, African Americans, and Latinos—called the PHQ-9 (see Appendix C). The PHQ-9 is a self-test for depression that can be completed before seeing a doctor (at home or in the waiting room). It lists the cardinal signs of depression, including low mood, loss of pleasure, guilt, hopelessness, disturbances in sleep and appetite, worthlessness, and wanting to die.

Scores on the PHQ-9 range from 0 to 27. A score of 10 or higher indicates that depression is highly likely, and a score of 20 would be

like having a blood pressure of 190/120—a real cause for worry. Whatever the score, however, only the doctor makes the diagnosis, just like
when your primary-care doctor determines if you have hypertension or
diabetes after getting the results of a blood-pressure or glucose test.

For the diagnosis of depression to be properly made, symptoms
must persist for more than 2 weeks, resist changes in environment or
changes to daily life, differ from a person's normal mood, cause significant distress, *and* result in a loss of everyday functioning. If all of these
conditions are met, then the person is probably experiencing a major
depressive disorder.

TYPES OF DEPRESSION

The kind of depression I just described is the most common type, but the
disorder can take other forms, too.

Psychotic Depression. Sometimes depressive illness can be so severe
that the mood disturbance is accompanied by a loss of reality, manifested
in delusions (typically of being a wretched person) and auditory hallucinations (typically blaming and degrading). This form of depression is
associated with higher rates of suicide. Treatment for psychotic depression usually requires the use of an antipsychotic medication in addition
to an antidepressant or the use of electroconvulsive therapy (discussed
later in this chapter).

Atypical Depression. This is when a person's depressive symptoms
are reversed—when appetite and sleep are *increased* instead of decreased.
And although the person may be sleeping far more than 8 hours a night,
he or she will still drag about with a leaden sense of fatigue. With this
type of depression, the person also has a heightened sensitivity to interpersonal slights and often feels rejected. Atypical depression can be
responsive to the class of antidepressants known as "selective serotonin
reuptake inhibitors" (SSRIs), as well as to the (now very infrequently
used) monoamine oxidase inhibitors (MAOIs).

Dysthymia. *Dysthymia*, a Greek word meaning ill or abnormal mood,
refers to a chronically low mood state that is present on most days and
lasts for more than 2 years. With dysthymia, a person's feeling a low-level
depression just never seems to go away. People affected by dysthymia

also suffer from low self-esteem and usually imagine the worst of things to come. When someone with dysthymia develops a major depression, he or she is said to suffer from *double depression*.

SUICIDE

No mental disorder is more associated with suicide than depression is. An estimated 9 of 10 people who kill themselves are suffering from a mental disorder, principally depression. Depression is a deeply painful disease: Psychic pain is no less severe than bodily pain, and some say it's even *more* painful. It is the combination of hopelessness—the conviction that there is no exit—with mental pain and unbearable, severe anxiety and anguish that fuels the wish to die and the act of suicide. Being alert to these harbingers of self-destructive behavior may help your loved one stay alive until the treatment sets in.

You may have seen news programs or articles that claim that antidepressants "cause" suicide—*don't be put off by them*. Although some studies have suggested that antidepressants may increase the risk of suicidal behavior in some patients, the risk of *untreated* depression is *far* greater than the risks of antidepressant treatment.

> More people, especially adults over 24, die from *not* having their depressive disease treated than from any medication effects. Don't let your loved one be such a casualty!

DEPRESSION AND GENERAL MEDICAL ILLNESSES

Depression is strongly linked with physical illnesses, especially common illnesses like diabetes, chronic heart and lung diseases, asthma, Parkinson's disease, stroke and cancer. Individuals with depression are:

- *twice* as likely to develop coronary artery disease,
- *twice* as likely to have a stroke, and
- *four* times as likely to *die* within 6 months from a heart attack

As if that weren't enough, people with chronic physical diseases and co-occurring depression have significantly increased healthcare usage and expenditures, as well as disability costs. As you may imagine, these patients often have great difficulty adhering to their prescribed treatments.

- Depressed patients are *three times* as likely as non-depressed patients to be noncompliant with their medical treatment regimen, resulting in increased physician and emergency-room visits and hospitalizations.
- Healthcare expenditures are more than *four times* greater for people with diabetes who also have depression than for people with diabetes who do not have depression.
- People who are depressed but not receiving depression care use *two* to *four times* the healthcare resources of other health-plan enrollees.
- Individuals with major depression average *twice* as many visits to their primary-care physicians as non-depressed patients do.

As you can see, diagnosing and treating depression—as early as possible—can reduce patient (and family) pain, disability, and unnecessary healthcare costs.

DEPRESSION AND PUBLIC HEALTH: A CASE STUDY

In 2004, frustrated by the ongoing poor detection and inadequate treatment of depression, I decided to spearhead a public health campaign about depression in New York City, where I was the mental health commissioner. Together with a group of colleagues, I began the NYC Depression Screening and Management Campaign. On hundreds of subways and kiosks throughout New York City, we placed posters that asked: *Have you asked your doctor about a simple test for depression?*

That was when I had my 15 minutes of fame. The *New York Times* thought the idea newsworthy and put it on page 1, above the fold, on April 13, 2005. Since then, step by tiny step, due to the work of many doctors, nurses, and health leaders around the country, depression screening and evidence-based management have been implemented in a growing number of primary-care settings.

Public health officials are now moving more forcefully to integrate the provision of health *and* mental health as a standard of care in primary-care settings. Screening for depression is on its way to becoming a standard of quality care, and when depression is present, specific treatment care paths and patient self-care practices follow suit. In fact, in my job as medical director for mental health in New York State, in collaboration with the NYS Department of Health, we have begun a statewide initiative to do so. With further advances in healthcare reform and a national investment in electronic medical records, the implementation of proper screening and evidence-based treatments will only grow, enabling more people with depression to be identified and properly treated.

TREATMENT

In the United States, more than half of people with any mental disorder are seen and treated in the general medical sector—by family doctors, primary-care physicians, and pediatricians. This is especially true for the non-psychotic illnesses, like depression, where those affected often prefer to receive care from a familiar doctor, in a familiar setting, where there is apt to be less stigma.

Most people with depression never see a mental health professional. In any given year, less than a third of adults suffering with depression receive treatment, and of those who *do* receive treatment, most receive inadequate care. Taking missed diagnosis and poor care together, *approximately 75 to 80% of those with treatable and often debilitating depression do* not *receive effective care.* Such poor results would cause public outrage if the illness were asthma, cancer, or heart disease. You don't want your loved one to be a part of that statistic, especially because depression treatments work.

Indeed, the treatment of depression is highly effective. Of patients with clinical (major) depression, *a full 75%* can improve or recover with appropriate diagnosis and treatment. Often, treatment combines both medication and psychosocial treatments. For people with moderate to severe depression, the additive effect of therapy results in greater adherence to medication treatment and self-care. Therapy and medication together can often improve both the biological symptoms and the interpersonal problems that plague a person with depression.

Medication

Antidepressant medications are the mainstay of medical treatment for depression, especially for moderate to severe depression. Since Prozac was first released in 1988, antidepressants have been consistently and increasingly prescribed by primary-care physicians and mental health care providers. One in 10 Americans is now taking an antidepressant. But although more people are taking antidepressants properly and effectively, many people in need still do not receive them. Conversely, there is also a problem with over-prescribing antidepressants to patients with mild or transient mood problems that could improve with support or therapy, or simply abate over time.

Although we know that antidepressants are effective at treating symptoms of depression, no one in the medical community is exactly sure how this happens inside the complex and still-mysterious brain. Antidepressants appear to act on brain chemicals called *neurotransmitters*, such as serotonin, norepinephrine, and dopamine, helping to improve the effects of these chemicals. Newer theories postulate that antidepressants stimulate nerve growth and enhance connectivity between neurons.

The most commonly used antidepressants are the *selective serotonin reuptake inhibitors* (SSRIs) and the *serotonin and norepinephrine reuptake inhibitors* (SNRIs). These names hint at an understanding of how the medications work—but "hint" is the operative word. Neuroscience has yet to definitively comprehend a great deal about how the brain functions, including how antidepressants work. But not knowing definitively how something works is not the same as not knowing what to do: Antidepressants can be very helpful, especially for people with moderate to severe depression and psychotic depressive states.

The SSRIs and SNRIs, which have fewer negative side effects, have virtually eliminated the use of older antidepressant medications, such as the tricyclics and the monoamine oxidase inhibitors (MAOIs). However, it is important to keep in mind that tricyclics and MAOIs can be useful to someone who does not respond well to SSRIs or SNRIs. For example, the MAOIs can work well for atypical depression, and both tricyclics and MAOIs can work for treatment-resistant depressive states.

Ask your doctor which type of antidepressant he or she is recommending, and why. You probably already know many of their names from television ads and magazines. The SSRIs include fluoxetine (Prozac), paroxetine (Paxil), sertraline (Zoloft), citalopram (Celexa), and escitalopram (Lexapro). The SNRIs include venlafaxine (Effexor), duloxetine

(Cymbalta), and mirtazapine (Remeron), though this last medication acts differently from the first two. Bupropion (Wellbutrin), an effective but less commonly used medication, affects dopamine as well as norepinephrine. Other antidepressants also exist, and may be useful to your family member, alone or in combination with another antidepressant.

Many of these medications are available in generic form, which is less expensive and more likely to be fully covered by your insurance company. Newer forms of antidepressants are in development by pharmaceutical companies, but so far they're mostly "me too" drugs that work similarly to existing medications. What does *not* appear right around the corner are medications that work in different ways on the neurochemistry and circuitry of the brain.

A final issue to address on the subject of antidepressant medications is the "trial and error" process that's often required to find the right one. This process can be frustrating for both patients and families, who desperately seek relief from symptoms. Adding to the frustration is the fact that many antidepressants require 3 weeks or longer for their effects to appear, meaning that patients sometimes must wait months, as different antidepressants are tried, to see significant improvement of their symptoms. If you find yourself in this situation, try to be patient and supportive of your loved one, who already may be feeling hopeless because of his or her depression. Again, we don't really understand why one medication works better than another: Perhaps it is genetics, or perhaps it is how the drug is metabolized in the body, or perhaps it is something unique in a person's neurochemistry or neurogenesis (creation of new brain cells). Until we know more, trial and error can be a necessary element in treatment (as it is for many physical and mental conditions).

A Note About Side Effects

Antidepressants are generally very well tolerated medications. But like all medications, they do have side effects. Some side effects, like reduced libido, sexual difficulties (in men and women), or weight gain, discourage some patients from continuing on the medication. The more frank your loved one is about side effects, the more likely your doctor will be to find a way to prescribe medication that is both effective *and* tolerable.

The Depression Patch

After many years of study, the FDA approved the use of a depression "patch" in 2007. The patch, which contains the MAOI selegiline, is placed on the skin once a day for absorption. Selegiline was previously prescribed orally as an antidepressant, but patients had a hard time adhering to dietary limitations (which were necessary to prevent a hypertensive reaction if certain foods were eaten). The use of an MAOI patch may be a good alternative for patients who do not respond to SSRIs or SNRIs, especially those people with atypical depression.

Vagus Nerve Stimulation

In 2005, the FDA approved the use of vagus nerve stimulation (VNS) for severe depression that did not respond to multiple and varied treatment interventions, and that lasted for more than 2 years. In VNS, a tiny pulse generator is surgically implanted in the skin of the chest; then an electrical wire run from the generator to the vagus nerve in the neck triggers this nerve to send signals to the brain. Originally approved for epilepsy, VNS was subsequently proven to have some effectiveness for persistent and unresponsive severe depression. So far, VNS has a limited application, and only some insurance companies will pay for it. Research is underway to be able to stimulate the vagus nerve through the skin, rather than using the invasive technique that exists today; if successful, this procedure could provide an important breakthrough for people with intractable depressions.

St. John's Wort

Western medicine is increasingly open to complementary herbal and Eastern therapeutics. St. John's Wort (hypericum), derived from a naturally occurring herb, was initially identified as having antidepressant effects in people with mild to moderate depression. The efficacy of St. John's Wort has not been consistently confirmed in large-scale studies; but that may be due to the studies' limitations rather than those of the herb.

It's important to note that St. John's Wort can *reduce the effectiveness* of a variety of prescribed medications (including oral contraceptives, anticoagulants, and antiviral agents). Make sure your loved one tells his or her physician about *all* supplements and alternative remedies that are being taken, including St. John's Wort, so the prescribing clinician can assess the potential for any problematic drug interactions.

Electroconvulsive Therapy

Electroconvulsive therapy, or ECT, involves sending an electrical current into a patient's brain to induce a seizure (called a "grand mal seizure"). ECT may seem like an extreme option, but if your loved one has a severe and persistent major depressive disorder, the likelihood of response to ECT is 80 to 90%. As many as 50% of people who do not respond to antidepressant medications can benefit from ECT. For people with severe, unremitting depression, or psychotic symptoms, or persistent suicidal thinking, ECT often can provide relief from their symptoms in just days or weeks.

ECT is quite safe. First, the patient receives anesthesia, so that he or she will remain unconscious throughout the procedure. Muscle relaxants are then used to prevent the major motor movements of a seizure; a person will still show some minor twitching of the toes and eyes. Electrodes are then attached to either one or both sides of the skull, and an electrical current, of a preselected intensity (the "dose"), is sent into the brain. After a few minutes, the ECT session is over and the patient begins to come out of anesthesia. Patients undergoing ECT can see some positive results within several treatments, but further treatments in a series of often 6 to 12 sessions are needed to establish and sustain gains. The beneficial effects of ECT may not last, however, so your family member may still need an antidepressant medication (or lithium) after the treatment is completed.

Despite ample evidence of its effectiveness and safety, ECT still remains a controversial treatment. In some states, activists press for its abolition.

Although ECT does have side effects, its speed and unique effectiveness can be lifesaving. Some common side effects include memory problems and brief confusion after a treatment. There are also reports of long-term memory loss and cognitive difficulty; thankfully, techniques have been developed to minimize these problems. Careful consideration of how the ECT is administered (on what side of the brain, at what intensity) can help lessen potential side effects.

Special considerations for ECT apply to patients under 18, especially because studies on this procedure for this age population are so limited.

Repetitive Transcranial Magnetic Stimulation

In 2008, the FDA approved the use of repetitive transcranial magnetic stimulation (rTMS) for adults with depression that is unresponsive to conventional treatments. Although the precise way that rTMS works to alleviate symptoms remains unknown, it is a "noninvasive" treatment option, which means there is no surgical or physical intervention. Instead, magnetic fields are applied right above the scalp to produce weak electrical currents in the underlying brain tissue, with little risk and few side effects. This procedure is still an emerging technology whose application and effectiveness will probably become better established in the years ahead.

Light Therapy

The use of bright lights to ward off or mute depression has been around for a long time, especially for those who suffer mild depressive symptoms in winter or when the sun is in short supply (e.g., in northern regions of the world). The daily use of high-intensity light for the "winter blues" (also called "seasonal affective disorder," or SAD), or to help a depressed patient during literally dark days, is something for your loved one to consider. So-called Happy Lights are readily available on the Internet or over the counter at many retailers. Choose carefully, in consultation with a doctor or nurse, to ensure that the proper light spectrum is delivered. Antidepressants can produce significant sensitivity to light, so, as with any treatment, be sure to discuss any potential problems with your doctor.

Psychotherapy

All psychotherapy starts with building a trusting relationship between the patient and the doctor. This *therapeutic alliance*, which is fundamental to the efficacy of any therapy, can only be achieved when a patient trusts that a doctor understands him or her, and has the patient's best interests at heart.

I discuss the different types of psychotherapy extensively in Chapter 8, so I won't describe them here, except to mention which types are most often used to treat depression. The two types that are most well researched and effective for depression are cognitive-behavioral therapy (CBT) and interpersonal therapy (IPT). Although psychodynamic psychotherapy is used widely in the United States, its research base is not as extensive. That doesn't disprove its effectiveness, however—it only means that it isn't as well researched. Some individuals do very well with psychodynamic therapy. We simply need more evidence to prove its effectiveness, and to identify which patients may be best suited to this form of treatment.

> ### Patient Preference Matters
> Most experienced therapists will use a mix of therapies for their patients, depending on that patient's needs at different times in the course of his or her illness and treatment. Patient preference about what form of therapy feels right is very important, because it plays a significant role in how engaged patients become in the treatment process. Location and logistics may also affect what therapy your loved one receives, especially in more rural areas that may lack therapists trained in a specific approach or therapists who understand your culture or speak your language. There is very promising work underway to develop i-CBT (Internet-delivered CBT), especially for people with mild to moderate depression who have an active linkage with professionals if the need arises.

RECURRENCE

Although depression is highly treatable, it is also a *recurring* disease. As I mentioned earlier, more than half of patients who experience a depressive episode will suffer another bout of depression; if someone has two or more episodes, the likelihood of yet another episode (recurrence) is very high. Individuals who experience ongoing dysthymia are also at a higher risk for recurrent depression.

The recurrent nature of depression makes it similar to many chronic health conditions that beset our society. Heart disease, asthma, diabetes, and arthritis (to name a few) can all become lifelong health problems that require good self-care, vigilant disease management, and the best the medical profession has to offer. Learning to live with and manage a chronic disease is what countless people do in order to live a full life in today's world. Your loved one can do it, too.

Acute Stress Disorder and Posttraumatic Stress Disorder

A person who has undergone a *trauma* is someone who has experienced, witnessed, or was confronted with an event involving actual or threatened death (or serious injury) to self or others. At the time of the trauma, that person felt intense fear, helplessness, or horror. However, people's responses to these situations are varied: Not everyone exposed to a severe traumatic event will develop acute stress disorder (ASD) or post-traumatic stress disorder (PTSD).

ASD always comes on soon after the traumatic event, whereas PTSD emerges after a month or lies dormant for months or even years before symptoms occur. PTSD is the more persistent and severe response to trauma, and ASD always precedes it. This means that detection of ASD provides opportunities for early intervention to stop the progression to PTSD. Military forces and disaster-response teams around the world are searching for the best interventions to do so.

The risk of developing ASD and PTSD can be mitigated by *protective factors* (such as supportive families and communities as well as faith) and *resilience* (which I'll discuss in a moment).

What kinds of events may cause ASD or PTSD? The *DSM* defines a traumatic event as one that threatens the life of (or causes serious injury to) a person or other people around that person. This includes:

- Natural disasters, such as earthquakes, tsunamis, hurricanes, fires, floods, and tornadoes
- Manmade disasters, like terrorist attacks or arson
- War, particularly instances involving atrocities or horrific deaths of fellow soldiers or civilians
- Crime, including torture (all too common among refugees), rape, and physical or sexual abuse

There are instances where the activating trauma may appear less extreme, but for reasons likely related to both the event and the person who experienced it, PTSD still develops. This condition, like so many mental disorders, exists on a continuum from milder to severe, as do the possible events that induce it.

A RESILIENT CITY: MY EXPERIENCE AFTER 9/11

In 2002, my work took me to New York City as director of mental hygiene services (mental health, addictions, and developmental disabilities) in the Department of Health and Mental Hygiene. The city had received a large FEMA grant to respond to the psychological consequences of the 9/11 terrorist attacks. My agency was charged with overseeing the city's response, in collaboration with the New York State Office of Mental Health. By the time the grant expired at the end of 2004, 1.5 million New Yorkers had received outreach, crisis counseling, and education from what was called Project Liberty.

I saw the pervasiveness of the psychic distress that trauma can produce—as well as the startling power of human resilience. I also learned that terrorism does more than destroy buildings or take lives: It destabilizes the psychological equilibrium of a community, city, or country. That is how trauma, especially intentional trauma, works its evil.

But in the aftermath of 9/11, New York City demonstrated how remarkably resilient its residents were. Although some people developed disorders, like ASD and PTSD (as well as depression and substance-use disorders), most did not: After a period of distress passed, they returned to their normal lives. Their lives were different because of their experience, but they were not ill from it.

Colleagues at Columbia University and the New York Academy of Medicine studied what predicts resilience after disaster. Among their important findings were that women proved less resilient than men, ethnic minorities were less resilient than the general population, higher education correlated with higher resilience, and loss of income, limited social support, and the presence of a chronic physical or mental disease did not auger well for resilience. These findings were empirical, that is, they did not claim to know why these differences occurred. We can, however, infer that the differences relate not specifically to the people themselves but to their social circumstances—circumstances that either had already limited their resources and options or did so after the trauma.

Much remains to be understood about resilience from any trauma or disaster. What we *do* know is that the more we can support one another and understand and respond to family needs and the needs of our neighbors and community, the more likely we will be to manage trauma, with unfortunate distress but without disorder.

WHAT MIGHT ACUTE STRESS DISORDER LOOK LIKE TO YOU?

A clear and major stress has happened to someone you love. He or she survived a serious accident, was directly exposed to a horrific natural disaster, or was assaulted. The person is deeply shaken and can't stop thinking about the event. Your loved one may have difficulty sleeping and may be "jumpy" or irritable. Taking care of everyday business is hard and socializing is no longer fun. The person may smoke or drink more and withdraw from others.

DIAGNOSING ACUTE STRESS DISORDER

Again, the essential elements that provoke ASD are exposure to a traumatic event and the experience of intense fear, helplessness, or horror. The symptoms of ASD include dissociation (where someone feels and appears very distant or shut off from what is going on), reexperiencing the event, anxiety and arousal, avoidance, and emotional distress; these symptoms impair functioning at school or work, and within the family. For the diagnosis to be made, the condition must come on within 4 weeks of the trauma and last more than a couple of days. If significant symptoms persist for longer than a month, it's likely that the ASD has progressed to PTSD.

WHAT MIGHT PTSD LOOK LIKE TO YOU?

Your loved one was exposed to a life-threatening or horrific event, which may have happened in recent months or may have happened in the past—even years ago. You see the person become inward, isolated, and preoccupied, with difficulty concentrating on and completing tasks. Your loved one has changed profoundly, leaving you confused and even afraid.

Some people will startle very easily, at something as minor as the sound of a door closing or a telephone ringing. Some will be highly vigilant, as if a sniper were on a rooftop nearby. If you can get the person to talk about what is happening, he or she will describe feeling scared, numb, or both. Images of the trauma erupt into the person's conscious mind, sometimes without a clear trigger. Sleep is terribly restless and full of anxious dreams. Alcohol and drug abuse is very common, and if a person smokes cigarettes he or she will smoke a lot more. Suicidal thoughts are common. (In fact, the number of completed suicides among veterans of Iraq and Afghanistan far exceeds the deaths suffered in combat.)

DIAGNOSING PTSD

As with ASD, someone suffering from PTSD has been exposed to a traumatic event that evokes fear, helplessness, or horror. Symptoms of PTSD include reexperiencing the traumatic event, avoidance of cues of the trauma, emotional "numbing" that can become pervasive, and persistent symptoms of heightened arousal.

PTSD symptoms must persist for over a month for the diagnosis to be made. Unlike ASD, PTSD may appear quickly in the wake of a trauma or sit dormant, only to arise months or years later, typically after some destabilizing event or illness. PTSD that arises well after the event is referred to as *delayed-onset PTSD*. Along with alcohol or drug abuse, the presence of other mental disorders (like depression or bipolar disorder) is a powerful risk factor for the development of PTSD after a traumatic experience. These factors also forecast that treatment will be more challenging.

In order to assess a person's resilience and responsiveness to treatment, it is crucial to know whether the person has experienced any trauma prior to the most recent one (and what it was and when it occurred), how the person responded, and what support (or lack of it) he or she received from family, friends, and community. As a family member, this is where you can provide the greatest insight for your loved one and the physician.

A well-validated screening tool is the PTSD Checklist (see Appendix C). A version also exists for military personnel. In addition, the American Psychiatric Association (APA) has put forward a set of principles to guide interventions for PTSD and ASD. The APA's guidance can help you consider what your family needs to do in the wake of trauma and its disorders. The APA principles are:

- Reduce the severity of symptoms using effective treatments, including crisis counseling, medications, and therapy.
- Prevent or lessen trauma-worsening, co-occurring disorders by early identification and treatment of these conditions—the most common being depression and alcohol and substance use.
- Enhance functioning in adults and promote normal development in children and adolescents by aiding and guiding individuals to return to daily routines and resume functioning as soon as possible.
- Strive to prevent relapse by understanding triggers of trauma and acquiring skills to manage them.
- Help search for meaning and reparative ideas and beliefs about the traumatic event so that individuals can put their experience into perspective and master their reactions to it.

TREATMENT

As with many disorders, a combination of medication and psychosocial treatments is often the best course for both ASD and PTSD.

Psychosocial Treatments: Outreach and Crisis Counseling

Outreach brings services to victims of trauma in their natural environments—in their communities, schools, faith-based institutions, and homes. Crisis counseling, recognized by FEMA as a core post-disaster service, is the provision of face-to-face, short-term education and support to return to pre-disaster functioning. A central tenet of crisis counseling is conveying to victims that their distress is a *normal* reaction to a deeply *abnormal* situation.

In addition, *psychological first aid* is an important intervention for trauma victims. A calm setting and a supportive environment are key elements in the provision of psychological first aid, which aims to foster belief in the prospect of recovery. Thus, psychological first aid is often delivered in the affected community, making use of local members to establish trust and to ensure cultural and linguistic competence. Healthcare workers are tasked with first making sure that all patients are physically and psychologically safe. When possible, individuals showing extreme reactions are identified and referred to professional treatment.

Workers in the affected community then provide education about the event and updates about relief efforts, as well as actively listening to the stories and distress that affected individuals wish to convey. Clear and accurate information from reliable sources is a critical anxiety-reducing activity in post-disaster situations. With a foundation of safety, support, and education, healthcare workers seek to create social connectedness and promote a sense of personal and community effectiveness.

Psychotherapy

Exposure to a horrific event is fundamental to the development of a trauma disorder. This means it's also fundamental to the treatment of that disorder. Effective psychotherapies for PTSD rely on varying levels of reexposure to reduce symptoms and promote recovery. Using principles of cognitive-behavioral therapy (CBT), victims are educated about the effects of trauma, taught relaxation techniques, and then progressively reexposed to the trauma either through imagery or, if possible, by directly entering situations that produce a stress response (such as revisiting the location of an assault). The reexposure is done very gradually so that the patient isn't retraumatized. By carefully preparing and then reexposing the patient to the traumatic event, CBT allows the patient to learn a new, less destructive response to the event. CBT is further discussed in Chapter 8.

With support from the U.S. Department of Defense and the Veterans Administration, fascinating and possibly effective work is underway to study virtual-reality exposure treatments for combat trauma-related disorders. This innovative work builds on video game technology, familiar to younger people, and places those individuals in simulated environments remarkably similar to what they have faced in combat. Other forms of therapy have also been tried for trauma treatment. Mostly anecdotal evidence exists on the effectiveness of a technique called "eye movement desensitization and reprocessing" (EMDR), and some patients have found psychodynamic psychotherapy to be beneficial. However, the respective efficacies of these techniques have yet to be established by controlled studies.

Medication

Several different kinds of medications are used to treat ASD and PTSD, depending on the patient's symptoms and the severity and duration of the disorder.

Tranquilizers and Hypnotics. Tranquilizers (such as lorazepam and clonazepam, in the class of medications called *benzodiazepines*) and hypnotics (short-acting sleeping pills) can be useful for brief periods of time when people are experiencing ASD. If symptoms persist, however, it is generally preferable to substitute these medications with antidepressants or beta blockers.

Antidepressants. Antidepressant medications are often used for severe ASD and for PTSD. The SSRIs and SNRIs (described earlier in the chapter in the section on depression) have been proven effective for non-combat-related PTSD in civilians exposed to disaster and trauma. Reports on the effectiveness of these medications in combat-related PTSD, however, still vary. Families of war returnees should seek consultation with clinicians and centers experienced in working with veterans to get the best information to help your loved one.

Beta Blockers. Beta blockers are also often used for severe ASD and for PTSD. These medications interfere with the nervous system's "fight or flight" response and thus help with symptoms like hyperarousal, anxiety, nightmares, and sleeplessness. An advantage of beta blockers is that they aren't habit-forming, like tranquilizers and hypnotics may be. Propanolol and related beta blockers are effective medications that may be helpful to your loved one.

Prazosin. This medication has been used specifically for nightmares. It was used many years ago at relatively low doses as an antihypertensive medication; doses used for trauma-induced dreams are generally higher.

Trauma is ubiquitous. For some it will cause a period of distress; for others it will induce a disorder. By identifying the trauma and its emotional impact, you can make a difference in how your loved one experiences the event. Early intervention and effective treatment—critically supported by family love, hope, and faith—are our best weapons against the consequences of disaster, terrorism, and trauma.

Obsessive-Compulsive Disorder

Obsessive-compulsive disorder (OCD) is another relatively common anxiety disorder. It runs in families and shows remarkable genetic influence: Identical twins are both affected almost 90% of the time, and fraternal twins almost 50% of the time. The greater the presence of OCD in a family, the more likely it will appear in other family members, and with an early onset.

WHAT MIGHT OCD LOOK LIKE TO YOU?

You may not notice this condition in a loved one until it becomes more serious or disabling. People with OCD generally recognize that their repetitive thoughts and behaviors are irrational, so they do their best to hide them. What you may see are excessive concerns about cleanliness and order, or very rigid ways by which a person must do something (like wash or eat), which, if not followed, cause them great distress. Your loved one may repeatedly wash his or her hands, or touch the same object, or seem to count when doing something. The person may avoid touching various surfaces or dread becoming contaminated from some surface or microorganism. These symptoms progressively interfere with functioning. Very severe OCD is disabling and cannot be hidden by the person suffering.

DIAGNOSING OCD

OCD is defined as the presence of obsessions, compulsions, or both.

Obsessions are thoughts or impulses that eat away at someone's mind, even though that person knows the thoughts are unreasonable. Obsessions are more than just worries like *Did I remember to leave a note for my friend who's staying at my apartment?* Rather, they often manifest as anxious thoughts, such as: *Did I turn off the stove?* (even though the person has checked it 25 times), or *Will I be exposed to infection if I touch any surface in the classroom?* Daily efforts to push these ideas away are seldom fruitful, and exhaustive time is spent dwelling on them.

Compulsions are actions a person takes, repetitively, in response to a particular idea despite knowing that these are irrational and foolish behaviors. Often, compulsive behaviors are done in secret to avoid mockery or scrutiny. Examples include: *I will count to 44 forty-four times; then I can leave the house safely. If I touch my index and thumb fingers while saying the Lord's Prayer then nothing bad will happen to my children. Even though I've already washed my hands for 10 minutes, I must wash them just one more time and then I can return to work.*

OCD can be a crippling disorder. Although a person may know his or her thoughts or actions are irrational, the capacity to resist them is but a weak reed against the demand of the symptoms. Eventually, anxiety mounts to unbearable proportions if the idea is not focused upon or the compulsion not ritually performed. In time, functioning becomes impaired, as does the ability to maintain normal relationships, thereby threatening everyday life.

There are screening instruments for OCD, including the Yale-Brown Obsessive Compulsive Scale (Y-BOCS) and the Obsessive-Compulsive Inventory (OCI). See Appendix C for more on these tests.

It's also important to remember that OCD commonly co-occurs with other psychiatric disorders, especially depression, eating disorders, attention-deficit hyperactivity disorder, and alcohol or drug abuse. Make sure your loved one receives a comprehensive evaluation that investigates for the presence of other psychiatric conditions, because if a co-occurring disorder isn't identified and properly treated, then neither condition stands a decent chance for improvement.

TREATMENT

The standard of care in the treatment of OCD is cognitive-behavioral therapy (CBT) combined with antidepressants such as the SSRIs and SNRIs (discussed earlier in this chapter). The two forms of treatment complement each other. In some cases, however, just one treatment may be used, such as when the disorder is milder, when CBT isn't available, or when the patient has a strong preference for one treatment over the other.

Medications
The doses of antidepressant medication for the treatment of OCD tend to be higher than the doses used for depression, though starting doses

are often lower to allow a person to tolerate the medication and its side effects.

Patients who are unresponsive to simpler medication regimens may benefit from treatment that involves more than one class of medication—for example, combining a benzodiazepine tranquilizer with an SSRI. Severe symptoms may require low-dose antipsychotic medication.

If you can, talk with your loved one and the treating doctor about what progress to expect in order to determine if the chosen medications are working. OCD can be deeply rooted in brain neurochemistry and circuitry and may resist even well-delivered initial treatments. Specialty psychopharmacological consultation may be needed to achieve desired results. Interesting research is underway with other means of biological intervention, such as transcranial magnetic stimulation (rTMS; discussed earlier), to offer alternatives to the great number of affected individuals.

Psychosocial Treatment

The mainstay of psychosocial treatment for OCD is cognitive therapy. (Psychodynamic therapy and psychoanalysis are not effective for OCD.) That said, a talking therapy alone, however structured it may be, is not enough for people with OCD. They need to act, to overcome their obsessions and compulsions, in order to recover. They need to master their obsessions and compulsions in the real world. This is called *behavior modification*.

A good example of cognitive therapy with behavior modification is what's known as *exposure response prevention* (ERP). With this method, patients identify a specific problem—say, fear of touching a surface in a public area—and then are taught to imagine touching that surface. Then, in a progressive way that evokes tolerable anxiety, the patient begins to confront the fear of touching by actually touching. "Response prevention" literally means preventing the previous response to the fear—whether that response is to avoid touching a surface or to engage in rituals about the touching. With successful ERP, the patient's compulsions can be greatly reduced or even alleviated.

ERP is very hard, and it takes determination and support. Medications and training to reduce anxiety with relaxation techniques and progressive exposure help a person do what previously could not be done. Don't let your loved one just *talk* about overcoming compulsions—recovery requires *action*. Sometimes, group treatment is helpful in enabling people with similar anxiety problems to support one another in doing what they all know needs to be done.

A good source of information for families who are assisting their loved one in recovery from OCD is the Obsessive Compulsive Foundation (see Appendix B).

Panic Disorder

Carl, a 24-year-old dressed in expensive jeans and T-shirt, arrived in the emergency room of a community hospital late on a Saturday afternoon. Brought by several friends from a nearby shopping mall, he was breathing rapidly, appeared flushed, and broadcast a sense of distress. "I'm having a heart attack!" he told the triage nurse. "I think I'm dying!"

Carl complained of shortness of breath, a pounding heart, and pain in his chest. He was perspiring and unable to sit still. Despite his distress, he appeared to be a healthy young man, a student or a young professional. Carl's friends said they'd been at lunch to cheer Carl up because his girlfriend had broken up with him earlier that week. After lunch, he told them that he didn't feel well. Shortly after that, he said he needed to go to a hospital right away because he could be having a heart attack.

Carl wasn't having a heart attack, although it felt and looked much like one. He was having a panic attack. Emergency rooms see cases like this all the time. Sometimes friends bring someone in; sometimes it is family members who accompany the patient. But everyone seems to share the state of urgent distress that the symptomatic person is experiencing. I recall one person brought to an emergency room by the police after he ran a tollbooth and a red light in a state of panic, trying to get to an emergency room because he, too, believed he was having a heart attack.

WHAT MIGHT A PANIC ATTACK LOOK LIKE TO YOU?

A panic attack is a formidable event. The explosion of body and mind is something to behold, no less experience. Suddenly, a feeling of intense, escalating fear overtakes someone. The person's heart pounds or palpitates, and he or she can feel nauseous, start to sweat or tremble, labor to breathe or start to choke, experience chest pain, or feel as if he or she is having an out-of-body experience. Not everyone will have all of these symptoms, but experiencing even a few symptoms is terrifying, and often people quickly conclude that they are dying or losing their mind.

DIAGNOSING PANIC DISORDER

Every year, about 1 in 50 adults suffer a panic attack. However, it is important to remember that not everyone who has a panic attack has panic *disorder*. A diagnosis of panic disorder is made when the person has experienced recurrent, unexpected panic attacks *and* is fearful of future attacks, worries about the consequences of future attacks, or significantly changes his or her behavior because of the attacks.

Before concluding that a person's panic symptoms are indicative of panic disorder, a psychiatrist, physician, or mental health professional needs to rule out any medical condition that could be producing these alarming symptoms.

Among the physical conditions that can produce panic-like symptoms are thyroid diseases (both hyperactivity and hypoactivity), low blood sugar (hypoglycemia), cardiac arrhythmia, a rare tumor of the adrenal gland (known as "pheochromocytoma"), and diseases of the vestibular (balance) system like Meniere's disease.

Even when these conditions are medically assessed and ruled out, people with panic disorder tend to persist in attributing their symptoms to a physical illness, sometimes insisting that more tests be done. This is a measure of how powerful the bodily symptoms they experience are. Supportive but firm information from the treating doctor (and loved ones) can help avoid further unnecessary, expensive tests, and focus the treatment on the actual disease.

As I just mentioned, people with panic disorder also develop persistent concerns about reexperiencing the attacks, or dying from them. They may begin to change their behaviors and habits in an attempt to avoid another attack. For example, if the first attack occurred at a busy shopping mall, as Carl's did, the person may avoid shopping malls or even other public places, such as grocery stores, theaters, or restaurants. As the disorder progresses, the avoidance behaviors become more extreme, sometimes to the point where the person won't leave the house at all. When the fear of attacks results in a person staying home to avoid having an attack, the disorder is called *panic disorder with agoraphobia*.

TREATMENT

Both medication and psychotherapy are effective in treating panic disorder. Because both approaches work, the patient's preference becomes an important factor in choosing the type of treatment.

Medication

Studies have shown that both SSRIs and SNRIs (discussed earlier) reduce symptoms of panic disorder. Tricyclic antidepressants are also effective, but their considerable side effects and risk of death from overdose make them a second choice of treatment, at best. Controlled studies have also demonstrated that benzodiazepines alleviate symptoms of panic disorder, but concerns about tolerance (needing higher doses to achieve the same effect) and dependence (where the body becomes dependent on the drug and experiences withdrawal when blood levels drop) keep them from being the first treatment choice. Sometimes tricyclics will be used if an SSRI, SNRI, or psychotherapy is not effective, or as a bridge while other treatments are being implemented. Finally, MAOIs can also be useful, but their dietary requirements and the danger of hypertensive crises limit their use (with the exception of the patch, discussed earlier).

For people with panic disorder, antidepressant medication may be difficult to tolerate at first. Side effects, especially increased feelings of anxiety or restlessness, nausea, or dizziness are very common in people with panic disorder. Starting at low doses and increasing slowly ("start low, go slow") can often help people get through this early phase of sensitivity to side effects.

Psychosocial Treatment

Panic disorder is especially responsive to cognitive-behavioral therapy (CBT), discussed in Chapter 8, when provided by a well-trained and experienced mental health professional. CBT has the greatest evidence for efficacy as a therapy for people with panic disorder.

Another effective therapy is called *exposure response prevention* (ERP). This psychotherapy, discussed in the earlier section on OCD, involves systematically exposing a person to triggers for worry, anxiety, or panic. There is some evidence that forms of psychodynamic therapy that center on panic can also be helpful; however, evidence of their effectiveness is limited.

Eye movement desensitization reprocessing therapy (EMDR) and supportive psychotherapy are not effective for panic disorder.

Again, the SSRI and SNRI medications and cognitive-behavioral therapy have the best-established evidence for effectiveness in treating panic disorder, which is why they are considered "first-line" treatments. If one first-line treatment does not work, you should encourage your loved one to try another first-line treatment—or, if the person is using only medication or only therapy, to add therapy or medication. Panic disorder is highly treatable using these well-studied approaches. If initial efforts do not succeed, don't give up! Urge your loved one to ask the treating clinician about finding another treatment option.

Generalized Anxiety Disorder

Business school had been Robert's dream since high school. He had an aptitude for math and an entrepreneurial spirit; he imagined starting his own business, even though he had no idea what that business might be. Robert's plan seemed to be working out. He worked at a financial-services company for 3 years, did well on the GMAT, had a good interview, and was accepted into an Ivy League business school.

Then, rather suddenly, Robert began worrying about starting school, doubting whether he'd be able to succeed. He also began to worry about whether he was doing well in the job he was already in. He became concerned that friends and coworkers might notice his apprehension and think poorly of him. The transition to business school increasingly frightened him—he even wondered if he could fall ill from the stress of beginning the next chapter in his life.

Robert's anxiety became a part of his everyday life; he couldn't get it to go away. Fearful of starting school, he asked to defer his admission. Months passed, and Robert's condition worsened.

It's normal to feel anxious about any big change in one's life. But Robert's anxiety went well beyond that. He wasn't just worried about the transition to school—he was experiencing generalized anxiety disorder (GAD).

WHAT MIGHT GENERALIZED ANXIETY DISORDER LOOK LIKE TO YOU?

If your loved one has GAD, he or she will appear apprehensive or afraid almost every day. The person will speak of being worried about many different things—health, work, money, relationships, safety; in fact, the list can grow over time. You may also notice that worries that get resolved are just replaced by new worries. For example, your daughter may be worried about making the track team, but upon hearing the good news that she *has* made it, she immediately starts worrying about future meets, having enough time for schoolwork, and whether she'll like the other team members. The worries may also seem to have no real cause—your spouse may worry that you'll be unfaithful during a business trip despite your marriage being strong and trusting; your son may worry about passing an exam despite having a straight-A average. To manage the persistent worry, your loved one may withdraw from friends, school, and work. Alcohol or street drugs may be used for temporary relief from feeling highly nervous. No reassurances seem to work—in fact, they sometimes can make the person's worry greater.

DIAGNOSING GENERALIZED ANXIETY DISORDER

Excessive, persistent worries that diminish functioning are the cardinal symptoms of GAD. Other symptoms include problems with concentration and sleep, restlessness or jumpiness, fatigue, and irritability. As with panic disorder, other psychiatric and medical conditions need to be ruled out before coming to a diagnosis of GAD.

GAD is quite common, appearing regularly in primary medical doctors' offices and slightly less often in the offices of psychiatrists and other mental health specialists. Fortunately, people with GAD are more likely to seek help and adhere to treatment regimens than are people with other kinds of mental disorders.

TREATMENT

Treatments for GAD are similar to those for depression and other anxiety disorders (see those sections earlier in the chapter). Medications, especially SSRIs and SNRIs and sometimes benzodiazepines, are effective. These medications should be combined with psychotherapy, especially short-term, focused cognitive-behavioral therapy or interpersonal therapy (see Chapter 8). Many self-management techniques can be very helpful, including exercise, yoga, meditation, limiting use of alcohol, and attention to sleep and diet.

Don't let GAD take the life out of your loved one! This is a condition that can be managed and mastered.

SECTION II:
Borderline Personality Disorder, Narcissistic Personality Disorder, Anorexia Nervosa, and Bulimia Nervosa

In this section I'll discuss personality disorders and eating disorders. Personality disorders are enduring patterns of maladaptive behavior that come on by adolescence. People with personality disorders create significant problems for themselves, their families, their friends, and the community. Their pattern of dysfunctional behavior, and often a perception of themselves as victims, persists throughout life and is typically quite inflexible. Perhaps the most difficult aspect of personality disorders is that people who suffer them generally do not think their character is a problem. In fact, they often regard others as the source of their troubles.

There are many types of personality disorders. I'll focus on two because of their prevalence and impact on families and communities: borderline personality disorder (BPD) and narcissistic personality disorder (NPD). BPD tends to be a highly visible condition because people with this disorder are prone to self-injury and suicidal behavior; the disorder may also involve transient psychotic symptoms. NPD is renowned for the way people with this condition exploit others.

Eating disorders—anorexia nervosa and bulimia nervosa—are all-too-frequent, profound disruptions in many families' lives, usually emerging when a daughter (or occasionally a son) is an adolescent. These conditions are described below, but they may also co-occur at the same time or over time. Families need help from smart professionals to understand these debilitating and sometimes deadly illnesses, so that they can intervene effectively.

Borderline Personality Disorder

Olivia arrived at the ER near the college she attended around midnight. Upon admission, she told the triage nurse: "I've been depressed since Thursday." She went on to say that she'd been feeling "all speeded up," with difficulty falling asleep and some early-morning awakening in recent weeks, following a breakup with a boyfriend she had only known briefly. The relationship had ended after Olivia posed semi-nude for a film her boyfriend's friend was making.

Olivia offhandedly remarked to the nurse that "it might be fun to die" and said she had thoughts of killing herself by jumping out of the window of a moving train. Further, she reported two transient experiences in which she thought a person on the television was talking to her. She also recounted feeling depressed for much of her life, feeling "dead inside." She said that as an adolescent, she had been promiscuous and had many stormy relationships with boys, adding, "When you get to know someone, you find out they are as screwed up as you are." In the brief time she was in the ER, Olivia had periods of crying, anger, and thinly veiled seductive behavior. She acknowledged regular use of alcohol, Vicodin, and marijuana.

When Olivia's family arrived to take her home, they were anxious and exasperated. They were alternately angry and empathetic toward her, and were eager to speak with the clinician on duty to get some direction about what to do next.

WHAT MIGHT BORDERLINE PERSONALITY DISORDER LOOK LIKE TO YOU?

Having a relationship—whether it's a work or family relationship, or friendship or partnership—with someone with BPD can be challenging, to put it mildly. Your loved one, friend, or colleague may seem delighted with your company one moment and furious with you the next. You may feel like you're constantly walking on eggshells, never knowing what mood the person will be in. Anger toward you or others in the person's life may be intense, seemingly out of proportion to the situation at hand. Similarly, the person's despair over setbacks or losses may seem extreme. If your loved one is a partner or spouse, you may be growing weary of his or her constant career changes or insistence on moving to yet another house, city, or state. If your loved one is a son or daughter, you may be worried about his or her problems maintaining friendships, frequent school transfers or dropping out, and risky behaviors.

People with BPD may change their appearance or other aspects of their identity with startling speed and ease. One month they're a vegetarian with plans to study acupuncture; the next they're eating chicken wings at the local pub and talking about opening a BBQ restaurant. This is different from the normal identity experimentation of youth in that it is rapid, incomplete, and continues on past adolescence. People with BPD also tend to be impulsive and reckless—for example, racking up credit card bills on shopping sprees, going on drinking or drug binges, or having risky sexual encounters. Even scarier, they may engage in self-harming behaviors such as cutting or burning themselves, or even consider or attempt suicide, especially in the wake of a disappointment or failed relationship. Many of these problems start in early adolescence and are not ones the person simply grows out of.

If you're living with someone with BPD, you probably feel like you're on a never-ending rollercoaster ride, spending all your energy dealing with whatever the crisis of the moment is. What's more, your efforts to speak to your loved one about his or her problems may prompt a wild and contentious response, with blame for the problems being placed anywhere but on the person him- or herself.

DIAGNOSING BORDERLINE PERSONALITY DISORDER

Few psychiatric disorders come with the seemingly ever-present emotional and interpersonal storms that characterize BPD. People with BPD have a persistent inability to manage feelings, tolerate stress, or be comfortable alone. They have trouble sustaining trusting and stable relationships, and they're likely to turn to self-destructive behaviors when disappointed, angry, or hurt. Those who suffer from BPD have considerable difficulty taking responsibility for their behaviors, instead projecting blame for their circumstances or behaviors onto others.

Underlying the chaotic and disruptive behaviors of BPD are profound problems with self-image and self-worth that date back to early life; sometimes these problems are the product of early trauma and emotional deprivation. Feelings of emptiness, intense and uncontrollable anger, and despair add to the compelling distress of a person with BPD.

External and internal issues like these create great challenges for families and friends of people with BPD. Clinicians who undertake long-term treatment of BPD understand that their patient will bring those challenges into the therapeutic relationship.

BORDERLINE PERSONALITY AND CO-OCCURRING CONDITIONS

People with BPD frequently experience depression or abuse alcohol and drugs. Some highly psychologically vulnerable people with BPD can have brief episodes of psychotic thinking. Therefore, careful assessment is needed to separate out any co-occurring conditions from BPD and to make a comprehensive treatment plan that targets other co-existing issues.

SUICIDAL THINKING

The intermittent eruption of suicidal thinking and behavior in people with BPD can test a family's resolve. It is important to try to distinguish chronic suicidal ideas (wanting to be dead) from acute suicidality (which can come after a significant stressor).

Families need to work with trained professionals to differentiate these two states, and to develop ways to help mitigate whatever state exists in their loved one. Therapists who work with borderline patients make self-destructive behaviors (including suicidality) a centerpiece of the therapeutic work.

CAUSES OF BORDERLINE PERSONALITY DISORDER

Early theorists tended to blame parents for BPD, describing them as not sufficiently nurturing or stable. This diagnosis, like some of the early theories of schizophrenia, has not been proven and is unfair. Although some people with BPD may indeed have had neglectful or unstable parents, others have had supportive, loving ones.

There is a considerable body of clinical literature on people, especially women, who reportedly suffered emotional and physical (often sexual) trauma as children or adolescents. Many BPD patients whose histories support this experience can benefit from trauma-based programs.

Recent scientific investigations into this condition and other character and behavioral problems stress that there are important biological or constitutional traits that a child brings into the world from a very early age, which cause the youth serious distress and can challenge effective and loving parents. No single theory explains the complexity and diversity of this condition. It is important that parents and other family members not blame themselves. To the extent that their loved one will permit, they can offer support for healthy behavior and personal development.

TREATMENT

Effective treatment for BPD needs to be comprehensive and targeted to specific symptoms and behavior patterns. Families, patients, and clinicians should expect that improvements will take time—years, as a rule.

Medication

Medications target specific symptoms, and this has particular relevance in the treatment of borderline patients. In choosing a medication, the patient and doctor should identify the primary symptoms the patient is experiencing and wishes to ameliorate. This symptom-specific approach also allows all parties to track the medication's effectiveness in controlling target symptoms, and to make adjustments as needed.

Antidepressants. Antidepressants are useful when there is evidence of a co-occurring major depressive disorder; usually one of the SSRIs or SNRIs (discussed earlier in the chapter) are tried first. For BPD patients who have symptoms associated with atypical depression, such as hypersensitivity to others, chronic feelings of lifelessness, and increased eating and sleeping, MAOIs may be helpful, but they carry greater risk if not responsibly used. Tricyclic antidepressants are not known to be very effective and are more dangerous in overdose.

Antipsychotic Medications. Antipsychotics can help with transient psychotic symptoms and may be useful in reducing self-destructive behavior, quieting paranoid thinking, and helping control impulsiveness. Antipsychotics have significant side effects, however, which need to be carefully weighed with the patient. If antipsychotics are used, very low doses typically suffice. Clozapine may have a place, under special circumstances, when comprehensive approaches have not been successful; this medication, as noted in Chapter 7, has been shown to reduce suicidality and aggression.

Mood Stabilizers. Mood stabilizers can be useful for patients with significant mood swings; lithium, a tried-and-true medication (and one that many believe reduces suicidality), may be the first to consider—though it can be lethal in overdose. In fact, all mood stabilizers carry serious risk in overdose, making consideration of risk versus benefit paramount.

Benzodiazepines. As a rule these should not be prescribed. They can disinhibit behaviors and produce tolerance and dependence.

Psychosocial Treatments

Individual psychotherapy is the mainstay of treatment for people with BPD. Longer-term therapy is needed in light of the chronic nature and severity of this disorder. A specialized form of cognitive-behavioral therapy called *dialectical behavior therapy* (DBT) has emerged as a very helpful approach to treating this condition. It is discussed in Chapter 8, as is a variant called *dynamic deconstructive psychotherapy* (DDP). Both treatments require special training for the clinicians who use it, but those who have taken the time and gained experience see its merits. Other therapies focus especially on interpersonal relationships, the bedrock of a borderline person's psychic stability (and instability).

Trauma-focused therapies can be important for patients who have been traumatized. In my opinion, no uncovering of trauma or its working through is possible until a person has achieved significant clinical and functional stability, of considerable duration, to undertake the stress of exploratory trauma therapy.

Treating BPD patients is hard work. Some therapists and doctors are highly skilled and temperamentally well suited for work with borderline patients. If your loved one finds one, try to help him or her stay the course. Therapists who are supportive and good at problem solving can make a profound difference in a person's life.

Family Support, Education, and Intervention

Although it can be hard for some BPD patients to recognize (or appreciate), an informed and supportive family can be their greatest asset. Families can provide emotional and material assistance and serve as a safe environment during treatment and recovery.

But having a borderline patient at home, living with a family, can be very difficult, especially in the face of a patient's anger and blaming, or periods of self-destructive behavior. When a family takes a stand about responsible behavior, or expects something—however reasonable—from their loved one, it will seem to carry risk; every time limits are set, there can be the danger that, this time, the patient's acting out could jeopardize his or her safety or even life. Sometimes the toughest moments for families can be when they decide to say "no" and stop whatever supports they may be providing that might be enabling their loved one's self-destructive behaviors.

Thankfully, families can learn to take carefully considered stands that demonstrate their commitment to do what is in their loved one's interest and long-term benefit. Good therapists know the value of committed families and will find ways to work with them over time, seeking to overcome patient protests about family members when they occur.

Narcissistic Personality Disorder

Greek mythology tells the story of a great hero, Narcissus, known for his personal beauty and contempt for others. The gods deliver their just punishment by having Narcissus gaze upon himself in a forest pool, where he discovers that his love for himself is unrequited. In despair, he kills himself.

George, a man in his mid-thirties, came to me for consultation after his boss told him that he had to go into therapy or he would not be able to keep his job. The CEO of George's company believed in the value of mental health services, for all levels of the company's personnel. At our initial meeting, I had the feeling that George not only didn't want to be talking to me but also thought I was useless and did not merit his time or attention.

Through our conversation, I found out that George's wife had left him after he spent her savings and became involved with another woman. George told me that he did not see any problem with his behavior in his marriage or at his current job. I asked him why his boss would be so insistent on therapy. He replied, "That idiot doesn't know how to manage, and, worse, he doesn't want to listen to me when I tell him how to do things." When I asked George if there might be something valuable to be learned from his boss, I felt his disdain for me and for anything I had to say. Even though his boss was literally holding his job over him, George could not fathom that someone else might have a valu-

able opinion, or a way to help him improve his life or relationships—not to mention hold the lifeline to his employment.

After a few meetings that George came to grudgingly, I cautioned him that it seemed his job was in peril. I suggested that, together, we might be able to figure out why he was having a hard time at work, and what he might do to save his job. After I said this, he stood up precipitously, called me a fool, and left my office. Although I was stunned by the suddenness of his actions, I wasn't really surprised. He did not return my calls and I never saw him again.

WHAT MIGHT NARCISSISTIC PERSONALITY DISORDER LOOK LIKE TO YOU?

For those with a family member who has NPD, you are apt to feel very challenged in controlling your feelings and maintaining support for your loved one. Although the person may begin by complimenting you and trying to curry favor, he or she can soon turn on you—usually at the first moment you don't agree with him or her or do what he or she wants. He or she is remarkably self-centered and shows little or no interest in you, unless you have something he or she wants. People with NPD typically see the world as owing them something; they project a sense of entitlement and can be readily exploitative of others. Efforts to appeal to fairness or empathy go unheard.

DIAGNOSING NARCISSISTIC PERSONALITY DISORDER

As the example of George illustrates, NPD features self-importance, lack of consideration of (and empathy for) others, and often a tendency to take advantage of others. Not surprisingly, this behavior leaves a long trail of troubled and fractured relationships. People with NPD seldom show the impulsive and self-destructive behaviors common in BPD, though I have seen examples of suicide attempts when patients with narcissistic personality see no way to escape the consequences of their choices or failures.

CAUSES OF NARCISSISTIC PERSONALITY DISORDER

Psychological literature, especially psychoanalytical theory, suggests that early emotional deprivation fosters the development of NPD. This theory is based on retrospective views by the affected individuals, who themselves are generally not reliable historians because of their tendency to feel slighted and blame others. However, this theory does help to explain the self-doubt that can underlie narcissistic behavior, as well as why narcissists do not have the emotional resources to think about and care for others.

TREATMENT

Narcissists rarely seek treatment because they believe that they are "above" such a bother. When pressured into treatment by family or unfortunate circumstance, it can be possible to leverage that moment to help someone gain perspective and perhaps change behavior.

Psychodynamic therapy and psychoanalysis are standard treatments for those with NPD. Treatment, provided as individual therapy, is long-term. Although people with NPD may act arrogant and self-confident, these behaviors hide an underlying fragile sense of self, and this is what the therapy targets. Once patients become more emotionally mature and able to build more mutually supporting relationships with others, therapists can help them tolerate the reasonable expectations and frustrations inherent to all human bonds.

Anorexia Nervosa

Rachel was 16 when her family doctor referred her to the psychiatric service of a general hospital for treatment. Rachel was just over 5 feet tall and weighed a frightening 78 pounds.

A quiet, studious girl, Rachel gave new meaning to the word "tidy": Everything was orderly in her life—her room, her clothes, her homework, her doll collection, everything. In school, Rachel did well, in large part because of how diligent and organized she was. She preferred schoolwork to time with friends, and stayed at home most nights to take care of her two younger sisters and do household chores to help her parents, who both worked. She didn't date.

When Rachel was 15, she began picking at her food. Although she was at a healthy weight, she started complaining to her mother that she was fat, that her hips were too big, and that her stomach protruded. Rachel avoided contact with others at school, and at home retreated to her room as much as possible. There, she would relentlessly follow exercise videos, sometimes for hours on end. When the toilet in the bathroom she shared with her sisters became clogged, Rachel blamed her sisters for using too much toilet paper. But she knew it had clogged because of her self-induced vomiting after her parents pressured her into eating meals.

Over the subsequent months, Rachel's weight began to plummet, and her menstrual periods became infrequent. The more weight Rachel lost, the more she believed she was overweight. She responded to these beliefs by further restricting her food intake and obsessively exercising. One day, Rachel's mother saw her getting dressed and realized how much weight she'd lost. She brought Rachel to the family doctor to assess her medically and arrange a referral for psychiatric care.

Although she had lost over 25 pounds in less than a year, Rachel saw no reason to be admitted to the hospital. In fact, she tried to jump from the car on the way there, to escape the "jail" she believed she was sentenced to enter. Rachel's parents signed her into treatment, starting her on the journey of recovering her life.

WHAT MIGHT ANOREXIA LOOK LIKE TO YOU?

Eating disorders typically begin in adolescence and early adulthood, so they are apt to emerge while a teenager is still living at home (or recently off to school). But don't all teenage girls diet and obsess about their appearance? How can you tell when dieting or exercising has gone too far?

There's a difference between common teenage obsession with appearance and the behaviors and thoughts associated with anorexia. A family may see overzealous dieting where weight loss is so extreme that efforts are made to hide it below baggy clothes or to avoid being touched lest protruding bones be felt. Family members may observe increased and alarming levels of daily exercise, for three-, four-, or five-hour stretches, or multiple times a day. Also, eating behaviors tend to become secretive, with the youth not wanting to join family meals, or picking at food so that it mostly remains on the plate. Periods of time in the bathroom after a meal may indicate self-induced vomiting. Comments about weighing too much or being fat despite what you see as growing emaciation are also telling. Weight loss is the cardinal sign of anorexia, with a young woman losing 20 or more pounds and progressively looking skeletal. Sometimes the eating disorder is a way of managing weight for a sport, like wrestling in boys or ballet or other dance forms in girls.

For some young people the symptoms of anorexia—overzealous dieting, compulsive exercise, and periods of bingeing and purging— are transient and pass like other phases in a young person's life. If your daughter or son is showing signs of these symptoms, you need to be deli- cately concerned and watch to see if the condition worsens and begins to affect relationships and functioning.

Evidence that anorexia has set in is when weight plummets, exer- cise dominates the day, mealtime is avoided at all costs, and school and friends fade into the background as the condition makes normal life no longer possible.

SEEKING HELP

When a loved one has anorexia, the sooner you respond, and the sooner treatment begins, the greater the likelihood of improvement. Taking control of the situation and getting your loved one into treatment is, of course, more possible with adolescents who are living at home; as the person with an eating disorder ages, or is out of the home, taking control becomes more difficult. Colleges and universities now experience very high rates of students with eating disorders, and are an important resource to a family. If the eating disorder has resulted in dangerously low weights or electrolyte problems (which can be fatal), you'll need to resort to hospitalization, preferably on a voluntary basis, if professional outpatient treatment is not sufficient.

I have seen families take charge, standing their ground and insisting on treatment and a plan for recovery from the disorder. I have also seen instances where the person affected was left to control her own destiny, regardless of the gravity of the condition; this has, at times, proven cata- strophic.

One of the biggest challenges with anorexia is dealing with your loved one's skewed perception of reality. No matter how skeletal your loved one looks, she or he remains absolutely convinced that more weight needs to be lost. And the more malnourished the person becomes, the more vulnerable she or he is to this skewed thinking. This means that getting your loved one to agree to seek treatment can be extremely difficult. From your loved one's point of view, the problem is *too much* weight—so why would she or he go to a doctor, who will insist on weight *gain?*

When a person has anorexia, the family members (parents, siblings, and even grandparents) need to come together and take responsibility for their loved one. In order to support the ill person, the family needs to behave like the loving and caretaking unit it is meant to be. As obvious as it may sound, you may need to say: *What we see you doing is not healthy. You could even be doing things that could endanger your life. We love you, and cannot stand by and let you hurt yourself.* Or: *We can't wait anymore for what you said you would control. We see how your life is out of control. We see that you have lost more weight [or don't have the energy for school, have stopped seeing your friends, never come to meals and hide in your room, or whatever behavior is specific to your situation].* You can conclude by saying: *We are going to arrange for you to see our family doctor, or a therapist, or a school counselor. Do you have a preference?*

This kind of firm but loving approach with your family member may come naturally to you and your family, though you may need support and counseling to stay the course in the face of resistance from your loved one. If it doesn't, and you find yourself having difficulty communicating with your loved one, you may need family therapy to help you better connect with and support your loved one, as well as remain determined to get that person into treatment.

DIAGNOSING ANOREXIA NERVOSA

Again, there's a difference between common teenage preoccupation with appearance and a diagnosable eating disorder. To be diagnosed with anorexia nervosa, a person must lose at least 15% of her or his bodyweight *and* have developed an intense fear of becoming fat. Eating itself—putting food into one's mouth—generates immense anxiety. It's not unlike a serious phobia, but here the feared situation is eating. In addition, all kinds of measures (like vomiting, inducing diarrhea with emetics, or exercising for hours to the point of collapse) are used to compulsively guard against weight gain. Patients will often deny that there is any problem, and their denial often paradoxically increases with starvation. This picture is not that of adolescent concern about appearance: This is the disorder of anorexia.

Anorexia is a two-headed monster. One type of anorexia is called the *restrictive type*, in which food intake is limited without bingeing or purging with laxatives, enemas, diuretics, or self-induced vomiting. The other type of anorexia is called *binge eating* or *purging*, where these behaviors have become a regular part of weight control. Often these two types coexist.

A number of screening instruments exist for anorexia, including the brief Eating Attitudes Test (EAT) and the Eating Disorder Inventory (EDI). (See Appendix C.)

WHO'S AT RISK?

We used to believe that only girls developed anorexia, particularly girls of economic privilege in Western cultures. Not anymore. We now know that boys are also affected by eating disorders, and that cases appear worldwide, throughout diverse cultures, ethnicities, and economic strata.

I have seen children as young as 10 and adults as old as 60 with a serious eating disorder. Anorexia nervosa typically comes on at some point in the teenage years or early twenties, but preteen cases have been reported—these younger cases are often associated with obsessions, compulsions, and depressed mood. Older women can also show signs of anorexia, often after a great stress, like loss of a loved one.

The earlier the onset of the disease, the greater the impact is on normal growth. Anorexia can result in stunted physical development, and its victims often have thin bones that fracture more easily. Eating disorders also erupt in the college years, especially among girls going away to school. Thankfully, school health and counseling services are usually attuned to the problem, particularly in girls who live in dorms where their weight loss or purging behavior becomes noticeable to others.

Both anorexia and bulimia are more common in competitive athletes, particularly girls who are dancers, gymnasts, and runners, and boys who wrestle or body-build. Often, eating disorders are multigenerational. Other risk factors include a tendency toward perfectionism, inflexibility, and distorted views of the body, as well as anxious tendencies and social phobias where contact with others generates intense fear.

TREATMENT

Don't be fooled by the arguments made by anorexic patients that they understand and can control their condition. They may believe their own logic, but you have little reason to join them in what is a profound self-deception. *The only measure of reality is how much the person weighs.* When weight loss exceeds 15% of body mass, and a variety of physical and mental problems gain the upper hand, it's time to get help—*immediately*. If there is no weight gain after concerted and intensive outpatient treatment, patients may need hospital care.

Anorexia nervosa benefits from comprehensive treatment that includes nutritional and psychosocial interventions. Before discussing these specific interventions, however, I'd like to go over general treatment goals.

Treatment Goals

The initial—and essential—treatment goal with anorexia nervosa is to assess the *physical health* of the patient, and to ensure that no grave medical complications have occurred (or will occur). Severe weight loss ushers in a variety of problems, including fatigue, intolerance of cold, difficulty concentrating, and intestinal bloating and pain. Additionally, abnormalities in heart function can produce slowing of the heart, drops in blood pressure (that cause dizziness), and impaired heart-muscle activity that can be dangerous. In rare but tragic instances, heart complications from untreated anorexia can be fatal.

Inpatient hospitalization on a medical (or psychiatric) unit may be necessary to control the medical complications of the illness. Early onset and severe weight loss are associated with the highest rates of mortality; anorexia ranks high among psychiatric conditions that result in death—either from the starvation-induced medical complications, or from suicide. The message here is to take this condition seriously, especially when it comes on early, with severe weight loss or metabolic irregularities from bingeing and purging.

The *second* treatment goal is to help the affected individual *regain a normal weight* and thus restore the bodily functions that happen naturally when we eat properly and are of normal weight. These include clear thinking, proper digestive-system functioning, normal growth and development, regular menstrual periods in girls and women, and normal hormonal levels in males of any age.

A *third* treatment goal is to help patients *recognize the disturbed and disturbing patterns of thought and feeling* associated with the eating disorder. This may be a protracted process, especially for those who have other associated conditions, including obsessive-compulsive and depressive illnesses, personality disorders, or corrosive self-esteem issues.

A *fourth* treatment goal, essential for youth and invaluable for many adults, is to *engage the family* in assisting with recovery by educating family members about their loved one's illness. Eating disorders can ravage families, but with professional help, recovery can be a healing process for everyone.

Once the anorexia is controlled, the *final* goal of treatment is *relapse prevention*. As with all mental disorders, the risk of relapse may continue for many years, especially when a person is exposed to known, destabilizing triggers or stressors (e.g, intimate relations, work stresses, or loss of support or a loved one).

Nutritional Rehabilitation

Paradoxically, starvation actually increases the body's resting energy expenditure. In advanced stages of the disease, an anorexic's body is in a constant state of starvation and is expending energy even when at rest. What this means for an anorexic's recovery is that she or he will need to eat greater amounts of food to gain weight than a healthy person. (Keep this in mind when battling with insurance companies who strive to keep hospital stays all too brief.)

For outpatients, a slow but progressive program of weight gain, limited exercise, and normalizing eating behaviors is more tolerable physically and emotionally than hospitalization is. The goal always should be a healthy weight—as determined by medical professionals, not the patient.

Individual Therapy

When someone is in a starvation state, support, reassurance, and explanation are essential. Because of the cognitive impairment starvation produces, formal psychotherapy has little effect, especially when weight loss is profound or precipitous.

Cognitive-behavioral therapy (CBT) and interpersonal therapy (IPT), discussed in Chapter 8, are effective, evidence-based treatments for anorexia. They are especially helpful for normalizing eating habits and preventing relapse. Individual or group psychodynamic therapy can provide psychological understanding of the anorexia and foster emotional development. Good clinicians often draw from all three models of therapy, selecting between them at certain moments in treatment.

Family Work

Anorexia can gravely impair a person's daily life: School and work are greatly affected and relationships with family and friends are often shattered. Yet those who are ill with anorexia suffer a profound denial of their illness and are unable to see its consequences. Further, they have a *true dread of eating and gaining weight.* This powerful combination produces some of the greatest resistance to treatment and recovery I have seen— in many instances, this resistance rivals even that of psychotic illness.

What's more, your anorexic family member may have an impressive capacity to sound so reasonable—and you may want to believe what she or he says. She may try to persuade you that she's fine, that she can gain weight but just doesn't want to, that she will gain weight (because you insist) but doesn't need any treatment to do so. Don't be fooled! Wait until you see real weight gain, a return to normal activities and school, and increased time spent among friends, to begin to relax your controls and let your child or loved one resume his or her important self-controls.

You need to be resolute about getting your loved one into treatment. As part of your loved one's support system, you will need professional assistance to understand the illness, know when to take a stand, strategize about what needs to be done, and participate in what will be a highly structured treatment that includes re-feeding and relearning how to eat normally.

For young people affected by anorexia, treatment and recovery cannot occur without the family. For adults with this illness, many a family member—parents, siblings, sometimes even an adult child—will be critical supports in the demanding work of recovery. A combination of psychoeducation and counseling will help many families figure out how best to aid their loved one in the process of recovery. Some families benefit from family therapy; in fact, some of the most established schools of family therapy had their beginnings working with families of anorexic youth.

Medication

Medication is never the primary or singular treatment for anorexia nervosa. But it may be helpful when there is a co-occurring mental disorder such as depression or anxiety disorder, including obsessive-compulsive disorder.

Infrequently, there can be evidence of psychotic thinking (a delusion) about a person's body or about food. This differs from the delusional thinking characteristic of schizophrenia or schizoaffective disorder— there are no hallucinations and the fixed idea is confined to weight and body image, without the perception of a paranoid or external control-ling force. It is best, if possible, to proceed with nutritional rehabili-tation before considering the use of a psychiatric medication. Many times, symptoms will abate when starvation is ended and the patient has obtained a normal weight. There is evidence that antipsychotic medica-tion, particularly olanzapine, may help with weight gain because of its effects in the brain.

High doses of antidepressants have also been used to treat patients with eating disorders. In addition to treating depressive symptoms, they may aid in weight maintenance.

Women who suffer low bone density as a result of hormonal and nutritional deficiency can be prescribed calcium and Vitamin D, in addi-tion to necessary weight restoration.

Support Groups

Support groups specific to eating disorders can be helpful, but they should not be used as an alternative to treatment. Some of these groups include Overeaters Anonymous (OA) and Anorexics and Bulimics Anon-ymous. Prudent self-help or 12-step groups should insist that a person with anorexia obtain professional services. Any support group that claims it can do the job alone is one you want to avoid.

A NOTE ABOUT DEALING WITH INSURANCE COMPANIES

Insurance companies often seem intent on denying hospital treatment for people with anorexia. Some of this may be related to opportunistic programs or ones that do not provide good treatment. Your battle sometimes may need to extend beyond your loved one to the insurance reviewers and their supervisors. Form an alliance with your caregivers and be relentless in challenging denial decisions. Fight back with clear information about necessity, specific information about what will be done, and timelines and goals. Go to the medical director of the plan if you need to. Usually, if your case is a good one you will win—but unfortunately not easily.

DON'T GIVE UP

There is great variability in the course of anorexia (and bulimia). Adult-onset eating disorders are associated with a more difficult and protracted recovery, but early intervention and ceaseless persistence make a difference. These disorders can be recognized, diagnosed, and effectively treated. However, even with good treatment, relapse is extremely common, regardless of age. Try not to be discouraged and *do not give up*. Your loved one needs to stick with treatment, work on recovering a life and finding hope, and over time, rejoin the family not as a person with an eating disorder but as someone who is healthy and functioning as a full member of the family.

Bulimia Nervosa

Eddie had always been a well-coordinated and active boy. But he was always a bit over-weight and concerned about his appearance. He fell in love with wrestling when he entered high school at 15, but was bigger in size and carrying more fatty weight (not muscle) than other boys his age, which meant he had to wrestle in the next weight class with older, more experienced wrestlers. Eddie would still usually win, but not as often as he wanted.

Then, Eddie discovered that he could manipulate his weight. If he used laxatives and made himself throw up on the days before an event, he could eat enough to train vigorously but still weigh in at one or two classes below his initial weight.

Eddie went on to win a variety of championships while keeping his eating disorder a big secret from everyone. He grew distant from his friends and was isolative and testy at home. Finally, months later, his coach discovered him throwing up in the bathroom after a disappointing practice.

The behaviors and thinking that mark bulimia are very similar to those of anorexia. (I therefore suggest reading that section in the chapter, even if your loved one isn't anorexic.) However, people with bulimia aren't always underweight—in fact, they usually are of a normal weight or even slightly overweight. This can make spotting the disorder more challenging.

WHAT MIGHT BULIMIA LOOK LIKE TO YOU?

As with anorexia, your loved one may exercise excessively and complain of being fat or say other negative, often distorted, things about her or his body. Eating also becomes secretive, and you may see trips to the bathroom after or during meals. Because bulimia involves excessive ("binge") eating, especially of sweet or high-fat foods, you may find evidence like wrappers or empty boxes—although the person may go to great lengths to hide them. Other red flags are calluses or sores on the hands and damaged teeth and gums (from repeated purging).

DIAGNOSING BULIMA NERVOSA

The cardinal feature of bulimia nervosa is *binge eating*. Binge eating is defined as eating a substantially greater amount of food than normal in a 2-hour period. Eating three donuts in a single sitting doesn't qualify as binge eating. But eating three *dozen* donuts in 2 hours does. During binge eating, a person feels out of control; stopping or limiting the intake seems implausible to her or him.

In addition, people with bulimia engage in a variety of behaviors to control weight, including taking laxatives, diuretics, and emetics, as well as self-induced vomiting. Often, people with this disorder will alternate binges and fasts; compulsive exercise is common. These bulimic behaviors can occur many times a week, even daily.

There are two variants of bulimia nervosa. The first is called the *purging type*, which involves regular use of laxatives, diuretics, enemas, or self-induced vomiting. The second type, *non-purging*, is when exercise and fasting are principally used to control weight. A person with bulimia can move quickly from one set of compulsive behaviors to the other.

The same screening instruments mentioned earlier for anorexia nervosa are used to identify people who may have bulimia nervosa.

TREATMENT

The treatment of bulimia should be comprehensive to increase the likelihood of improvement from this debilitating condition. This is especially the case when co-occurring mood, anxiety, personality, and substance-use disorders are present. Comprehensive treatment means a combination of nutritional rehabilitation; individual (or group) psychotherapy; family psychoeducation, counseling, or therapy; and, frequently, the use of antidepressant medications. Make sure your loved one is receiving comprehensive care.

Treatment Goals

The primary aim in working with someone with bulimia is to help that person diminish, or even fully eliminate, the bingeing and purging. These behaviors have taken over the person's life and stand in the way of healthy relationships and a productive school or work life. To eliminate bulimic behavior, the person must *find and sustain the motivation and will to participate in treatment and rebuild a life of normal eating.* Recovery requires hard work: Patients have to change the disturbed patterns of feeling and thinking that are driving their pathological eating behavior.

Like with anorexia, a *second* goal of treatment is to identify any *physical complications* resulting from the binge eating or purging. These include: worrisome disturbances in electrolytes (like low potassium and sodium), which can produce cardiac arrhythmias; intestinal problems like severe gastric reflux and intestinal pain, bloating, esophageal tears, and gastric and rectal bleeding; significant problems with concentration and thinking; dental decay; and generalized weakness and apathy.

A *third* treatment goal is to identify and treat any *co-occurring psychiatric disorders*. Among the more common disorders are alcohol and drug abuse, as well as mood and anxiety disorders.

Fourth is *educating and engaging affected families,* which is always necessary with young patients and often vital for adults as well. For couples in which one has bulimia, involving the partner can be especially critical.

Finally, as with anorexia and all eating disorders, people with bulimia need ongoing help with *relapse prevention*.

Nutritional Rehabilitation

Although many patients with bulimia are of normal (or near normal) weight, their nutritional state is far from healthy. They often suffer from a loss of electrolytes and depleted calcium due to food preferences or bingeing and purging, and they may lack protein and other nutrients as well.

Thus, nutritional rehabilitation for people with bulimia focuses on restoring normal patterns of food intake, with regular meals of sufficient food to satisfy physiologic needs, restore healthy nutrition, and maintain weight. For low-weight people with bulimia, progressive caloric intake needs to be planned and carefully introduced to overcome any dread of weight gain. A structured meal plan, diligently followed, is instrumental in reducing fasting, bingeing, and purging.

Individual Therapy

The complexity of problems often associated with bulimia calls for a treatment plan that addresses the specific needs of the individual affected. For example, one person may have problems with fasting, bingeing, and compulsive exercise. Another may abuse stimulants and laxatives and overuse tranquilizers and sleeping pills. Still another may have a co-occurring and persistent depression or anxiety disorder. With co-occurring disorders of any type, not addressing any one problem greatly limits recovery from the other disorders.

Cognitive-behavioral therapy is the best studied and demonstrably effective of the individual therapies for bulimia, though there is also support for interpersonal therapy. Psychodynamic therapies have been used in the treatment of bulimia but may be best for individuals whose acute eating symptoms are controlled and who still face problems with relationships, self-esteem, body image, and sexuality. To repeat, experienced clinicians often draw from all models of therapy according to the stage of recovery and the needs and preferences of each individual patient.

Group Therapy

Group therapy has been used extensively with people with bulimia. Group work can lessen shame, as a person shares the hidden behaviors with others with similar problems. Group therapy also draws from cognitive-behavioral therapy, interpersonal therapy, and dynamic models of therapy. It can also incorporate nutritional education and wellness instruction (see Chapter 11).

Family Work

Adolescents and young adults with bulimia who are living with or supported by their families will benefit from family psychoeducation to support their treatment and recovery. Married and older patients may also benefit from assisting families.

A combination of psychoeducation and counseling will help many families figure out how best to parent or aid their loved one in recovery from bulimia. As with anorexia, family therapy can be useful when specific problems in functioning as a family limit how they can help a member in need. If you are considering family therapy, don't be shy about asking a therapist what experience he or she may have working with families.

Medication

Individuals with bulimia experience significantly higher rates of depression and mood disorders than their unaffected relatives. Studies have shown that the use of antidepressants can be effective with bulimia nervosa, even when there is not prominent evidence of depression, in part because they can help to control the binge and purging behaviors. SSRIs, including fluoxetine, are often used in higher doses to treat patients with bulimia. Other serotonin receptor drugs and traditional tricyclic antidepressants have proven effective, though the latter tend to produce more side effects and are dangerous in overdose.

There are other medications that may be helpful but require consultation with a psychopharmacologist, including doctors familiar with addiction. The addiction model (compulsive, uncontrollable behaviors, with ardent denial, that do not relent despite serious adverse consequences to body, family, and purpose in life) may be useful in understanding and treating symptoms of bulimia.

Support Groups

Like with anorexia, support groups may be helpful but are not a substitute for professional treatment. Overeaters Anonymous (OA) draws individuals with bulimia, possibly because of its highly structured approach to eating and group support. Twelve-step recovery programs may also be helpful with recovery from many compulsive and self-destructive conditions. But, again, do all you can to ensure that your loved one is receiving professional treatment and is not reliant on support groups alone.

It can also be a good idea to attend a support group yourself (with or without your loved one) to see firsthand what this group experience provides.

SECTION III:
Schizophrenia, Schizoaffective Disorder,
Acute Psychotic Disorder, and Bipolar Disorder

This section focuses on serious and persistent mental disorders that have as their hallmark periods of time when reality is impaired as a result of psychosis. These conditions can persist, recur and, unless they are identified and effectively treated early on, carry considerable risk of functional and social disability.

Schizophrenia

Schizophrenia has long been considered a debilitating condition. In the late 1800s, Emil Kraepelin, a famous German psychiatrist, labeled it *dementia praecox*, suggesting an early and progressive "dementing" illness. Today, we know that is not the case.

Over two million Americans—and about 1% of the worldwide adult population—will suffer from schizophrenia in their lifetime. Schizophrenia is a serious illness, and it requires a thorough diagnostic process and a carefully constructed and maintained treatment plan. Over 100 years of studies show that people with schizophrenia can recover. They can have lives of health and productivity *with illness*. Recovery takes work, family support whenever possible, good treatment, and time—but it is possible.

WHAT MIGHT SCHIZOPHRENIA LOOK LIKE TO YOU?

This illness tends to come on slowly, in adolescence and young adult-hood, with progressive withdrawal from family and friends. You may see a lack of attention to showering and wearing clean clothes. The person developing schizophrenia spends more time alone and abandons many of the activities he or she previously engaged in, including sports, music, and time with friends. You may have the feeling that your loved one is acting like a stranger—an eerie sense that you are losing the person even though he or she is there. Your loved one may start to dress oddly, wearing unusual or even bizarre clothing, or start a lot of body piercing or tattooing. He or she may become preoccupied with ideas about "special" things happening yet offer few if any details. You may notice the person becoming highly anxious or worried about dangers to him- or herself or family members. The person will seem preoccupied with what he or she is thinking, perhaps responding to things you cannot understand. You may detect significant use of marijuana or alcohol, covertly taken. Habits around sleep may change, including staying awake at night and sleeping during the day. Schoolwork or job performance becomes impaired. If you try to talk with your loved one about what is happening you are likely to be dismissed or even yelled at—something you haven't see before.

Then, one day, sometimes even years later, an acute psychosis emerges. Your loved one becomes extremely paranoid, is responding to threats you cannot detect, to sounds he or she is hearing but you are not. The person may run from the house, be agitated or even threatening, and resist your efforts to help.

DIAGNOSING SCHIZOPHRENIA

People should not be diagnosed with schizophrenia until they show 6 months of persistent symptoms characteristic of this illness *and* evidence of a loss of social, educational, or vocational functioning. A psychotic illness that is transient—or in which there is no persistent loss of func-tioning—is *not* schizophrenia. If your mental health clinician says your loved one has schizophrenia after only a few weeks of symptoms, even delusions or hallucinations, ask him or her to think again.

Let's take another look at Tony, whose story was introduced in Chapter 5. As you'll recall, Tony's mother had taken him to an outpatient clinic after becoming worried about changes in her son's behavior.

After his evaluation at the clinic, Tony became progressively more agitated and paranoid about the devil, who he believed was occupying his home and was posing a danger to his life and soul. Tony stopped going to school and isolated himself in his room. From time to time, he would yell out or beat the walls, especially at night, frightening his family. Tony seldom changed his clothes or washed, and he had little to no appetite. Months passed with no improvement. When his parents mentioned that he might need to take medication, Tony first resisted and then refused outright. He told them he could not be sure who they were.

Six months later, Tony broke into the local church. The priest heard his screams and called the police. At the emergency room, Tony was admitted to the psychiatric unit of the hospital.

Tony's admitting diagnosis was schizophrenia, acute episode. He showed what are called the cardinal *positive* symptoms of schizophrenia: *hallucinations* (sensory experiences in which the person hears, sees, or smells things that aren't there) and *delusions* (a disorder of thought). Delusions usually take the form of feeling controlled by external forces (being persecuted or plotted against, or having ideas put into one's head). Tony was agitated, and his functioning had deteriorated substantially; he no longer ate or bathed on a normal schedule, and he had stopped going to school. Because Tony's symptoms had lasted for over 6 months and were not the result of a drug-induced state or a physical disease, he met the diagnostic criteria for schizophrenia.

Schizophrenia also involves what are known as *cognitive symptoms*. Cognitive symptoms are disturbances in thinking. A person's thoughts may be disorganized or illogical, and it may be hard for you to understand them. Memory may be poor and distraction is common. Sometimes there is what's called *poverty of thought*, where a person's mind seems blank or there appears to be little responsiveness to what is going on in the immediate environment. Perhaps the most challenging cognitive symptom is *lack of insight*. This means that the person isn't aware that he or she is ill or thinking or behaving oddly. Lack of insight is especially prevalent during acute periods of psychosis, and it presents a unique predicament: Because the person is certain he or she isn't ill, the person doesn't see any need for treatment, and he or she may wonder why others are demanding it. This often leads the person to assume that doctors and family members who insist on treatment are part of a persecutory plot.

What are called *negative symptoms* tend to come on later in the course of illness, sometimes years after the positive symptoms. Negative symptoms include a loss of will, where a person is apathetic and unmotivated. The person may also exhibit a flat or expressionless emotional state, and what is called *paucity of speech*, in which the person says few words, and only when prompted. Sometimes negative symptoms can be caused or worsened by certain antipsychotic medications, so it is important to update your loved one's clinician about any changes you see in his or her behavior.

Schizophrenia is a serious mental illness not only because of the incapacitating nature of some symptoms but also because of its effects on the brain if treatment is delayed. As I mentioned earlier in the book, psychotic episodes are bad for the brain: Untreated psychotic illness is associated with loss of brain cells. As with all illnesses, seeking the proper treatment early on can avoid losses in functionality and improve the odds of your loved one's long-term success. Studies have shown that when treatment of psychosis is delayed, a person generally becomes more symptomatic and more likely to become disabled. Sadly, many people with schizophrenia refuse treatment for long periods of time, which exposes them to the deleterious effects of the disease on the brain. By encouraging and supporting your loved one to get and stay in treatment, you will, quite literally, be helping to save the person's brain.

ONSET

Schizophrenia typically begins in late adolescence or early adulthood, although there are instances of late-onset schizophrenia, where someone becomes ill for the first time in his or her fifties or sixties.

CAUSES OF SCHIZOPHRENIA

Schizophrenia is a very varied disease; psychiatrists have been creating categories of the illness for a very long time. Some forms of the illness have greater positive symptoms, others more negative; some people are very paranoid, others preoccupied with religious and spiritual matters;

some show prominent mood symptoms and some seem to have lost their feelings; some people reconstitute more quickly than others; some have a family history of serious mental illness, some do not.

The variety of expressions of the illness suggests that there is no one cause of schizophrenia. Yet its prevalence of 1% of the global adult population has been remarkably stable for generations. Because there is a low birth rate among people with schizophrenia, its persistence must be explained by more than genetics alone, though there is good evidence for a genetic component to its causation.

Researchers have done twin studies—where identical twins have the same genetic makeup and generally the same environment—to try to assess schizophrenia's heritability. These studies have shown that, when one twin has schizophrenia, the likelihood of the other (healthy) twin getting it is about 50%. There appears to be a vulnerability conferred by certain genes, but this only means that a person's risk for falling ill is increased; it does *not* mean that the person will become ill.

Researchers have also searched for environmental influences that may affect the development of schizophrenia, but there are no definitive findings. Some theories about environmental causes suggest that viral exposure in the uterus, as well as maternal starvation and malnutrition, can put babies at risk for developing the disease. However, not all babies who encounter these challenges in the womb go on to develop schizophrenia. Fortunately, older theories that blamed mothers and families have been dismissed as invalid and unfair.

There are, however, certain known stressors that can unleash the illness in a genetically vulnerable person. Malnutrition, exposure to toxins (including inhaling solvents), and a destructive and critical peer group can all be stressors. A significant stressor is the use and abuse of drugs—particularly hallucinogenic drugs and the heavy use of marijuana (especially synthetic marijuana)—which can be especially dangerous to the brains of youth at risk for schizophrenia. Emergency rooms around the world see young people who show up with a drug-induced psychosis that does not abate when the drug has been eliminated from their bodies. Instead, the psychosis persists, and becomes indistinguishable from schizophrenia.

Genetically vulnerable people can be reactive to family troubles and dysfunction, but *families do not cause schizophrenia*. In fact, the family can often be an ill person's best ally when the illness strikes and in the years thereafter. Families can play a protective role by engaging in responsible parenting and providing a supportive environment to a child or family member at risk for recurrence of acute episodes or for becoming disabled.

TREATMENT

In the treatment of schizophrenia, the most effective approach is comprehensive care with both biological treatments and psychosocial treatments. Biological treatments primarily include medications. The more well-known psychosocial interventions (and mainstays of many clinical programs) are case management, self-management, problem-solving therapy, and cognitive-behavioral therapy.

In general, the greatest reduction in relapse occurs when medication is coupled with case management. And relapse rates *continue* to drop when these core interventions are matched with family education, therapy, and social-skills training. Don't settle for limited programs of medication alone, or medication and case management. The more comprehensive the treatment, the better the chances that your loved one will be on a successful road to recovery.

Biological Treatments

Antipsychotic medications are standard practice in the treatment of schizophrenia, yet they are plagued by controversy and problems. Most people with schizophrenia cannot function without antipsychotic medications, especially in the early years of the illness when they suffer from positive symptoms, like hallucinations and delusions. Antipsychotic medications help to control these symptoms, enabling patients to think more clearly and be less fearful, which helps patients to take advantage of psychosocial treatments and supports. Without antipsychotic medication, a relapse into psychosis is highly likely. However, patients' reactions to the medication's side effects and their lack of insight about being ill make noncompliance extremely common.

There also are now a number of promising alternative biological treatments for schizophrenia, including the use of omega fatty acids and an antibiotic (minocycline). With more time and research, we'll have a better understanding of their value and be in a position to weigh benefit and risk.

Prescribing Principles*

Select a medication that proves the most effective for the patient's symptoms and functioning.

Find the minimally effective dose. Lower doses cause fewer side effects, involve fewer medical complications, and reduce possible drug interactions if other medications are used.

Avoid use of multiple antipsychotic medications, when possible. Treatment with multiple antipsychotic medications is more expensive and produces more side effects and more drug interactions. Plus, the more pills a person is supposed to take, the harder it is to be compliant.

* Based on the New York State Office of Mental Health guidelines

Case Management

People with schizophrenia (like others with serious and persistent mental illness) often need support, direction, and assistance with meeting the demands of everyday life. A case manager is a type of life coach who helps a person organize the day, make and attend appointments, complete the endless forms needed for social services and medical coverage, and live effectively in the community. The need for a case manager will vary over time, with a greater need earlier in the course of a person's illness and during times of distress when acute and disorganizing symptoms recur. Case managers need to work very closely with therapists and psychiatrists; if they don't, then bring this up with the case manager, or the leader of the treatment team.

Assertive community treatment (ACT) is an intensive form of case management that includes a doctor and nurse who provide services in the patient's home. ACT supply varies from state to state and county to county. ACT teams are highly intensive services, meant to prevent or replace inpatient treatment, so they are limited in number and need to be carefully used for only as long as necessary.

Self-Management

This treatment is about the patient taking responsibility and control over his or her life. Illness—especially chronic illnesses like diabetes, hyper-tension, and schizophrenia—can be best managed by the person who is ill, not passively left to others to control. Self-management techniques include planning how to spend the day; making decisions about whom to see or not see (for example, seeking the company of people who are supportive and avoiding those who aren't); deciding what to eat, how to exercise, and what activities to do; and, finally, adopting healthy habits like refraining from smoking, taking medication, avoiding destabilizing drugs and alcohol, and engaging in active problem solving. (I'll talk more about self-management in Chapters 8 and 11.)

Problem-Solving Therapy

Resilience is a hallmark of mental health. Basic to resilience is the capacity to problem solve when faced with challenges in relationships or work. Problem-solving therapy is just what its name implies: It is learning to respond to difficulty using problem-solving skills rather than avoidance and denial, blame, discouragement, or defeat. Problem solving is a learned skill. As I mentioned earlier in this book, good therapists are good problem solvers and can help others learn problem solving for themselves.

Cognitive-Behavioral Therapy

Cognitive-behavioral therapy (CBT) is discussed in detail in Chapter 8. I mention it here because it is has become a standard of care in Great Britain to help control delusional thinking. CBT can be used to help a person reconsider fixed, false ideas that are interfering with day-to-day living. It is a valuable approach to helping a person gain perspective and function in ways that are less influenced by paranoid or other delusional thinking.

PORT

The schizophrenia Patient Outcomes Research Team (PORT) is an invaluable source of information about what has been shown to work in the treatment of schizophrenia. Not all treatments are reviewed by the PORT because there may not be studies sufficient to do so—but that doesn't mean that those treatments don't work. It simply means the data is not sufficient to comment on them.

The principal psychosocial treatments recognized by PORT include:

- assertive community treatment (ACT)
- supported employment
- family interventions
- skills training
- cognitive-behavioral therapy
- psychosocial interventions for alcohol and substance abuse

Refer to this list when you're trying to ascertain whether your loved one is getting evidence-based, comprehensive care. If your loved one isn't receiving one of the treatments on the list, ask someone on the treatment team why.

Schizoaffective Disorder

In the 1930s Dr. Jacob Kasanin coined the term *schizoaffective disorder* to refer to the combination of psychotic symptoms characteristic of schizophrenia and the presence of mood symptoms characteristic of depression or mania. Because many people suffer from both psychotic and mood problems, this diagnosis is widely used and serves to support targeting both psychotic and mood symptoms for treatment. Some doctors consider schizoaffective disorder a form of schizophrenia; indeed, it has many of the same symptoms, the same age of onset, and the same probable causation. I list it here as a separate condition because of how frequently the term is used.

WHAT MIGHT SCHIZOAFFECTIVE DISORDER LOOK LIKE TO YOU?

The principal symptoms just described for schizophrenia, including withdrawal, loss of functioning, and disordered thinking and behavior, are still what you will observe. But you are also likely to see your family member or friend show significant depressive feelings, including low mood, sadness, and pessimism. The person may feel terribly discouraged and say that life isn't worth living or that he or she would be better off dead. In some cases, excitement will sometimes take over the person's mood; your loved one will be hyper, unable to sit still, and will talk excessively and quickly. He or she may also speak about having big, often unrealistic plans to do things that seem to you out of his or her reach. These moods can last for days or weeks, sometimes longer, especially the depressive states.

DIAGNOSING SCHIZOAFFECTIVE DISORDER

A diagnosis of schizoaffective disorder is often made when a person meets criteria for both schizophrenia and a mood disorder, and when a diagnosis of either schizophrenia or a mood disorder alone does not seem to sufficiently encompass the range of symptoms a person displays.

TREATMENT

The specific treatments for schizoaffective disorder overlap with those of schizophrenia. Again, both medication and psychosocial treatments are needed. When used together, these treatments provide additive benefits.

Biological Treatments

If your loved one has schizoaffective disorder, a doctor may suggest a combination of medications—antipsychotic medications for the psychotic symptoms of hallucinations, delusions, and thought disorder, *and* an antidepressant or mood-stabilizing medication to treat the mood disorder.

There are two different types of medications that treat mood symptoms: *antidepressants* and *mood stabilizers* (see Chapter 7). Antidepressants include the various SSRIs and SNRIs mentioned in the section on depression. The mood stabilizers you may hear suggested include valproate, carbamazepine, lamotrigine, and the veteran drug lithium (which, in my opinion, is highly underutilized in today's practices). Antipsychotic medications are also discussed in Chapter 7. Clozapine is often used to control symptoms of both schizophrenia and schizoaffective disorder.

A note for women of childbearing age: We now know that valproate, an anticonvulsant frequently used to treat mood disorders, is *teratogenic*, meaning that it may disrupt fetal development. A pregnant mother who takes valproate is exposing her fetus to a higher risk of developmental and birth abnormalities. In addition, lithium has long been known to expose a fetus to a heart abnormality, which may be one reason for its diminished use among younger women. Any woman of childbearing age who may be treated with these medications should have a pregnancy test and a clear discussion with her doctor of the choices, risks, and benefits from any medication.

Psychosocial Treatments

Although there is limited research specifically about psychosocial treatments for schizoaffective disorder, the same principles of comprehensive and evidence-based treatment noted for schizophrenia and mood disorders apply.

Acute Psychotic Disorder

Mary, a college student, was brought to the emergency room by her parents after her roommate had called them to say that Mary was "pacing around, not sleeping, and talking nonsense about voices telling her she is no good." There was no evidence that Mary had been drinking or using drugs. Her vital signs and appearance gave no suggestion of any acute medical problem, though the emergency room physician performed a physical exam and ordered a variety of blood tests. After the doctor had finished the exam, he called me in for a consultation.

I took Mary and her parents to a quiet room. I listened to her and then asked questions about what she was experiencing. Mary said that a man's voice was telling her that she was "ugly" and a "horrible girl." She was scared and couldn't sit still.

After observing Mary's discomfort and with the assessment mostly done, I asked Mary if she would be willing to take a medication that would make her less frightened and restless. She agreed. I explained that a nurse would bring a tranquilizer pill that would help her feel better within an hour.

I also told Mary that she was having a severe stress reaction, and that I knew from her parents that her behavior was markedly different from her usual self. I said that I thought this reaction would pass quickly and that the medication would help in the short-term as she figured out what had happened.

While waiting for the medication to take effect, I began to ask about the weeks before Mary's episode in order to obtain a good medical history. I learned that Mary had ended a short but disastrous relationship with a young man who had quickly become emotionally abusive to her. At the same time, Mary's schoolwork was suffering because she couldn't focus on her studies, and she was having difficulty sleeping and concentrating during the day. The night before the psychotic symptoms began, Mary's ex-boyfriend had shown up at her dorm insisting on seeing her. Mary refused, but the incident had rattled her and she couldn't sleep at all that night. By morning, she was experiencing the full-blown symptoms of an acute psychotic disorder.

Acute psychotic disorders are uncommon, but when they come on, they can do so intensely and rapidly. Acute psychotic states typically affect individuals in their twenties and often follow a stressful event, like the breakup of a relationship, a family fight, the loss of a job, or a traumatic accident.

When a woman has an acute psychosis after giving birth, it is called a *postpartum psychosis* and should be differentiated from other forms of acute psychosis.

WHAT MIGHT AN ACUTE PSYCHOTIC EPISODE LOOK LIKE TO YOU?

Your otherwise well family member or friend will suddenly seem "out of his mind." He or she will behave in a markedly different way, almost overnight. The person may do bizarre things like walk in the street without clothing or call elected officials, or may talk incoherently, sing or yell, or seem fearful or expansive. People experiencing an acute psychotic episode are usually very agitated, unable to sit still and unable to sleep. And although it's clear to you that something is seriously wrong, your loved one has very limited insight and may not think there is a problem. All of these behaviors occur after some highly troubling event has caused your loved one's world to come crashing down.

DIAGNOSING ACUTE PSYCHOTIC DISORDER

The acute psychotic state can include hallucinations, delusions, disorganized thinking, incoherent talking, volatile moods, disorientation, impaired attention and memory, and bizarre behavior. An acute psychotic disorder is brief, in the clinical sense—it only lasts for up to 30 days, and often much less. Although those 30 days might feel interminable to you, there is an end in sight. If the psychosis lasts longer than 30 days, it means that another condition is affecting the person, and other diagnoses need to be considered.

It is important to distinguish an acute psychotic disorder from *toxic* or *medical* states, especially those induced by:

- Drugs like PCP, methamphetamine, cocaine, ecstasy, steroids, hashish, and marijuana (especially synthetic marijuana, sometimes called Spice, K2, and many other names), often mixed with alcohol or prescription narcotic and sedative drugs
- A medical condition, like an infection producing a high fever, an acute and hyperactive thyroid or adrenal disease, a head injury, or a blood vessel rupture in the brain

These conditions are acute physiological (organic) medical states and must be properly diagnosed and treated.

It's also important that the patient is asked about suicidal thinking or extreme fearfulness during an acute psychotic episode, as both of these can result in self-destructive behavior or violent outbursts, the latter the result of the person's attempts at self-protection from what he or she perceives as a threatening situation.

Scary as an acute psychotic state may be for family members and friends, this is the time to be reassuring and hopeful with your loved one. It's better to wait to talk about problems—even problems that may have triggered the psychotic state—until the person has the psychic where-withal to tolerate looking at difficult matters.

ONSET

Younger people, often in their twenties, are the age group most likely to experience an acute psychotic disorder, and these disorders are more common in women than in men. The onset of acute psychotic disorder is rapid: With little warning, acute symptoms of psychosis (like hallucinations and delusions) erupt, and a person becomes markedly agitated and volatile. The severity of the psychotic state is not a predictor of whether the patient will recover. As with other psychotic illnesses, the sooner someone can be treated, the more rapid the recovery will be.

CAUSES OF ACUTE PSYCHOTIC DISORDER

Unlike acute drug-induced or medically induced psychoses, acute psychotic states do not have a clear cause. There may be a genetic or biological vulnerability in some individuals, which can be set off by a significant life stressor. People with poor coping skills and weak supports are more vulnerable to severe reactions.

TREATMENT

As I mentioned, these acute psychotic states are brief, with most people experiencing a full recovery in days or weeks. However, treatment may need to be extended for months, depending on what triggered the eruption of the illness. Like with all psychotic conditions, treatments for acute psychotic disorders fall into two categories: biological and psychosocial treatments.

Biological Treatments

The sudden extreme distress and agitation of this condition, coupled with the loss of reality and hallucinatory or delusional experiences, makes the use of an antipsychotic medication an appropriate intervention. Antipsychotic medications are highly effective in reducing psychotic symptoms within hours or days. They also lessen agitation and fearfulness, which has the added benefit of reducing the risk of danger to self or others that might result from a person's responding to psychotic ideas.

Low doses of antipsychotic medications are generally effective and produce fewer side effects. Anti-anxiety medications (like clonazepam or lorazepam) can also be very helpful in low doses and are sometimes used concurrently with an antipsychotic medication. Don't be surprised if the doctor suggests continuing the antipsychotic medication for days or weeks after the symptoms abate: Continued antipsychotic medication may help prevent relapse. Ongoing visits to the psychiatrist or prescribing physician or nurse are essential in order to monitor symptoms as well as side effects from medication, which can cause problems of their own (like sedation, stiffness, or restlessness).

It is imperative that people experiencing an acute psychotic disorder completely abstain from drug and alcohol use, regardless of whether those substances were a contributing factor to the original psychotic episode. Try to envision a brain already racing and in an acute psychotic state. Adding the effects of alcohol, marijuana, cocaine, or other drugs only introduces more undue stress and disequilibrium into the brain's disturbed environment. Ask your loved one what *he* or *she* imagines the effects of drinking or drugs might be, so that you can help the person decide to stay sober.

Psychosocial Treatments

Information, clarity, and support are the tenets of psychosocial intervention for this condition—*both* for the person who is ill *and* for that person's family. The person experiencing an acute psychotic episode needs to understand simply and clearly that this is a *severe stress reaction* that will be over in a few days or weeks. In the short term, families need to have good information about the illness and its prognosis. In the longer term, the patient and the family need to consider how to reduce the stressors that may have contributed to the initial episode.

While your loved one is in treatment for an acute psychotic episode, it is vital that the family be a supportive unit. This is not the time to confront your loved one about what he or she may have done, or to criticize any problem or failure on his or her part. People in this state of mind are already overwhelmed—they are in a psychotic flight from an unbearable reality. Your family member needs your patience and empathy.

Once the crisis has passed and the acute psychosis has resolved, you and your loved one can consider what therapy might be helpful in moving forward. Together, you want to think about how the person can put the episode in perspective and improve coping skills so that the risk of relapse is reduced. If psychotherapy has already begun, the focus needs to be on identifying and reducing potential stressors. The therapy should continue until your family member has achieved perspective and stability.

Bipolar Disorder

Nearly 1% of people suffer from bipolar disorder (sometimes referred to as "manic depression"). Bipolar disorder is a serious mood disorder that produces major mood swings that include mania and depression.

It usually comes on in a person's early twenties and can last throughout adult life. Although a diagnosis of bipolar disorder can seem like a life-long burden, patients with a good support system and who are active in managing their illness can live full and productive lives.

Without treatment, bipolar disorder can have a devastating effect on the person and the person's family and relationships. Divorce rates among people with bipolar disorder are two to three times that of other couples. In addition, it can be hard for people with untreated bipolar disorder to hold down a job or function in the community at a productive level.

WHAT MIGHT BIPOLAR DISORDER LOOK LIKE TO YOU?

Again, bipolar disorder involves both depressive and manic states. Review the section on depression to see how that aspect of this disorder may look. Here, I'll talk about what you might see during a manic episode.

Over the course of days to weeks, your loved one starts sleeping less and less. He or she seems to have boundless energy and is full of ideas. At first, the person may be infectiously funny and pleasant to be around, but over time that mood becomes more irritable and unstable. Your loved one may start drinking more or using drugs secretly. If the person was on medication for bipolar disorder, he or she has probably stopped taking it because it is apt to curtail the person's sense of empowerment. Money may be missing from where you keep it or from your bank account. Bad judgment is common during an emerging or full manic state: Your loved one may spend money recklessly and engage in risky behaviors, including casual (and unprotected sex), gambling, driving at high speeds, and frequenting neighborhoods and settings where no good is known to happen. Your loved one may accuse you of being boring, oppressive, or ruining the person's life or hopes. As time goes by and the condition goes untreated, the excitement mounts and your loved one is unable to get anything done; behaviors become progressively more threatening to the safety and wellbeing of the family. No amount of commonsense talk seems to make any difference.

DIAGNOSING BIPOLAR DISORDER

The defining state for the diagnosis of bipolar disorder is the presence of a manic episode. The person may have had depressions in the past, but it is not until mania also appears that a diagnosis of bipolar disorder can be made.

Mania is a state of great emotional and psychological intensity. For the diagnosis to be made, a person has to: feel an inflated sense of self, feel a diminished need for sleep, be talkative (sometimes to the point where ideas exceed their capacity to be expressed), be hyperkinetic (have excessive and sometimes uncontrollable activity or muscle movements), and be highly distractible. These symptoms must persist for a week or longer. School or work functioning plummets. Judgment is typically seriously impaired.

The lack of judgment that stems from a manic episode can cause considerable damage to the lives of loved ones and friends. As I mentioned, the manic person may spend money without care, gamble, or engage in impulsive sexual or other irresponsible behavior. Mania challenges the patience and love of every family.

Some people with bipolar disorder will have a manic episode before experiencing any depressive episodes; other times the mania follows depressive episodes. In fact, the diagnosis can be made even when the person hasn't had any depressive episodes. To reiterate, the defining criterion for the diagnosis is a manic episode. If a person doesn't have a manic episode, he or she doesn't have bipolar disorder.

When bipolar disorder shows persistent evidence of psychotic symptoms that decrease a person's ability to function in a family, among friends, and in work or school, this may indicate the presence of a schizoaffective disorder (discussed earlier).

ONSET AND CAUSES OF BIPOLAR DISORDER

Bipolar disorder usually comes on in a person's early twenties and lasts throughout his or her adult life. As with the other psychotic illnesses I've discussed, both genetic and environmental factors appear to contribute to development of the illness.

TREATMENT

Your loved one's doctor will recommend a course of treatment based on whether the bipolar condition requires *acute* or *maintenance* care:

- *Acute treatment* refers to what is done to control and manage the destabilizing and disruptive symptoms of mania (or the depressive phase of the illness).
- *Maintenance treatment* (also called *continuation treatment*) is the ongoing care for this often chronic and recurring disease. Instances of a single, isolated lifetime manic attack do exist, but as a rule people with this disorder experience more than one episode.

Acute Treatment

Acute treatment is determined by the presence of one of three states:

- Acute mania (or mixed mania and depression)
- Depression in bipolar disorder
- Rapid cycling disorder

Acute Mania. Mania is an intolerable condition, both for the patient (eventually) and their loved ones. Mania is not a wonderful, never-ending high: It is an *overwhelming state of excitement, agitation, and irritation* where your loved one will have little or no insight into the severity of the illness. Acute mania is usually treated in a hospital because of how chaotic, uncontrolled, and resistant a manic person can be.

When symptoms of excitement and sleeplessness are severe, the doctor's goal is to quiet the mania with a combination of a mood-stabilizing medication (like lithium or valproate) and an antipsychotic agent. Extreme agitation or restlessness may be treated (briefly) with a benzodiazepine, like clonazepam or lorazepam. Less severe manic (or mixed manic and depressive states) may respond to the singular use of a mood stabilizer or an antipsychotic medication (some antipsychotic medications have achieved FDA approval for the treatment of mania).

If your family member was taking an antidepressant, you can expect the doctor to discontinue it. Although depression is common in people with bipolar disorder, treatment of depression with antidepressants alone, especially during a manic episode, can actually have the opposite of the intended affect, further destabilizing the manic state. Even when in a stable state, people with bipolar disorder who are prescribed antidepressants (for intermittent depressions) often have them combined with mood stabilizers. *Rarely are antidepressants the only treatment for bipolar disorder.*

Severe states of mania that threaten to exhaust a patient to the point of physical danger—including cardiac or vascular collapse—can be effectively treated with electroconvulsive therapy (ECT), though it is very uncommon for medications alone to be insufficient. ECT may also be a safer treatment option for people whose medical conditions limit the use of antipsychotic and anti-manic medications.

Depression in Bipolar Disorder. Depression in a person with bipolar disorder presents a medication challenge because some antidepressants can increase the risk of unleashing a person's vulnerability to developing mania. Research evidence supports the use of lithium for bipolar depression; other possibilities exist but may require consultation with a doctor who is an expert in psychopharmacology.

The presence of psychotic symptoms like depressive delusions or hallucinations generally calls for the use of antipsychotic medications (or ECT).

Rapid Cycling Disorder. Rapid cycling disorder is a highly disturbing form of bipolar disorder. It is diagnosed when a person shows frequent (as many as four or more) manic or depressive episodes in one year. For example, there could be a depression that improves but is quickly followed by a manic or hypomanic (less intense mania) episode, which is then followed by another depressed or excited state.

The use or abuse of drugs and alcohol (especially heavy use) can induce mood fluctuations that spur the onset of rapid cycling. The gravity of rapid cycling on a person's functioning, as well as on family and friends, calls for bipolar patients to maintain sobriety, if at all possible. If antidepressants are thought to worsen rapid cycling, they should be stopped, if possible.

Lithium and valproate are effective treatments for rapid cycling bipolar disorder. However, this condition is difficult to control, and often requires a combination of mood stabilizers and antipsychotic medications—as well as disciplined self-management.

Maintenance Treatment

After an acute manic episode, a person with bipolar illness is at a high risk of relapse in the 6 months after the episode abates. In order to avoid another episode, your loved one needs to continue treatment *after* symptoms have gone away, even if he or she may feel completely normal.

Lithium and valproate show the best evidence of effectiveness in maintenance treatment. A specialty psychopharmacologist may be able to suggest other medications or combinations of medications. If your family member was treated with an antipsychotic medication (in addition to a mood stabilizer) for mania during the acute episode, you will want to question its use once the mania abates.

In the maintenance phase of bipolar disorder, *psychosocial treatments* can have great value.

Illness Education and Self-Management. This generally is taught in the beginning stages of psychotherapy. Lack of insight (not understanding that one has the illness, especially the manic aspect), as well as a persistent yearning for the high that mania provides, results in problems engaging and retaining patients in treatment. Illness education and self-management training can help to mitigate these problems.

Ongoing Psychotherapy. The more skilled a person becomes in navigating human relationships and daily work or family stresses, the more likely it is that the disorder will remain manageable. Ongoing psychotherapy that focuses on interpersonal relations and everyday problem solving can be very helpful.

Case Management or Assertive Community Treatment (ACT). Individuals whose bipolar disorder creates persistent functional impairments in school, work, and relationships (and results in hospitalizations or emergency room visits) may require a more intensive and comprehensive treatment. Case management or ACT may be needed for a period of time to help the person stay in treatment, continue to take medications, and pursue the hard work of recovery.

Twelve-Step and Other Recovery-Oriented Activities. Identifying the presence of a co-occurring alcohol or drug disorder is a critical aspect of the evaluation and treatment of a person with bipolar disorder, because neither condition can improve unless both are identified and treated. Twelve-step and other recovery-oriented activities may be an essential component of your loved one's recovery.

Family Psychoeducation and Support. Because this illness is so hard on family members and friends, family psychoeducation and support is something you should seek. The National Alliance on Mental Illness (NAMI), The Depression and Bipolar Support Alliance, and other support and advocacy organizations can help you learn what helps and what disturbs the illness, how to identify early warning signs of relapse, and what you can and cannot do to help your loved one. You are not alone; many other families face this illness, too.

Medications:
What to Know, What to Ask

Once you find a clinician who practices the principles of good care, you and your loved one will face the complex questions of whether to use a medication, which one (or ones), at what dose, and for how long, among other considerations. In fact, the choice of a medication, starting with whether to use one or not, may be one of the most important decisions you will face.

Most treatment recommendations, especially for a serious or persistent mental disorder, will include the use of medication. This chapter discusses which medications are typically used for certain disorders, how they may work, and the critical balancing of benefit, risk, and side effects. I'll also offer suggestions on how to talk with the prescribing doctor about medications, and I end the chapter by going over commonly asked questions. This chapter should not serve as a substitute for speaking with the treating clinicians—you should always go to them to seek information and answer questions. Rather, my aim is to better inform you for those moments.

It is an understatement to say that psychiatric medications have come to dominate the treatment of mental conditions. One very good reason for their highly common use, controversy notwithstanding, is that psychotropic medications are effective, even lifesaving, for many people—especially for patients with moderate to severe psychiatric conditions. With the proper medications and other treatments, these individuals can avoid hospital stays, succeed in their efforts to build their lives, reduce the burden they may create for their loved ones, and achieve what we all want—namely, to have a life rich with relationships, work, and purpose.

As you and your loved one pursue the road of recovery, you'll need to keep asking the right questions, and make sure that you are getting answers that you understand. You and your loved one want to feel confident that your doctor is suggesting medications because scientific research has shown they're effective—not because the medication is being heavily marketed. You also want to make sure that your loved one (and you, if possible) is treated as an equal partner in making decisions about his or her health.

Choosing A Psychiatric Medication

It's important to remember that not even experts in the medical community fully understand exactly how medications work in people with mental illnesses. As I mentioned earlier, the brain is a complex, mysterious organ, and we still have much to learn about it. In fact, the medical and research community continues to debate whether some psychiatric medications work *at all*. The debate is perhaps the most contentious when it comes to antidepressants and antipsychotic medications, some of the most widely used medications *in the world*.

The medical research community is searching for a greater understanding of how medications work, and for more effective medications. Yet, an important and reassuring study on the effectiveness of psychiatric medications, published in *The British Journal of Psychiatry* in 2012, answered an ever present question: How well do psychiatric medications work? In a carefully constructed research study called a "meta-analysis" (where the results of many studies are compiled and examined to answer specific questions), the authors provided "the first . . . panoramic overview of major drugs." Researchers looked at 48 different drugs used to treat 20 general medical diseases and 16 different drugs used to treat 8 psychiatric diseases. The researchers concluded that psychiatric drugs, overall, were *as effective* as those used in general medicine.

Although some individual drugs for a few medical conditions outperformed the psychiatric drugs they studied, as a whole, the two groups were about the same in terms of their effectiveness. For those affected by psychiatric illnesses, this research tells us that when it comes to benefits, psychiatric medications hold their own when compared with general medical medications in the treatment of diseases that affect so many people.

The authors of the study also noted that the benefits of medications can *accrue* over time. This stands as a reminder for families that continuous (ongoing) medication use can make more of a difference, supporting the principle of continuous treatment.

How do these medications work? A variety of theories exist about how psychiatric medications may affect brain chemicals (like dopamine, serotonin, and norepinephrine), help brain cells regenerate, and improve brain-cell circuitry (how they pass messages). But theory is not proof. What we do know is that there are abnormalities in how the brain works with psychiatric illness, and that these medications can improve symptoms.

How do doctors decide which medications to prescribe for which conditions? In the case of mental illnesses, it isn't because we understand the underlying mechanisms of the diseases they aim to improve or their therapeutic actions in the brain (or body). Rather, it's because findings have shown that the medication helps people with their condition. Psychiatric medications are perhaps best understood as not addressing specific psychiatric *diseases*, but rather as addressing specific *symptoms*. I want to repeat this point: When chosen and administered properly, *medications improve symptoms*. Antipsychotic medications can reduce agitation and hallucinations in people with a variety of disorders, including schizophrenia, bipolar disorder, and postcardiac surgery ICU delirium. Antidepressant medications can be useful for patients with depression, anxiety, and some pain syndromes. Mood stabilizers can help a variety of psychiatric and medical/neurological conditions where moods fluctuate abnormally.

In considering a psychiatric medication, therefore, a patient and doctor should be clear and specific about what symptoms need to be "targeted"—that is, what symptoms the patient and doctor want to improve. Knowing the targets of the treatment will help you decide which medication to use and whether it is working.

It's extremely important to maintain open communication with the doctor. Some people take the initiative to search on-line for information—finding sources that range from the credible to the absurd—but regardless of the amount of research you do on your own, you still need a doctor with expertise, experience, and objectivity who will recommend a medication treatment, write the prescription, and guide the care. Some people also feel too shy or afraid—or too emotionally overwhelmed—to be able to be an informed consumer who actively discusses treatment options with the doctor. The stigma associated with mental illness often compounds this problem. But it's important to try to overcome these fears. The more you know about treatment options, the more you can advocate for your family member and ensure that treatment will be successful.

ADVERTISING AND PHYSICIAN DETAILING

Good doctors and nurses (and there are many!) want to reduce psychic pain and accelerate recovery in their patients, so they are often looking for a medication that's new or different or better or faster. Unfortunately, one result of this well-intentioned attitude is that they may prescribe a drug that a pharmaceutical representative or advertisement has promoted even if there is little or no evidence that it might be a better choice for your loved one's specific symptoms. The same problem can happen when doctors want to be responsive to patients or family members who ask for a new or specific medication.

Physician Detailing. "Physician detailing" is when foot soldiers for pharmaceutical companies visit doctors' offices or hospitals and urge them to prescribe their company's drug. Increasingly, hospitals and professional practices are limiting company representatives' access to doctors and prohibiting the pharmaceutical companies from giving "presents," however small (like pens, pads, and food). However, many pharmaceutical representatives also provide free "samples" or supplies of certain medications their company manufactures. Doctors can use these samples to start patients on medications, or to supply people who may not be able to afford to pay at pharmacies.

That said, physician detailing can be a real problem, with doctors selecting medications based more on pharmaceutical information and incentives than on scientific evidence of their effectiveness (or safety). In 2009, for instance, the pharmaceutical giant Eli Lilly was ordered by a Pennsylvania court to pay a fine of $1.4 billion for marketing its antipsychotic medication Zyprexa (olanzapine) to psychiatrists and other physicians to use for what are called "off-label" indications. In other words, Eli

Lilly was marketing the drug to doctors as a treatment for diseases, like dementia, where no evidence of its effectiveness had been established. By "marketing," the court meant that Eli Lilly had handsomely paid a few very influential psychiatrists, "thought leaders" in their fields, to speak about the drug's utility to their peers at upscale restaurants and professional meetings sponsored by Eli Lilly. In 2012, GlaxoSmithKline agreed to plead guilty and pay a $3 billion fine for illegally marketing drugs and withholding safety data. There are other examples as well.

The Ethics of Clinical Trials. Pharmaceutical companies also have been a mainstay in funding the required clinical trials of drugs before they are approved for use by the FDA. These trials also help to fund the work of psychiatrists who lead this type of research, raising many questions about the ethics of clinical trials. We know, for example, that drug companies have had too much control in determining which clinical studies they publish, holding back what they don't want the public to know about their product.

Psychiatry (and medicine in general) has been tarnished by its close interaction with pharmaceutical companies. Can you trust your physician or psychiatrist to come up with the correct diagnosis and proper, evidence-based treatment? You and your loved one want to try to answer that question.

You are on firm ground asking about how your doctor has come to a recommendation about a medication for your loved one. A good clinician will be able to discuss the evidence supporting the chosen medication, as well as provide the risks and benefits, along with other options.

Direct-to-Consumer Advertising. Beware: You are also in the marketing crosshairs of the pharmaceutical industry. Direct-to-consumer advertising (DTC) is a new and powerful tool shaping American prescribing practices. These are the ads in magazines and on television and radio that urge you to get help for depression, anxiety, urinary frequency, osteoporosis, arthritis, sexual dysfunction, and many of the other human conditions from which we suffer.

DTC has been shown to generate greater sales than marketing directly to doctors. Thus, the pharmaceutical industry has retooled some of its sales efforts so that you'll ask for a drug by name when you go into a primary-care doctor's office. If you name a specific drug, the doctor is pretty likely to give you what you have asked for. Specialty doctors, like psychiatrists (myself included), are apt to behave the same way because we know that "patient preference" is a big factor in whether or not people follow through with treatment.

WHAT TO ASK

Being an informed consumer is key. Encourage your loved one to ask the following questions when the doctor suggests a medication (or ask them yourself, if you can):

- "Why did you select that medication for my condition?"
- "Why did you choose this medication over another one?"
- "What benefits can I expect from this drug, and how long will I have to wait to see them?"
- "Are there other approved medications, or other treatments, for my condition?"

These questions will help you understand not only why the doctor is advising one drug over another, but also what *alternatives* there are to this medication.

Your doctor should be able to answer these questions in a brief and understandable way. If he or she doesn't, keep asking. Some doctors will provide information sheets about a medication or treatment, which can be very helpful. You can also find important information online as well as from the resources in Appendix B at the end of this book.

Treatment Works

I want to repeat that treatment approaches for mental illnesses are *no different* from treatment approaches for other serious and persistent medical illnesses such as heart and lung diseases, diabetes, asthma, and cancer. There are scientifically based medication treatments that work for the wide array of mental disorders. There is reason for hope if your loved one receives and remains committed to proven treatments, including medications for many people.

It is my view that psychiatric medications are both underused and overused: Too many people with mental disorders who could benefit from medications do not receive them, and too many people who do not require medications are taking them. This is true for a wide variety of drugs, including antidepressants, psychostimulants (for attention-deficit hyperactivity disorder), tranquilizers, and sleeping pills. Another point I want to make is that psychiatry has become far too reliant on medication treatment. Frequently, medications are an invaluable component of good care, but as a rule medication alone is not enough. If your loved one is only taking medication, especially for a serious mental illness, then you need to ask why. Medications and therapy (including talking therapies and rehabilitation programs, discussed in Chapter 8) can complement each other, delivering greater benefit than either alone.

Sometimes the first medication that is tried will work, and sometimes a person has to keep looking for the right medication. Don't give up, and don't let the prescribing doctor give up. If the first choice is not effective or produces too many side effects, there need to be systematic, sequential trials. What this means is that the doctor and patient both keep trying one medication after another—in *adequate doses* (sometimes this means increasing a dose; it also means not using doses higher than needed) and for an *adequate duration* to determine if a good response will be achieved. Doctors, as well as the patient and family, should keep a careful record of what has been tried, at what doses, for how long, and with what response and side effects.

When you and your loved one do see results, that is *not* the time to stop treatment. Treatment should usually be continued for some time, depending on the condition. Medication treatment might last a couple of years, or longer, to establish the benefits in an enduring way. As time passes, your loved one will be able to discuss with the doctor whether he or she needs to continue on the medication, at what dose, and for how long. Not everyone needs long-term medication treatment. But deciding to reduce doses or discontinue a medication must always be done with the doctor. A patient's reducing or discontinuing a medication on his or her own can have disastrous—sometimes even fatal—results.

Again, keeping communication open with the doctor is crucial. Finding the right medication, and the right dose, might take a little time.

But by being patient and persistent, you, the patient, and the doctor will be able to get your loved one headed on the road to recovery.

Classes of Psychiatric Medications

Psychiatric medications are grouped into the following six classes:

- *Antidepressants* are used for depression (moderate to severe, as well as chronic depression), anxiety disorders (including generalized anxiety, OCD, and PTSD), and a variety of dysphoric (painful mood) states found in people with personality disorders.
- *Antipsychotics* are used to treat psychotic symptoms that occur in schizophrenia, schizoaffective disorder, mania, and a host of brain disturbances produced by infection, trauma, or ingestion of drugs.
- *Psychostimulants* are used for attention-deficit hyperactivity disorder and narcolepsy.
- *Mood stabilizers* are used for bipolar disorder, schizoaffective disorder, and mood instability produced by organic and neurological mental conditions, and for severe forms of personality disorder.
- *Anxiolytics* (anti-anxiety medications) are used for many anxiety disorders as well as for situational stress.
- *Central nervous system depressants* are used as sleeping pills and for anesthesia.

Within each of these classes is a wide array of individual medications that can work slightly differently and often have different side effects. If you go online to find out more about these classes of medications and the specific medications in each class, go to reliable websites, such as the National Institute of Mental Health (NIMH), NAMI, and the Network of Care. Be sure to look for dates of issue on the information you are reading, because details on these medications, including benefits, side effects, and doses, can change over time.

Onset of Action

Onset of action simply means how long it takes for a medication to produce an effect. Some medications, like tranquilizers, have a quick onset of action, whereas others, such as antidepressants, can take longer. Your loved one may have to take a medication for several weeks before you'll see positive results.

Ask the doctor: *How long before I know if the medication is working?* Doctors ask this question when they are patients themselves. You can, too.

Medication Schedule

Can your loved one realistically follow the instructions for taking the medications? Patients and families need to consider the schedule for taking the prescribed medications. Time and time again, I have seen hospital patients placed on medication regimens that no one could follow on one's own at home. For example, a patient may be scheduled to take five or six different medications three or four times a day. Who can maintain this type of schedule at home? When working? Or having a social life?

The more pills they have to take in a day, and the more different times in the day they have to take them, the less likely people will be able to comply. A complex schedule is even less likely to work if a patient has difficulty concentrating, has problems believing he or she needs the medication, has a lot of side effects, or feels like a burden to others.

As a general rule, fewer medications are better than more medications. Simpler schedules of once or twice a day are far better than complex regimens. And the minimally effective dose is always better than a higher dose.

If your loved one has been prescribed multiple medications, ask the doctor whether it's possible to take fewer. And if the schedule is one you think your loved one won't be able to manage, ask your doctor whether it can be simplified. If your loved one is being treated by several prescribing physicians (such as a primary-care doctor and psychiatrist), it's best if those doctors can be in communication with each other. If that isn't possible, make sure you or your loved one is informing each of what the other is prescribing.

Side Effects and Adverse Effects

As I mentioned earlier, medications are chosen to "target" certain symptoms. But most medications will have effects other than those on the targeted symptoms. These are called *side effects*. Depending on a patient's particular needs, sometimes a medication's side effects will be beneficial, such as an antidepressant taken at bedtime with sedating properties. Other times a side effect will be of little or no consequence—or last only briefly. Still other times the side effects will be problematic, making it important that you know about them.

Adverse effects are side effects that are dangerous. It's especially important to ask the doctor about these.

> **Common Side Effects of Psychiatric Medications**
> Weight gain
> Drowsiness
> Restlessness
> Muscle tension or stiffness
> Blurry vision, dry mouth, constipation (often occur together)
> Sensitivity to sunlight or sunburn
> Rash

Questions to ask:

- "What are the side effects of the medication you are suggesting?"
- "Are there any serious, or life-threatening, problems with this medication?"

Not everyone gets side effects, and side effects do not always interfere with everyday life. Of course, an ideal medication is one with substantial benefits and few or no negative side effects. But ideal medications are like ideal homes or cars—not very common. Instead, what we often see is the good (benefit) in a balance with the not-so-good (negative side effects). Individuals are then left to decide what to do, which can be confusing for a patient who wants to get better but doesn't want his or her quality of life to diminish even further from side effects. Thankfully, many side effects improve over time (days to weeks), or can be managed by lowering the dose, by changing the time of day the medication is taken, or even by taking other medications that reduce or counteract the side effects. I have also seen many people learn to live with side effects because of the benefits they achieve from taking a medication.

If your family member or friend is having problems with side effects, *write them down* and be sure to *raise them* when meeting with the doctor. Your doctor wants to find the right medication—a medication that improves a patient's symptoms without causing too much trouble in other aspects of the person's life. Psychiatrists (and primary-care doctors prescribing psychiatric medications) have learned a great deal about how to minimize side effects, so don't hesitate to ask for help!

ADVERSE EFFECTS

Adverse effects are serious problems that need immediate attention from your healthcare professional. Some of the uncommon but serious adverse effects include:

- *Dystonic reaction.* This is a sudden spasm of muscles in the neck, back, tongue, or eyelids. It can be very frightening but is rarely dangerous. It is typically brief, and is reversible with time or medications that end the spasm. Dystonic reactions are far less common today because of the limited use or lower doses of certain antipsychotic medications (like haloperidol).
- *Neuroleptic malignant syndrome.* This is a very rare, potentially life-threatening reaction to antipsychotic medications. This syndrome comes on over the course of one or more days and consists of fever and muscle stiffness. This condition is a *medical emergency*.
- *Seizures.* Some medications can lower the "seizure threshold," or the level at which an individual person's brain will have a seizure.

People with underlying seizure disorders are most prone to this adverse effect, which warrants *immediate medical attention.*

- *Agranulocytosis.* This is a *very serious* adverse effect that requires immediate attention. It is when your bone marrow stops making a certain type of white blood cell that is essential to fighting infection. A rare adverse effect of the antipsychotic medication clozapine, agranulocytosis usually comes on early in the treatment. In the past, the use of clozapine was very limited because of fears of this reaction; today, careful blood monitoring has made it possible to spot this reaction and end it, thus increasing the safety profile for this medication.

  Because clozapine is the only antipsychotic medication proven effective in people with schizophrenia (and schizoaffective disorder) who do not respond to other medications, it could be an important medication to consider, as long as you weigh the risk and benefit, and everyone is engaged in careful monitoring to minimize risk.

As I mentioned, adverse effects are rare. But a person must be alert to his or her body and get help if the unexpected happens.

Drug Interactions

Another important matter to discuss with the doctor is *drug interactions*— the chemical reactions that medications can have with one another when a person takes them simultaneously. For example, different types of antidepressants taken simultaneously can induce sudden spikes in blood pressure or a syndrome called "serotonin syndrome," which is characterized by fever, confusion, increased heart rate, sweating, twitching, and tremor. Certain medications can have additive side effects like fatigue or sleepiness when they are combined (like taking anxiolytics with an antipsychotic). Some medications can increase or decrease the blood levels of other medications, causing more problems with side effects (when levels are increased) or lessening the benefits (when levels are reduced). Finally, certain medications prescribed by a primary-care doctor for physical conditions (like heart disease) may have interactions with medications prescribed by a psychiatrist, and vice versa.

The list of drug interactions is so extensive that doctors, nurses, and pharmacists usually have to look them up. It is up to the patient, and the family when possible, *to inform all doctors prescribing medications of all the medications a person is taking.* Pharmacists are very knowledgeable about drug interactions and can be very helpful to you and your loved one. Generally, doctors will ask too, but sometimes they don't.

INTERACTIONS WITH ALCOHOL AND ALTERNATIVE MEDICINES

A very common but not regularly discussed drug interaction is between alcohol and prescribed psychiatric medications. Alcohol, even a single glass of wine (generally regarded as beneficial to most people's health), can interfere with the therapeutic action of many prescribed medications or make one glass of wine feel like two or three. Be sure that your loved one discusses the use of alcohol with his or her doctor. Depending on the person, the medications, and the capacity for moderation, not all doctors will prohibit the use of alcohol.

The use of alternative medicines, like herbal medications and a variety of fish oils and antioxidants, is extremely widespread in the United States and many other countries. Often, little is known about the side effects and risks of herbals and other compounds sold in health-food stores and on the Internet, even if they have apparent benefits. The interactions of alternative medicines with prescribed medications are virtually unknown because there are no carefully controlled scientific studies. However, if your loved one is taking these compounds, or is planning to, urge the person to discuss it with the doctor. At the very least, patients and families can monitor the benefits and side effects of alternative medications and supplements, and learn together.

Dealing with Medication Problems or Emergencies

What do you do if there is a problem with the medication, especially a serious problem that can't wait until the next appointment? The patient and family need to discuss this potential scenario at the time the medication is prescribed—not wait to deal with it until the middle of the night when the problem is upon you. You need to know how your doctor runs his or her practice. Some doctors are willing to be contacted during business hours, nights, and weekends. Some will have coverage arrangements with other doctors, as often happens in a group practice. And some will be part of a clinic that may or may not have evening and night-time coverage. The way to find out is to ask.

When problems with a medication come on suddenly or are severe, unknown, or frightening, most experienced clinicians will tell you to go to the nearest emergency room. If you can't get in touch with your clinician and you're worried that your loved one is having what appears to be a serious problem with a medication, it may not be prudent to wait to get the clinician's advice—just take the person to the hospital.

Paying for the Medication

Even if a doctor may think a particular medication is best, you still need to know: *Will we be able to afford it?* There is no shame in asking about the cost of a medication, or in talking about how the cost will affect your family member or your family. If the payment, or copayment, of a medication is likely to result in you or your family member not buying it—and not taking it—what sense is there in being silent? This is not a time for pride to preclude success. Ask your doctor to help you find a medication that your family can afford.

Another question to answer is: *Does my insurance cover it?* Many insurance payers, including Medicaid and Medicare, have what are called *preferred (limited) formularies*—selected medications that are approved and covered by insurance. A preferred drug on a formulary is one that the insurer has decided to (more fully) cover for payment. An insurer's decisions to limit what medications are covered are usually determined by evidence that a more expensive drug has not been proven more effective in treating a certain condition than a less expensive one. This is especially the case with brand name medications, when generics are far less costly: The insurer will cover the generic but not the brand name drug.

Be sure that the medications your doctor wants to prescribe are included in your insurance company's drug formulary. Most pharmacists can tell you if your medication is covered. You also can obtain this information by calling your insurance carrier or going to their website.

A Brief Recap

Before going on to the $64,000 question—whether the treatment is *working*—let's briefly summarize the questions your loved one (or you) should ask when being prescribed medication:

- "What symptoms are we trying to target?"
- "Why did you select this medication for my condition?"
- "Why did you choose this medication over another one?"
- "Are there other approved medications, or other treatments, for my condition?"
- "What benefits can I expect from this drug?"
- "How long will I have to wait to see those benefits?"
- "How many times a day will I have to take this medication, and if it's more times than I think I can reasonably handle, can the medication schedule be changed?"
- For patients on multiple medications: "Can any of my medications be discontinued so that I don't have to take so many?"
- "What side effects does the medication have?"
- "Are there any serious or life-threatening adverse effects?"
- For patients experiencing side effects: "What can be done to help these side effects?"
- "Are there any drug interactions between this medication and other medications or herbal remedies I'm taking or plan to take?"
- "What interactions does this drug have with alcohol?"
- "What should I do if there is a problem with the medication, especially a serious problem that can't wait until the next appointment?"
- "How much does this medication cost, and is it covered by my insurance plan?"
- For patients who can't afford the medication: "Are there other, less expensive drugs that you could prescribe instead?"

The $64,000 Question: Is the Treatment Working?

A simple, practical approach to being able to answer the question of whether a treatment is working is to identify, from the start, what the patient (and family) is seeking.

As I said earlier in this book, I like to ask patients not only *Why are you here?* but also *What is it you want to accomplish?* Is a person's goal to be able to sleep better? feel hope? be less angry? have better family relationships? return to work or do better at school? have a date? When beginning a treatment, your loved one needs to think about his or her goals. Perhaps the doctor, therapist, or program will ask. But if they don't, don't let their oversight keep your loved one from identifying why he or she is there. Most people are pretty good at getting what they want—if they are clear about their goals and persistent in their pursuit.

At the outset of treatment, try to identify the markers of success for the patient, the family, and the clinician. Be explicit, write them down, and come back to them on a regular basis to determine if what everyone seeks is being achieved. If the medication (or other treatment) hasn't helped you achieve those goals after a reasonable amount of time, it's time to start discussing alternative treatment approaches with the doctor.

Treatment Research

Some families will hear or learn about the research underlying a treatment, or encounter opportunities to participate in research. For those who do, I offer here some key concepts about psychiatric research.

The "gold standard" for psychiatric research is the results obtained under highly controlled situations where differences between one treatment and another can be scientifically determined. In a controlled research study, there are two different, randomly assembled patient groups: one group that receives the treatment, and another group that receives a placebo (the control group). The treatment provided is kept "blind" (not told or revealed) to the participants as well as to the clinicians providing care; only the researchers know which patients have received treatment and which have received a placebo. This type of research is called *randomized controlled efficacy research.*

The participants in the study, or the *subjects*, are "randomized," which means that only chance—not choice—determines whether they get active treatment or placebo. In order to limit factors that might make the results difficult to interpret, there also are stringent criteria for participants. These criteria often eliminate people with co-occurring medical or substance-abuse disorders, people who are considered too old or too young, people who are unable to travel to the university setting, and the like. Such ideal conditions seldom exist in real life. Thus, although results gathered in efficacy research are apt to be "pure" from a scientific standpoint, they can be limited in their generalized application. As a result, a great deal is learned about a treatment *after* it is FDA approved and released for general use.

Another form of research, called *effectiveness research*, seeks to determine whether a treatment can produce its desired results under real-life conditions. For example, instead of studying a limited group of selected individuals under laboratory conditions, a group of patients is selected from an actual clinical program, like an outpatient clinic, an Assertive Community Treatment (ACT) team, or a competitive employment program. Researchers then investigate what interventions are helping which individuals at what point in their illness or treatment. Sophisticated statistical methods (for example, *analyses of variance*) are used to sort out the different effects of different interventions.

The scope of effectiveness research is typically broader than that of efficacy research and thus may have more meaning when you are thinking about what might best inform the choice of the treatment for your loved one.

UNDERSTANDING CLINICAL TRIALS

There is a government site run by the National Institutes of Health (NIH) that provides information about ongoing clinical trials (http://clinical-trials.gov). The site has a set of frequently asked questions (FAQs) on what a clinical trial is, who can participate, what happens, the risks and benefits, trial protocols, and sponsorship.

This website also provides details about the purpose of an existing clinical trial, who is eligible for the study, and how to contact the research group for further details. You can select a study area (like postpartum depression, obsessive-compulsive disorder, or schizophrenia) and see details of work underway, including who is paying for the study or how to enroll (if they are recruiting participants). The information available on this site may be useful to you or your loved one if you are considering new options for treatment.

If you have specific questions about a particular researcher, especially about whether that doctor is receiving payment from pharmaceutical companies, you should be able to find out from this website or by looking at published works by that researcher. Professional journals now require that authors identify their sources of support as well as potential sources of conflict of interest.

Not all psychiatrists or other specialty doctors who do clinical research are in the pockets of pharmaceutical companies. In fact, very few are. That said, the reality is that in recent decades, a great proportion of the money available to study medications has come from the pharmaceutical industry. Clinicians and researchers need to be held to highly transparent reporting arrangements, which at least expose any possible conflicts of interest to consumers and potential participants. In addition, rigorous monitoring and enforcement of ethical standards can help the profession stay honest and true.

It isn't easy to sort through complex information and have the time (and confidence) to act when you have doubts about a research protocol. A number of national information sources, including the National Institutes of Health, the National Institute of Mental Health, the National Alliance on Mental Illness, and National Mental Health America, can help guide you.

Frequently Asked Questions

In addition to drawing on my own experience, I polled more than a dozen of my psychiatric colleagues to inquire about the questions they most frequently receive about medications. These are questions that patients typically have *and* questions that families have. I list both types of questions below. The responses are mine.

QUESTIONS FROM PATIENTS

What are the chances that my medication will or will not work?
This would probably be the most frequently asked question—if all who wondered dared to ask it. For a medication to be approved by the FDA, it must be shown to be safe and effective. "Effective" means that it outperforms the placebo effect, which can result in improvement in more that 30% of individuals.

A common example is antidepressant medication for depression, which can improve symptoms for approximately 75% of people suffering from moderate to severe illness. But the effectiveness of antidepressants depends on the right dose, taken responsibly for enough time, and in the absence of barriers to its effectiveness like alcohol or drug abuse. Antipsychotic medications are highly effective for acute treatment of hallucinations, delusions, and agitation, but additional interventions (see Chapter 6) are required to prevent relapse and recurrence of illness. Anti-manic agents may need to be paired with tranquilizing medications for acute manic states but are highly effective as maintenance medications. Medications have limited use in eating and personality disorders, with the exception of when another mental disorder co-occurs.

But medications do not cure mental disorders; they simply treat symptoms. Careful attention to a person's health and wellness, adequate sleep, good nutrition, moderate (or no) use of alcohol and no non-prescribed drugs, therapy, effort, and support are what everyone needs to manage an illness, be it a mental or a physical illness.

How soon will the medication work?
Some medications work in hours, like tranquilizing medications. Some take up to 6 weeks, or longer, like antidepressants. Some are meant to prevent relapse and recurrence, so they work over time. This is a good question to ask when the doctor is writing the prescription.

How will I know if it's working?
This is a crucial question. Again, I urge patients and their families to set specific goals for treatment. Medications target specific symptoms like sleep problems or anxiety or feeling very blue or agitated; speak with the doctor about what symptoms the medication is meant to manage so you

can know if it is working. Improvements in functioning at school and work both take more time to achieve and can be harder to measure, but if you clarify what you want to achieve and ask others you trust to also observe, you can get a good sense of whether your goals are being met.

Will this medication change my personality?

No. Your personality is you; it is how you have been since you were young. The effects of a medication can change how you feel (more focused, more energetic, more clear-thinking—or more restless, sleepier, or without sexual desire) but that is not a change in your personality.

Will this medication change my brain?

The goal of a medication for a mental illness is to change how the brain is working to help you feel, think, and behave more like you want to. There are also unwanted side effects (temporary brain changes) that result from the way the medication may affect other parts of the brain, like regions involved in appetite or alertness or muscle tone. There is no such thing as a perfect medication that has only benefits and no side effects, so it is up to you to weigh benefits and side effects and decide if a medication is right for you.

There are also some medications, taken for extended periods of time, that can result in permanent changes in the brain. The condition known as tardive dyskinesia (a late-onset movement disorder where the brain has been changed) can occur in people on certain antipsychotic medications taken in high doses or for long periods of time. Your doctor should explain long-term risks of a medication to you; this is best done when a person is not in the midst of an acute episode of illness.

If I take this medication, does it mean I'm crazy?

Talk of craziness remains an unfortunate residue of the stigma that continues to pervade how people think of mental illness. Mental illnesses are diseases of the brain and mind, not inexplicable happenings or failures of will and character. We need to think of taking medication for a mental illness as part of a comprehensive plan by which a person manages an illness and rebuilds functioning at school, home, and work as well as within relationships with family and friends.

Will I have to be on this medication for the rest of my life?

Not necessarily, but you should not stop a medication suddenly or without discussing it with your doctor. Over time, the dose a person takes can be reduced, and with planning, a trial off a medication can be tried. People whose illness has gone on for years or who have had repeated bouts of illness usually require taking medications for a long period of time in the same way that individuals with diabetes, high blood pressure, and asthma do.

My doctor wants to put me on two or three medications at once. Why?

A principle I have advocated for in this book is "as few medications and as low a (therapeutic) dose—whenever possible." *But* there are regular times that more than one medication is needed. Examples include combining a mood stabilizer with an antipsychotic medication, or an antidepressant with a sleeping pill (for a brief period of time), or adding a medication when the results you seek are not happening from one medication alone. Sometimes a doctor will suggest adding a medication to prevent or minimize the side effects of the principal medication selected. Don't be shy about asking why and insist on an answer that makes sense to you.

What if I miss a dose or a day?

People commonly forget a dose, even a day, especially if they are taking more than one medication. Usually, the best thing to do is to resume your usual schedule as soon as you can. If you've missed many days, check with your doctor to see if you need to build up slowly to the dose you were taking.

What happens if I stop taking the medication suddenly?

Many medications can produce unwanted effects if stopped suddenly. This does not mean that a person was "addicted" to the medication but rather that the body has become accommodated to it. These effects include upset stomach or diarrhea, headache, sleeplessness, restlessless, and many other symptoms. Stopping a medication suddenly also usually increases the risk of relapse (falling ill again). Don't stop suddenly. Speak with your doctor and make a plan if that is what you want to do.

Will I become addicted to this medication?

None of the antidepressant, mood stabilizing, or antipsychotic medications are addicting. Our bodies can develop tolerance (where a higher dose is needed to achieve the same effect) or dependence (where a person experiences withdrawal symptoms if the drug is quickly stopped), however, with benzodiazepine tranquilizers and some sleep medications (as is also the case with many pain medications).

Will the medication make me fat?

Many psychiatric medications bring with them the unwanted side effect of weight gain. But some medications in the same class (for example, in the class of antidepressant or antipsychotic agents) are associated with greater weight gain than others. A careful consideration of which medication to use, coupled with attention to diet and exercise, can minimize weight gain. With all medications, potential benefits have to be weighed against potential side effects.

Can I drink while I'm on this medication?

Excessive drinking (or use of non-prescribed medications or street drugs) is not a good idea for a person whose brain is affected by a mental illness. For those who have a co-occurring alcohol or drug-use disorder, abstinence will be a necessary aim. In some instances, alcohol may interfere or alter blood levels of the medication, so it is important to check with your doctor. For people with no substance-use problem and mild to moderate or stable illness, I usually say that it may be possible to enjoy a drink. Try one and see how it feels—as a rule, for people on psychiatric medications, one drink can feel like two or three.

Will I still be able to feel "feelings" while I'm on this medication?

Some people experience what they describe as a dulling of feelings when taking antidepressants. If this happens, it is important to discuss the issue with your doctor rather than stop taking the medication or skip doses; there may be ways to reduce this problem, or you can try a different antidepressant that might not produce this effect. Antipsychotic medications, especially when used in high doses or when multiple medications are taken, can make a person feel tired and dull; again, discuss with the doctor how you might minimize this side effect so that you can live more fully. Anti-manic medications can decrease the "high" of that disorder—the expansive and excited states experienced during a manic episode—but this is not the same thing as not feeling. In fact, decreasing the high is part of the proper treatment of that ruinous illness.

Will this medication affect my sex life?

SSRIs and SNRIs can result in problems with sexual arousal as well as achieving orgasm in men and women. In some cases, a person's libido, or sex drive, is reduced, but for people who lost their drive from depression, it can improve. There is one antidepressant, bupropion, that has not shown these problems, and for the other antidepressants there are ways to manage dosage or use short-acting medications that enhance sexual functioning.

Other types of medication (psychiatric as well as general medical) can also affect sexual desire and performance, so if that happens, speak with your doctor. Losing the pleasure of sex should not be a consequence of taking medication.

Can I combine this medication with the other medicines I take?

Maybe. Sometimes medications interact in ways that increase or decrease blood levels, increase side effects, or produce serious symptoms. Be sure that all your doctors, general medical and psychiatric, know what the others are prescribing and can tell you if the combination is safe. Bring a list of what you are taking to all your medical doctors and show it to be sure.

Are antidepressants any better than placebo?

Yes, they are for people with moderate to severe depression.

Can I take vitamins and nutritional supplements with this medication?

Generally there is not a problem taking vitamins and nutritional supplements with psychiatric medications. Bring a list of what you are taking and show it to your doctor to be sure.

Are there alternatives—natural substances such as St. John's Wort, or non-medication interventions—that change brain activity?

Yes. Some of these are described in the section on depression in Chapter 6.

For the most part, these alternatives can have value in mild to moderate and non-psychotic conditions. More severe disorders are far less responsive.

Are there alternatives like exercise, meditation, yoga, or acupuncture?
Yes, these can be very useful to complement conventional Western medications for virtually any mental illness. These practices, in and of themselves, often can help people with mild to moderate and non-psychotic conditions.

Will this medication take the place of counseling?
Medications and counseling assist each other; they do not replace each other. Some people with mild to moderate conditions can do well with one or the other, but they generally do better with both. For more severe or persistent conditions, a more comprehensive treatment plan is generally the most beneficial.

Do medications ever stop working?
Some people on antidepressants unfortunately experience that they seem to stop working—not right away but after a year or more. Because this is apt to be noticed when someone is not doing well, that is not the time to try to go medication-free. It is a time to try another medication, perhaps in a different class of antidepressant, which may work. It is also important to consider other causes of feeling depressed, like a physical illness, new medications for other conditions, or undetected alcohol or drug abuse.

I've just started dating someone and I don't yet want to tell him/her that I'm taking medication. When should I say something? What should I say?
You are correct that "right away" is not a good time. But don't wait too long. If you know you are interested in someone more than casually, and the feeling seems mutual, bring up that you are taking medication for a condition called [whatever your condition is], much like you would if you had diabetes or asthma.

I would like to get pregnant. Will this medication have effects on my fetus or baby?
Women of childbearing age who are considering a medication should be asked if they might be pregnant and, if they're uncertain, have a pregnancy test. A variety of medications can affect fetal development,

especially in the first trimester. If you are pregnant and have a mental illness that could benefit from medication, it is crucial to discuss benefits and risks with your doctor. At times, it may be necessary for a pregnant woman or her prescribing doctor to confer with an expert psychopharmacologist familiar with prescribing during pregnancy (and postpartum, for mothers who want to breast feed).

Is this medication expensive? Is there a generic version?

Yes, it may be expensive, especially if you have no insurance or your insurance plan does not cover it, or requires a substantial copayment. Be sure to check what your insurance covers and speak with your doctor, because the price could deter you from taking what could be of benefit. When medications are made by more than one company, they are sold as generics and the cost can come down substantially; some insurance plans insist on generics. Generic production is highly quality-controlled in the United States and many other countries, but not all; and despite good quality control there are differences between people that will mean some will do better on one brand than another.

Can the medication be detected in my blood?

Some people looking for work or in positions requiring regular blood testing will face this problem, because many psychiatric medications, like general medical medications, can be detected in the blood. Some organizations only test for drugs of abuse, so you want to know what substances are being tested for. In some instances it may be necessary to reveal that you are taking a medication—but stress that the measure of your performance is your work, not any condition or medication you may be taking.

Whom do I call if there is a problem?

Be sure to ask this question before there is a problem! There is great variety among doctors regarding how they respond to questions, both urgent and not. You deserve to know whom to call if you need to.

QUESTIONS FROM FAMILIES

If my child (or loved one) gets worse after taking the medication, how do I know whether it's due to a side effect or due to the progression of the illness?

Medications generally have specific side effects, which are well known. An illness has specific symptoms. By being familiar with the side effects of a medication and the symptoms of an illness, you can often tell the difference—but not always.

Talk with your loved one or friend when you are concerned. If you are meeting with the prescribing doctor, describe what you are seeing and ask what to make of it. Good medical care requires good observations from patients, families, and friends, and a doctor who will listen to and work with the patient to optimize the use of medication and the road to recovery.

Will this medication cause permanent changes in my loved one's personality?
As I mentioned earlier, no. A personality does not change; it is how a person has been since he or she was young and will continue to characterize who the person is. The effects of a medication can change how you feel (more focused, more energetic, more clear-thinking—or more restless, sleepier, or without sexual desire) but that is not a change in your personality. Illness doesn't change someone's personality, either—but it can certainly mask the wonderful person he or she is. Once the illness is treated, the person you know and love will emerge again as recovery continues.

My child refuses to take the medication. Can I hide it in his or her food?
Trust is the bedrock of every relationship. A family can feel very desperate and want to do something like this when they see their loved one suffering and failing. But the cost in loss of trust usually outweighs any (temporary) benefits.

I'm having a hard time getting my loved one to take the medication.
Do you have any advice?
I echo here what I just said: You cannot control much of what your family member, even a child, does. The more you focus on what your loved one wants and on his or her goals, the more you can influence that person to live a life that fosters recovery and minimizes risky behaviors and the chance of relapse.

What happens if my loved one drinks alcohol, smokes pot,
or drives while taking this medication?

Drinking and using drugs are risky behaviors for a person with a mental illness or for someone taking a medication that affects the brain. But again, you can't control much of what your family member does, so the best route is to focus on what your loved one wants in order to help him or her live a life that minimizes risky behaviors and the chance of relapse. Driving in itself is not a risky behavior if someone is not using intoxicants; however, if side effects (like sleepiness or blurred vision) occur, your loved one should discuss these with the doctor and refrain from driving until they are controlled.

Psychotherapy and Rehabilitation

Comprehensive care—care that includes medication, therapy, and sometimes rehabilitation and family psychoeducation—is often the best approach to treatment (see Chapter 3). Yet despite numerous studies supporting this fact, some clinicians are still biased toward one or another treatment. Although it's true that some conditions may improve with medication or therapy alone, the mental health community makes a mistake when it categorically identifies treatment choices as either medication *or* therapy.

Scientific breakthroughs in antidepressants, mood stabilizers, antipsychotics, and other psychiatric medications have brought relief to a vast number of patients. But drugs alone are rarely the answer for serious and persistent mental illnesses. As Nobel Laureate Eric Kandel and others have demonstrated, the brain can be equally altered by biological *and* behavioral interventions: Each complements and potentially augments the other. Their research makes a strong case for the benefits of therapy.

We know that medications change the brain. But how can *therapy* change the brain, too? Perhaps the simplest yet still elegant way to understand this is that all thoughts, feelings, and behaviors are mediated by brain neurotransmitters and nerve circuits. When we feel, think, or act differently, we are generating change in the chemistry and electrical pathways of the brain. CBT, for example, employs both changes in thinking and behavior in the treatment (therapy) that produce changes in the brain – both short term and enduring. It's a beautiful thing.

How Do Therapy, Rehabilitation, and Medication Complement One Another?

The need for therapy is further underscored by the accumulating evidence that many medications carry with them long-term side effects that can be harmful to our health—side effects such as weight gain, increases in unhealthy cholesterol and triglycerides, hypertension, and, over time, the development of diabetes. Medications, however, are often a vital part of a comprehensive treatment for serious and persistent mental illness. They must be carefully chosen and prudently prescribed according to the principles outlined in Chapter 7. Medications target specific symptoms, like anxiety, agitation, sleeplessness, depressed mood or mood instability, hallucinations, and delusions. But other problems are commonly present: These include difficulties in relationships, low self-esteem, negative patterns of thinking, loss of self-control resulting in impulsive, angry, or self-destructive behaviors, and many other problems in living. Therapy helps with problems in living, and thus can complement medications in many important ways.

Rehabilitation programs specifically aim to address functional losses that people with mental illness develop—or skills they have not achieved because their lives were derailed by illness. These losses are as varied as the ability to organize time, to follow a schedule, to sustain concentration, and to have a functioning memory of how to complete day-to-day tasks. Rehabilitation programs enable young people to stay or return to school; they enable people to keep their jobs or return to competitive employment positions by training or retraining them in the work habits and skills many of us take for granted as we go about our everyday lives.

Medications, therapy, and rehabilitation work on different and often coexisting types of problems, and augment one another to aid a person with mental illness in the challenging work of recovery.

Why Don't Psychiatrists Provide Psychotherapy?

Some psychiatrists *do* provide psychotherapy, but most don't. Why? There are a few different reasons. One has to do with the simple principle of supply and demand. There is a great need for medication treatment, but prescribing clinicians are limited in number. And whereas a psychotherapy session takes around 50 minutes, a meeting to prescribe and monitor medications takes only about 10–20 minutes. This means that psychiatrists can treat many more patients in a day if they are providing medication treatment, thereby better meeting the high demand for medication treatment. Psychiatrists in public mental health are principally employed to prescribe medication because of the very high need for this service and the limited number of doctors working in the public sector.

There are also financial reasons for splitting care between prescribing and non-prescribing clinicians—for both doctors and patients. Psychiatrists can earn a lot more money if they are seeing three, four, or even five patients in an hour than if they're seeing just one. And patients can save money by seeing a non-prescribing clinician for therapy, because these clinicians' fees tend to be much lower than those of prescribing clinicians.

What Makes Therapy Therapeutic?

Different forms of therapy—cognitive-behavioral and interpersonal, to name just a couple—are effective for different kinds of mental illness. (I discussed which forms are most often used for each disorder in Chapter 6.) But *all* therapies have a few essential building blocks in common: empathy, genuineness, warmth, active listening, positive regard, and trust. Without these building blocks, the therapy isn't going to be very successful, no matter what form it is.

Empathy. Empathy is built into our brains. We have what are called "mirror neurons" that permit us to feel and behave like the person (or people) we're with. Empathy is the capacity to feel what someone else is feeling. It is different from sympathy, where we feel sorry for another person. Empathy allows one person to live, however transiently, in the shoes of another; this creates a bond, and a basis for understanding and mutual problem solving.

Genuineness and Warmth. These are the essence of human connection. Sound clinical studies have shown that people return to doctors and therapists who are warm and genuine (real)—sometimes even when the clinician's technical skills are not very good. Warmth counts, especially when a person is exposing painful and persistent problems that cause suffering, guilt, and shame.

Active Listening. Active listening is the capacity of a therapist to listen attentively, not just talk. Your therapist needs to do more than just emotional handholding. Active listening means that the therapist actually hears what the patient says—*as well as* what the patient doesn't say but communicates through body language and other nonverbal cues. An active listener makes connections, asks good questions, pushes gently, insists on movement that is in a patient's interest, and limits avoidance (the natural human tendency to elude what hurts us).

Positive Regard. This is an acceptance of the patient without critical judgment. It also means believing the patient can change and have a better life. With some rare exceptions (e.g., sociopaths), the therapist needs to believe in a patient's goodness and provide hope for a better life.

Trust. Trust is basic to all good relationships. A patient must trust that the therapist will provide a safe, confidential environment that places the patient's needs before those of the therapist. Trust is the unshakeable belief that your therapist will not exploit you.

These building blocks work together to establish what's called the *therapeutic alliance*. The therapeutic alliance is perhaps the best predictor of response to psychotherapy. Developed between therapist and patient, this phenomenon is based in trust and built on the ability of the therapist to demonstrate that he or she can coach the patient across the most challenging of life's rivers.

When a therapeutic alliance exists, the patient feels deeply that his or her therapist will be there in a helpful, nonjudgmental, safe, and confidential way, no matter what happens. Many studies of psychotherapy—in clinics, inpatient settings, and other service sites—consistently demonstrate that the therapeutic alliance trumps credentials or training. Successful therapy is about the interpersonal experience with the clinician, not the diploma on the wall.

Therapy Is a Team Sport

Therapy requires active participation from both people seated in the room: *Both* the patient and therapist are responsible for making it successful.

The *patient's* responsibility is to:

- Develop and clearly state their goals throughout treatment.
- Take action (rather than just being passive recipients). Therapy takes work.
- Be honest, face facts, and learn to see when they are deceiving themselves.
- Ask questions, and expect answers, from themselves as well as the therapist.
- Regularly review whether therapy is meeting their goals.
- Seek outside support for their efforts from family, friends, and others, especially those who have experience with what they are going through.

The *therapist's* (or program's) responsibility is to:

- Put the patient's needs and goals first.
- Act with integrity, which means behaving ethically and never exploiting a patient emotionally, sexually, or financially.
- Protect the patient's privacy.
- Provide hope and encouragement.
- Engage the patient as a partner in the process.
- Master and deliver the specific skills of the therapy provided.
- Monitor therapy to assess if the patient's goals are being met.
- Establish and work to preserve the therapeutic alliance.

Types of Therapy

In this section I'll discuss:

- Psychodynamic Therapy
- Cognitive-Behavioral Therapy
- Dialectical Behavior Therapy
- Dynamic Deconstructive Psychotherapy

- Interpersonal Therapy
- Problem-Solving Therapy
- Group Therapy
- Family Psychoeducation and Family-to-Family Education Programs
- Family Therapy

PSYCHODYNAMIC THERAPY

Psychodynamic therapy is the "talking cure." It dates back to Freud, but it has come a long way since then. Psychoanalysis is an intensive form of psychodynamic therapy that involves frequent sessions over an extended period of time. Because of this time commitment and other aspects of this treatment (see below), most people choose to engage in regular psychodynamic therapy instead.

At the core of psychodynamic therapy is the view that unconscious feelings, drives, memories, and self-perceptions are the basis for our relationships and conflicts (within ourselves and with others). The theory proposes that we naturally protect ourselves from our internal cauldron of psychic activity by keeping much of it unconscious, lest it have us act in unconscionable ways or fill us with anxiety, guilt, and shame. But, according to this theory, the capacity of the "mental wall" (or psychic set of defenses) that retains the unconscious is limited: Feelings, wishes, and drives roil below the surface and cause distress. Sometimes they go beyond just causing distress, breaking through and erupting in less-than-desirable actions, maladaptive behaviors, and unbearable feelings.

The work of psychodynamic therapy is to *make the unconscious more conscious*. This allows patients to become self-aware enough to generate adequate control of the effects of unconscious thoughts and feelings, thereby depriving them of their power and influence.

Psychodynamic therapists are highly trained and skilled at developing an alliance with patients to uncover and understand the unconscious forces at work. The therapeutic alliance (patient-therapist relationship) is particularly critical in this form of therapy, because deep psychological exploration must be done in a trusting, safe environment that is free of judgment and blame. It's quite remarkable how a safe, therapeutic relationship can enable even very fragile people to summon the strength and sustain the energy for psychodynamic therapy.

Who Does Best With This Therapy?

Self-reflective and resilient patients are best suited for this form of therapy. It isn't recommended for people in the midst of acute mental illnesses, psychotic episodes, or overwhelmed by trauma.

The Therapeutic Process

As with any form of treatment, the patient should give informed consent at the beginning of therapy. For the therapist, of course, maintaining confidentiality is a fundamental rule and ethical obligation. Confidentiality, as explained in Chapter 10, is the patient's right to expect that what he or she says in confidence to a doctor will remain within the confines of the doctor-patient relationship.

In psychodynamic therapy, patients are ruthlessly honest with themselves and commit to *free-associating* (speaking what comes to mind without censorship). As a way of psychologically protecting themselves, patients will naturally exhibit defenses such as intellectualization, repression, denial, altruism, and somatization (when a psychological problem manifests as a physical one, such as a headache or gastrointestinal distress); therapy aims to help patients become aware of these defenses and understand what's causing them. Dreams are what Freud called the "royal road to the unconscious," and are instrumental to understanding our psychic lives.

As the therapeutic alliance develops, the therapist educates, explains, explores, encourages, (gently) confronts, and interprets feelings and experiences that are outside the patient's awareness (i.e., are unconscious). Past and present are woven together in the hands of a good therapist.

According to psychodynamic theory, the patient will experience what is called *transference*. This is when the patient transfers feelings about someone else in his or her life (often a parent) onto the therapist. These feelings may be fear, desire, envy, or anger, to name a few. The patient is supposed to talk about these feelings about the therapist but not act on them. Investigating transference is an important part of the therapy because how a person feels, thinks, and behaves often derives from early experiences, which can be buried away and out of conscious awareness. The transference allows the patient to discover and examine internal experiences as they arise in the therapeutic relationship.

(Therapists also can have unconsciously driven feelings about the patient. These are called *countertransference*, and the therapist is expected to recognize and manage them as a part of acting professionally and ethically.)

Like in all therapies, it is vital to *establish goals*. What problems does the patient want to work on and what does he or she seek to achieve in the therapy? When does the patient want these goals realized? As I've already said, goals not only help to ground the treatment but also serve as milestones along the way. Over time, the patient gains mastery over his or her feelings, actions, and self-image. Higher levels of adaptive functioning develop and psychic distress is mitigated.

Time Frame for Treatment

Psychodynamic therapy is generally conducted once (or more times) a week for months; the therapy can last up to a year or longer, depending on the patient's goals and how entrenched he or she is in the problems of life. Shorter-term psychodynamic therapy has become more popular and can be very effective in the hands of skilled clinicians and with patients with clear and focused goals.

Psychoanalysis: My Personal Experience

When it came time for me to enter therapy many years ago, I started in the deep end of the pool: psychoanalysis. Instead of beginning with a more focused, time-limited psychodynamic therapy, I decided to go for the full monty. I found a traditional Freudian psychoanalyst, a past president of Boston's major psychoanalytic institute. I was on the couch four times a week for 6 years. Even when I wasn't at my analyst's office, I was continuing our analytic work, waking at night to record dreams for our later exploration.

My dream life—which was rich then and has grown more so with age—was a centerpiece of my psychoanalysis. Dreams are revelatory of hidden wishes, drives, and fears. Dreams can demonstrate how we perceive and respond to others, going beyond transference reactions to give us insight into how we feel, think, and act.

For me, analysis was exceptionally helpful in improving my life in the areas of love and work. But I still wonder: What was it that helped? Was it the traditional technique of the analyst being out of sight (behind the couch), free association (saying whatever comes to mind), dream interpretation, or analysis of the transference? Or was it the long-term relationship with my wise and kind analyst, who could spot every psychological evasion in the book, and who demanded that I take responsibility for how I felt and lived?

My analysis was a journey into the mind, into the primitive ways we all can feel, judge, and behave. It helped me take the reins of life away from my unconscious and its misguided practices. Of course, central to my experience, and to the experience of any patient, was the alliance I had with the analyst. Whatever therapy a person decides upon, it is essential to build trust and confidence in the therapist.

COGNITIVE-BEHAVIORAL THERAPY

Cognitive-behavioral therapy (CBT) focuses on helping patients unlock the connections among thoughts, negative feelings, and self-destructive or problematic behaviors. By finding and diffusing the triggering beliefs and thoughts that produce negative feelings and undesired behaviors, CBT greatly improves a patient's functioning. For example, a person suffering from anxiety may believe that she "always makes a fool of herself" when she participates in social situations. This belief leads her to feel embarrassed and nervous around others, and these feelings lead her to avoid social situations. A CBT therapist might challenge this patient's belief by asking her to keep a record of all the times she is in a social situation, what she felt and what she did. This record would likely show that there were many times when the patient did *not*, in fact, feel awkward or do anything foolish, or if she did, she was able to master the moment. Correcting the inaccurate belief that she "always makes a fool of herself" helps correct underlying beliefs that can keep someone from participating in the social situations she's previously avoided.

CBT originated in the 1950s to treat depressive and anxiety disorders, but it's been used successfully for many other conditions, including personality disorders and eating and addictive disorders. More recently, it has found valuable application in psychotic illnesses.

CBT is typically a short-term treatment, and may or may not be combined with medications. There are no contraindications to its use with medications.

Who Does Best With This Therapy?

CBT can be of great help for people who have dysfunctional thoughts or beliefs that result in disruptive behaviors that harm their relationships with family, romantic partners, and schoolmates or coworkers. For example, someone with negative or self-critical thoughts (and thus low self-esteem) is apt to feel depressed and discouraged and will therefore avoid social situations or refuse opportunities at school or work. In the case of eating disorders, CBT can help correct misperceptions about the body that may cause anxiety and serve as a deterrent to regaining needed weight.

CBT also has been proven to help people with psychotic disorders. When applied to the symptoms of schizophrenia, CBT aims to alter problems of paranoia, isolation, and lack of motivation. Paranoia in particular can be greatly helped through CBT. If a person thinks he's being threatened or persecuted, he will isolate himself as a protective measure, which profoundly interferes with goals at work and within relationships. Skilled CBT therapists can help patients control their paranoid thoughts and thus limit how those thoughts affect their behaviors.

The Therapeutic Process

CBT starts by identifying the problem thoughts and beliefs. This stage is called *functional analysis*. It takes a trained CBT therapist and a motivated patient to do this work. The treatment then moves on to recognizing the behaviors that contribute to the patient's dysfunction. Finally, the patient learns to practice new ways of thinking and acting to improve his or her everyday life.

For example, a person with depression who thinks every obstacle is the end of the world (often called *catastrophizing*) first learns to recognize when this is happening and what the triggers are. Then he or she is helped to use new, more accurate thoughts to stop the freefall into despair. Finally, the patient learns what thoughts and actions can lead to successfully managing these moments in the future.

Time Frame for Treatment

CBT sessions are highly structured and time-limited, often taking place over 10 to 24 meetings. CBT programs for depression and anxiety disorders (mild to moderate in nature) also have been developed to be delivered on the web; these involve about 8 to 10 highly structured sessions done weekly (with homework between sessions) by a person who logs into a protected website.

DIALECTICAL BEHAVIOR THERAPY

Dialectical behavior therapy (DBT), developed and propagated by Dr. Marsha Linehan, is a special type of CBT. This type of therapy has special application in the treatment of people with borderline personality disorder (see Chapter 6), but it also has broader use in helping people with a variety of serious mood, impulse, and self-image problems. DBT assists people with managing feelings, sometimes opposite in nature like love and hate, without acting destructively or self-destructively. It enables individuals to observe themselves (mindfulness) and better tolerate disabling levels of distress. It is CBT plus mindfulness, emotional regulation, and tolerance of intense emotional states.

DYNAMIC DECONSTRUCTIVE PSYCHOTHERAPY

Another recently established evidence-based psychotherapy for people with borderline personality disorder and other (and related) personality disorders is called dynamic deconstructive psychotherapy (DDP). DDP builds on neuroscience research: Its premise is that, in individuals with symptoms of borderline personality disorder, some regions of the brain are underperforming (especially the medial prefrontal cortex), while others are overactive (including the amygdala and ventral striatum). Dysfunctions in these areas are associated with problems in identity, hyperreactivity, and impulsivity.

DDP treatment, developed and researched by Dr. Robert Gregory, is a weekly psychotherapy delivered for one year that weds neuroscience, psychodynamic theory, and philosophy (where the concept of deconstruction helps patients to be open to the existence of another person).

Although DDP sounds theoretically complex, studies show it is feasible to use and that patients can succeed in treatment (see www. upstate.edu/ddp). When borderline conditions are coupled with the additional challenges of substance abuse, eating disorders, and self-destructive behaviors (as they frequently are), DDP has been shown to be effective, especially in young adults.

INTERPERSONAL THERAPY

Interpersonal therapy (IPT) was developed in the 1980s by Drs. Myrna Weissman and Gerald Klerman as a brief therapy for depression; since then, its application has significantly broadened. IPT is now a well-researched therapy with proven efficacy for anxiety, depressive disorders, and eating disorders; it also has application for substance-use disorders. IPT focuses on helping people with the challenges in interpersonal relationships that arise for everyone, regardless of whether they have a diagnosed mental illness. It has proven utility across the life cycle, including for adolescents, adults, and older people.

Who Does Best With This Therapy?

Because IPT has broad value with problems that arise in everyday life, as well as in mental disorders, almost anyone can be a candidate for this treatment. That said, this psychotherapy may be best suited for people who are able to focus on relationships and who are prepared to see their role in the troubles they experience. Its brevity and focus make it easier to commit to, and there are clear goals and milestones. IPT is provided individually and in groups.

The Therapeutic Process

Initial sessions in IPT involve the therapist actively developing an alliance with the patient by identifying and naming the patient's problem and linking that to what is going on in the patient's life. The therapist explains the treatment as talking about concerns and problems in relationships (e.g., with a spouse or partner, parent, adult child, sibling, coworker, boss) that are current and important to that person. An expectation of feeling better is linked to solving these problems. IPT focuses on the present, not the past, and on current interpersonal and feeling states, not the unconscious. Subsequent sessions concentrate on what has been specifically selected as affecting the person seeking help: These can include role disputes, life transitions, grief, or interpersonal deficits (such as limited attachments to others, isolation, and loneliness). Role playing is common, allowing the therapist to demonstrate new ways of managing interpersonal encounters. The treatment assesses progress on an ongoing basis, every few sessions, and makes course corrections if needed. Final sessions, called the "termination phase," review what has been learned and accomplished.

IPT does not seek to modify any underlying personality problems but rather takes as its premise that improving relationships and role responsibilities will produce symptom relief and improve functioning and mood. The therapist is active, nonjudgmental, and an explicit advocate for the patient. IPT often is combined with medications for people with moderate to severe depressive, anxiety, or psychotic conditions. IPT is now being introduced into low-resource environments in developing countries to help meet the needs of people with mental disorders worldwide.

Time Frame for Treatment
A course of IPT typically lasts for 12 to 16 weekly sessions.

PROBLEM-SOLVING THERAPY

Problem-solving therapy (PST) dates back to a number of clinician-researchers in the early 1970s; it is now a standard therapeutic approach. PST does just what its name implies: It helps patients learn to respond to identified difficulties using problem-solving skills rather than resorting to avoidance, denial, blame, discouragement, or defeat.

Who Does Best With This Therapy?
Some people are fortunate and develop problem-solving skills early in life. But everyone can improve their problem solving, and learn to apply those skills to the demands of relationships and work. PST can be especially helpful for patients whose natural resilience to stress and repertoire of adaptive responses are limited.

The Therapeutic Process
From the first session, the therapist helps the patient identify major problems interfering with what the patient wants to achieve in life—whether

those problems are at school, work, in relationships, or with behaviors that cause emotional pain. The patient's problems are discussed in a systematic way, and the patient and therapist look for ways to solve them. The patient is expected to try to solve the identified problems in daily functioning; difficulties in actually solving the problems are, of course, a part of the therapy. Good therapists (of every school of therapy) are good problem solvers and can help others learn problem solving for themselves.

Time Frame for Treatment

A course of PST lasts 6 to 10 sessions, usually weekly, and can be resumed if needed.

GROUP THERAPY

Group therapy dates back over a century. In its original form, group therapy was a series of "medical education lectures" that helped families learn about their loved ones' illnesses. This work led to the development of psychoeducational interventions for patients and families, where people afflicted with a disease, and their loved ones, were taught about the condition, its effect on everyday life, and ways of effectively managing the disease.

Group therapy today is an umbrella term that refers to the provision of a number of specific therapies delivered in a group setting. Psychodynamic therapy, interpersonal therapy, cognitive-behavioral therapy, and even psychoanalysis have been delivered in groups. Groups can focus on specific problems, like grief, anger, or addiction; life crises, like divorce or aging; disabling physical illnesses, such as cancer or autoimmune disease; or interpersonal conflicts that impair work and love. Fundamental to group therapy is the view that patients can reinforce one another's strengths and help to confront and reduce one another's maladaptive behaviors. Therapy groups have strict rules about privacy and against fraternizing outside of the group in order to maintain the emotional safety and work ethos of the treatment. The therapist must be active in insisting that group members work with one another, and should not deliver individual therapy in a group setting.

Who Does Best With This Therapy?

Group therapy is especially effective for people with interpersonal problems, personality disorders, and addictive behaviors. Groups typically have 6 to 12 members. Although diversity of age and problems can be helpful, too much disparity can create difficulties in cohesion, which is essential to success in group therapy. In my opinion, group therapy is a vastly underutilized treatment. Far too few therapists are skilled in this mode of treatment and far too few patients make use of it. My own experience doing group therapy has shown me how lively and useful groups can be (for both patients and therapists).

Time Frame for Treatment

Group therapy can be short-term (6 to 12 weeks) or longer-term (months to a year or more) for those with deeply rooted interpersonal or addictive problems.

FAMILY PSYCHOEDUCATION AND FAMILY-TO-FAMILY EDUCATION PROGRAMS

Families need education and support to understand, respond to, and help a loved one with a chronic illness. Family psychoeducation for serious mental illness is one of a handful of evidence-based (scientifically proven) practices that can help families to support their loved one and take care of themselves. Family education is *not* therapy: The family is not in treatment. Instead, family members learn problem-solving and coping skills for the demands and stresses of a serious and persistent illness in the family.

If you are not engaged in family education around a serious mental illness you are not giving yourself or your loved one what you both need and deserve. There is no more shame in being in a family education group for mental illness than there is in learning everything you can about how to support heart-attack or cancer survivors.

I have had the privilege of sitting in on sessions of NAMI's family-to-family education program (FFEP). These are weekly 90-minute sessions that run for 12 weeks. The NAMI FFEP sessions are free, and they are led by two family members who have been trained and certified by NAMI to lead FFEP. There are often about 8 to 15 members in the group—few enough to permit helpful interaction. Sometimes groups are specifically for parents, or for siblings, or for children of a mentally ill relative; sometimes they are blended.

The groups have very specific rules about privacy, respect, and support written on a poster in the room. Each group member is given 5 minutes to speak about what he or she has been struggling with regarding the mentally ill relative. Other members of the group, including the two leaders, are active listeners, and offer remarkably practical and helpful ideas and resources. In my experience, there was no stigma and no blame. I found it very inspirational to see what NAMI and the people running these groups are doing.

One particular technique taught in some family education programs is called "listen-empathize-agree-partner" (LEAP). Developed by Dr. Xavier Amador, LEAP is an active form of listening and validating a patient's reality without having to agree with it. Families can learn to listen and empathize with their loved one's view of reality—even if that view is false—in order to better engage them in treatment. LEAP can be very helpful in teaching families how to respond to a loved one's lack of insight and refusal to get treatment. Dr. Amador's work is listed in Appendix B at the end of this book.

FAMILY THERAPY

Family therapy is a broad term that encompasses a variety of different treatment methods. Different "schools" of family therapy have been around since the 1950s. Family therapy approaches are built on psycho-analytic theory, small group dynamics, systems and linguistic theory, child guidance, and couples counseling. Whatever the school or form of family therapy, the underlying premise needs to be that a well-functioning family may be every person's greatest asset and strongest advocate; that certainly applies for people with mental illnesses.

Who Does Best With This Therapy?

When family problems are persistent and not responsive to family psychoeducation or brief counseling, then a course of family therapy, with specific goals and timelines, can be considered. Family therapy has been used to assist with eating disorders, behavioral problems in children, parent-child conflicts, divorce and loss, and long-term adaptation to chronic illness (including physical and mental disorders).

The Therapeutic Process

Although families are often assessed in the clinical care of a person with a mental illness, that is *not* the same thing as engaging in family therapy. And although many therapists meet with families, not all have been *trained* to work with families. Good clinicians want to understand their patient's family and how to ally with the family to enable the patient to benefit from all a family has to offer; this is the case when evaluating and treating a patient, when engaged in family psychoeducation, or when providing family therapy.

A family therapist tries to engage all members of the family in actively working to face current challenges, to communicate clearly and honestly, to function within respective roles (for example, to take on parental responsibilities if one is a parent), and to solve the problems that are keeping a family from functioning as an effective and loving group.

Time Frame for Treatment

Family therapy can be brief—even as few as two sessions. More often it is 6 to 10 sessions, but some families require more time.

Residential Rehabilitation Programs

Perhaps the best-known rehabilitation programs are "rehabs"—where people with alcohol and drug problems admit themselves for weeks or months to get clean, sober, and on the road to recovery. Among the better-known rehab centers are the Betty Ford Center, the Mayo Clinic, the Hazelden Foundation, and a variety of celebrity rehabs along the California coast (such as Promises and Passages).

But there are also rehabilitation programs for people with mental conditions. Many of these patients also have problems with the use and abuse of alcohol and drugs; when that is the case, effective mental health programs identify and engage the person in treatment for the co-occurring substance-use disorder.

EATING DISORDER PROGRAMS

When outpatient treatment is not sufficient to control a disabling and dangerous eating disorder (especially anorexia nervosa), the patient may need a course of residential rehabilitation.

Critical to a residential eating disorder program is its focus on nutritional rehabilitation (relearning how to eat normally); slow but progressive weight gain; cognitive-behavioral, interpersonal, and problem-solving therapies; and active involvement of the family (whenever possible). Medications can be used to treat a co-occurring mood or anxiety disorder but are not the primary treatment for an eating disorder.

As I note elsewhere in this book, it can be difficult to get insurance companies to pay for a residential eating disorder program. Be prepared to battle: Gather expert advice, establish clear goals and timeframes, insist on speaking with insurance-company medical leadership, and be persistent. When you have a good case for treatment, you can win against a skeptical insurance company.

POSTTRAUMATIC STRESS DISORDER PROGRAMS

PTSD is the product of overwhelming trauma often coupled with the absence of supports. We see PTSD in soldiers who have been exposed to deadly circumstances or witnessed horror, in victims of torture, in those who have been driven from their countries, in victims of sexual and physical abuse, and in those who have experienced natural or human-made disasters. Although many of the symptoms that these diverse groups suffer are similar, the patients' backgrounds and trauma experiences are often highly different. Therefore, the best rehabilitation programs for each group are quite different.

The U.S. Veterans Association (VA) hospitals offer some of the best residential programs for Americans who have returned from combat. Too few veterans, however, avail themselves of the assistance the VA can provide. Families are not eligible for VA benefits directly, but they can seek assistance for their loved ones or find services for themselves (or their family member) in other hospital and community clinics.

PTSD programs can last for weeks, months, or longer. Psychotherapy (especially CBT and exposure techniques), medications, and group therapy and support are central to treatment. Family involvement and support are crucial; it has been said that whatever happens to a soldier also happens to his or her family.

There are also PTSD programs that focus on victims of domestic violence and physical and sexual abuse. These programs may identify themselves as treating trauma and dissociative disorders. Trauma programs should begin with a focus on recovering basic, daily functioning, as well as on enabling a person to manage overwhelming feelings without engaging in self-destructive, addictive, or dissociative behaviors. Going into a partial hospital program (where a person goes up to 5 days a week for a half or full day but does not reside overnight) after a residential program can be very useful, because it allows intensive treatment to continue while a person is still living in the community, facing the daily challenges that she or he needs to master.

OBSESSIVE-COMPULSIVE DISORDER PROGRAMS

Highly specialized programs have been developed to assist people with severe and intractable OCD. Residential OCD programs are highly structured to assist patients in managing intense and seemingly irresistible thoughts and behaviors. CBT, exposure therapy, and medications are the most commonly used treatments.

Admission to OCD residential programs is limited to patients who have not sufficiently responded to evidence-based outpatient programs—and whose condition significantly impairs functioning at school or work or otherwise prevents the person from being a productive member of his or her family or community. Patients in these programs often have co-occurring anxiety, eating, or depressive disorders.

Access to OCD programs may require you to consult with an expert to determine if the outpatient care provided to date was of sufficient quality and duration. You may also need to consider what residential programs are available (locally or at a distance) to make the case to your loved one (and to obtain insurance approval) in seeking this level of care.

Transitional Residences

No matter how devoted a family may be, some mental illnesses prevent patients from living independently or with family members. People with serious and persistent mental illnesses (like schizophrenia, schizoaffective disorder, and severe bipolar disorder) may require living arrangements that also provide them with ongoing daily support.

Halfway houses, group homes, and supportive housing can be found through community mental health services. These forms of living arrangements are available in all states, though local investment in them varies considerably.

HALFWAY HOUSES AND GROUP HOMES

These are community settings where a patient lives with a small group of others who have a mental illness and are in need of daily (sometimes 24-hour) contact with counselors. These patients learn the skills needed to live more independently in the community. Halfway houses and group homes also provide shelter from the destabilizing effects of exposure to substance abuse or destructive relationships. However, these settings are not permanent housing: Group-living settings should always be used as stepping stones to independent living.

SUPPORTIVE HOUSING

Supportive housing has become a mainstay in enabling people with serious and persistent mental illness to live safely and effectively in the community. Supportive housing is when a person lives independently but with ready access to counselors and treatment. There is considerable evidence that many people can go directly into supportive housing without intervening stays in a group home or halfway house (direct admission to supportive housing is called "first-step housing"). Supportive housing is coupled with case management and community mental health and substance-use treatment—as well as with programs that enable a person to develop the skills to work or return to school. Appendix A has a walkthrough of a supportive housing program.

Nonresidential Rehabilitation (Skill-Building) Programs

In past decades, people with serious, persistent, and disabling mental illnesses entered what were called "day treatment programs." Patients would attend these outpatient programs for up to five days a week, often over the course of many years. However, there is little evidence to demonstrate that day treatment programs do anything beyond providing a protected setting, and although a protected setting is important, it's usually not enough to prepare patients for independent living. In order to achieve independent living, patients need skill-building programs.

The advent of the recovery orientation in mental health (see Chapter 11) has ushered in a more hopeful and constructive approach to rehabilitation. In New York State, recovery-oriented programs are called "personalized recovery-oriented services" (PROS). PROS programs deliver intensive skill-building services targeted at helping patients live independently and return to school or work. Skill building may involve lessons in how to organize time, concentrate on specific work tasks, or relate appropriately to others. These programs also give ongoing attention to living *with illness*—and to maintaining mental and physical health (as many people with serious mental illness also suffer from chronic physical disorders like obesity, diabetes, hypertension, and heart disease).

To find recovery-oriented rehabilitation programs in your community, you can contact county or state mental health agencies or community mental health centers. The availability of rehabilitative programs with a recovery orientation varies from state to state and even county to county, depending on local investment, understanding, and belief in recovery models of care. You can also turn to local NAMI affiliates for assistance.

The Buck Never Seems to Stop:
Paying for Mental Health Care

For many patients and their families, the mental health system can seem overwhelming. In this chapter, we'll take a closer look at the private and public mental health systems, as well as how the health-care industry affects mental health care and its costs.

"System" is something of a misnomer when it comes to describing the various, often uncoordinated components of mental health care in the United States. Although we have a heavily financed healthcare system, the mental health care services within it are far from perfect—and far from what patients and families need. What is needed is a system that is accessible, is patient- and family-oriented, intervenes early, and delivers evidence-based services.

President George W. Bush's New Freedom Commission on Mental Health, led by Commissioner Michael Hogan (then Commissioner of Mental Health for Ohio and subsequently for New York State), called for transforming the "intimidating maze of mental health services into a coordinated, consumer-centered, recovery-oriented mental health system" (see Appendix B).

The Commission's report underscored how fragmented mental health services are in this country. It noted a lack of comprehensive services for many high-need, underserved populations (like children and older adults), gaps in care for about every population, "wasted resources" (effective treatments that went unused or money that was spent on ineffective care), and a pervasive lack of a recovery-oriented ethos to patient care.

One of the biggest gaps in the mental health care system is follow-up care. An outpatient visit after discharge from a psychiatric hospital is hardly ever scheduled within a timely manner (i.e., within days), which results in poor patient attendance. The longer the time to the appointment, the less likely it is that a patient will attend that appointment. Problems with delayed or absent follow-up treatment no doubt have an effect on relapse: 20% of patients who are admitted to a psychiatric hospital are readmitted within 30 days, and 40% of patients are readmitted within a few months.

Another problem with mental health care is the lack of delivery of the comprehensive care that most patients need. People with serious mental illness often require medications, case management, therapy, recovery-oriented rehabilitation, and family psychoeducation. Just as it is easier to adhere to medication plans if there are fewer medications, it's also easier to participate in a comprehensive treatment plan if a patient only has to go to one place for those varied services. Unfortunately, comprehensive services are rarely provided by the same program, or at the same site. This not only affects patient attendance but also compromises the coordination and collaboration among services and clinicians that are vital to quality care. It is always more effective and convenient for patients when the team of doctors and healthcare professionals work together at one location.

Emergency services also must be improved. Many communities do not have emergency (crisis) services, so families must turn to a hospital in an emergency. Further, many community clinics regard the hospital as their coverage for nights and weekends; many a voicemail will direct desperate families to an emergency room instead of to an on-call mental health professional from their clinic. The result is that the patient is treated by ER clinicians—in an often frantic, chaotic setting—who are unfamiliar with the patient and his or her particular situation.

Acute-care hospitals (and emergency rooms) are notorious for inadequate discharge plans. Patient stays are now very short on psychiatric units, and contact with outpatient clinicians all too infrequent. Even when a patient already has treating clinicians—say, through a clinic outpatient program—the work done on the inpatient unit (generally geared to crisis intervention and medication management) is not well communicated with the clinicians who will work with the patient upon discharge. And when the patient has no established treating clinicians, the difficulty finding and linking the patient with care is further compounded. The inpatient staff rush to discharge a patient within the few days allowed by an insurance plan, leaving little time to establish substantive aftercare plans that the patient is apt to pursue.

This is what the President's Commission meant by gaps in care, system fragmentation, and wasted resources. As with all public health problems, an ounce of prevention (and early intervention) is worth a pound of cure. The use of emergency rooms and crisis inpatient stays is less than ideal for patients and their families—and they're bad for the public health system's bottom line. As a nation, we now spend huge amounts of money for acute psychiatric hospital care (in ERs and inpatient units) because, too often, there are no functioning, accountable, and responsive community-based mental health services.

Private and Public Mental Health Care

Private mental health care encompasses services provided by nongovernmental organizations; they are typically professionally run, not-for-profit organizations licensed by state agencies. Examples of private healthcare services include community general hospitals, academic (university) medical centers, community health centers, psychiatric hospitals, community mental health centers (or clinics), and mental health rehabilitation services.

Some privately owned services are for-profit. Today, there generally are few differences between not-for-profit and for-profit. Not-for-profit has come to mean trying not to lose money; for-profit institutions try to achieve minimal profit margins. The difficulty that mental health services have in generating market-competitive earnings helps explain the dearth of mental health services at many private, for-profit healthcare organizations.

Patients with the most serious and persistent of mental illnesses, and the fewest resources or community supports, often find themselves in the public system. Public mental health services are run by cities, counties, and states, or, federally, by the Veterans Administration or the Indian Health Service. Public mental health services are non-profits that are mandated to provide services to patients in need, regardless of a patient's ability to pay. These public services are known as "safety net" services, because they are meant to "catch" or serve people without health insurance, people with insurance for the poor and disabled, and others who would otherwise be limited in their ability to access care (like undocumented people or those leaving prisons or jails).

But the public health system does *not* have to be the last place families turn to for help—in fact, it *shouldn't* be. Many public mental health clinics, rehabilitation programs, and hospitals can be where a family turns for the most complex and persistent mental health problems. When you think of treatment for advanced cancer, for example, you may think of Memorial Sloan-Kettering or Dana Farber. When you think of severe heart disease, you may think of the Cleveland Clinic, New York Presbyterian Hospital, or Massachusetts General Hospital. The practice of highly expert care and advanced treatments is known as "tertiary care."

For many people with serious and persistent mental illness, particularly psychotic illnesses, the public mental health care system can and does deliver tertiary mental health care. If you are a family facing severe and persistent mental illness, you should consider state- or county-run hospitals and clinics. These publicly run services should make it their goal to become Centers of Excellence—to deliver the tertiary care that patients and families need.

Parity in Mental Health Insurance

In 2008, President Bush augmented the existing Mental Health Parity Act (MHPA, 1996) by signing the Troubled Asset Relief Program (TARP) into law. It may seem strange, but TARP did not just aim to help the country's financial crisis; it also was designed to help Americans avoid a mental health crisis. It did this by mandating *parity* for mental health. The bill requires that, over a number of years, companies that provide commercial health insurance to their employees also must provide mental health benefits equal to the benefits they provide for general medical (physical health) care. Parity means that the insurance benefit for mental health or addiction services must be identical to coverage for medical and surgical care in terms of numbers of visits, copayments, and annual limits.

Parity is an important and hard-won victory for mental health care advocates. But before we start celebrating, you need to know that, like many laws, the MHPA and TARP only go so far. Some illnesses, like PTSD, are not covered. In addition, companies with fewer than 50 employees are exempt from compliance.

Managed Care

Even when parity exists, insurers can still introduce *managed care*—a practice that is too often the scourge of healthcare clinicians and medical services. When done well, managed care can deliver care management, meaning that the insured patient receives more accessible, accountable, quality care. Unfortunately, however, managed care companies often demand considerable information before they approve payment for services, placing a huge burden on clinicians and families. Managed care is also well known for severely reducing payments to clinicians, claiming these payments to be the "usual and customary" rates for a particular service when, in fact, many clinicians say they are so low that they can't cover the costs of maintaining a practice. Insured individuals, families, and clinical care providers frequently have to fight endlessly with insurance or managed care companies to extract approval for good and necessary services. Sometimes, the saga of obtaining insurance approval for even minimal amounts of payment (for example, two days in a hospital, or more than eight outpatient visits) requires repetitive requests. Frugal insurance-approval techniques have discouraged many patients from continuing much-needed treatment.

The world of managed care—especially mental health managed care—has become so complex and problematic that it is now a sweet subject for stand-up comedians. But patients do need care management.

Good care management ensures that patients in need can access the best treatment with clinicians and services that deliver quality, continuous, and coordinated care (what you want for your family member). Public officials, healthcare providers, consumers, and advocates need to come together to insist on good care management and to make bad managed care a historical footnote.

Medicaid and Medicare

Medicaid is the state-sponsored health insurance for people living in poverty. Increasingly, Medicaid is also provided to children of uninsured (and underinsured) families. Medicaid pays for certain medical services (which vary by state), prescription medications, and nursing home care.

To qualify for Medicaid, a person must have very limited assets. Some people will "spend down" their assets by paying for care until they become eligible. The asset limit in some cases can be as low as $2000 (excluding the value of a home and possibly a car). Medicaid is undergoing further rule changes as a result of the Affordable Care Act. Most clinics and hospitals have financial-aid professionals to assist you and your family member in obtaining Medicaid and understanding the services it covers. Don't be reluctant to seek their help; benefits can be complex and require particular approvals that trained staff are familiar with from doing this work every day.

Remarkably, Medicaid is often the best insurance coverage for people with serious and persistent illness, including mental illnesses. It covers outpatient and inpatient treatments, as well as the rehabilitation services that can be essential in treating serious mental disorders. Medicaid "waiver" services (those outside of standard benefits, which vary from state to state) can provide children with comprehensive and coordinated community-based services that enable them to remain in the community, with their family, in order to avoid or abbreviate hospital stays. Medicaid also pays for medications—invaluable coverage for everyone with a serious illness.

If your family member is on Medicaid, seek assistance from professionals to help him or her remain eligible; losing eligibility can interfere with getting needed services. If you think your adult family member may be eligible for Medicaid, look into obtaining coverage. A social worker, a case manager, or administrative clinic (or hospital) personnel can help you understand eligibility and obtain Medicaid benefits. If you are the parent of an uninsured child, be sure to check with your child's treatment program or a trained benefits manager about Medicaid coverage.

Medicare is the federal health insurance program for patients over 65 and disabled individuals. Assessment for disability coverage under Medicare requires an extensive evaluation process; although some mental disorders qualify as a disability, a primary diagnosis of alcohol or drug addiction will not.

UNDERSTANDING MEDICARE

Medicare has different components, and you will need to understand parts A, B, and D.

Part A is hospital insurance. It pays for hospital treatment and short-term nursing home care. Part A also covers some home health-care and hospice services. Medicare Part A typically has a copayment and an annual deductible that the beneficiary is responsible for. These additional payments are covered for individuals on both Medicare and Medicaid (often called "dual eligible").

Part B is coverage for doctors, clinics, certain laboratory tests, and some forms of physical therapy. Part B is optional, which means you must specifically *opt-in* and pay a monthly premium to one of the many insurance companies that sell Part B coverage. There is also a small annual deductible.

Part D covers some prescription medications. This has been an important benefit to seniors and the disabled, but, again, it involves a monthly premium and an annual deductible.

There is also Medicare **Part C**, an option known as the "Medicare Advantage Plan," which is offered by private insurers. This coverage includes Parts A and B and often has other benefits, including prescription drug benefits. To purchase Part C, a person must have Medicare A and B and then elect to have this private plan instead. Medicare Advantage Plans often have limited networks of hospitals and doctors.

Medicare benefits for mental health are not as comprehensive as those of Medicaid in terms of what services are covered. Medicare often has copayments for inpatient, outpatient, and medication treatments that can be a hardship, especially for people on fixed incomes. In addition, coverage for mental health rehabilitation services is far more limited and may not exist for certain services. Be sure that you and your loved one seek good information and counseling about benefits if he or she is eligible for, or already receiving, Medicare.

Medicare recipients living in poverty may be eligible for Medicaid as well, which would cover that portion of the costs not covered by

Medicare. These individuals are called *dual eligibles* in the world of insurance coverage. You and your family member will want to have very good information about obtaining dual eligibility, which is complex and can be difficult to manage. Talking to a benefits specialist is a good idea.

What to Ask When You Have Insurance

Do not mortgage your house or take out loans to pay for mental health services that your insurance carrier should cover. Before you make an appointment to receive care, if at all possible, you want to have an answer to the following detailed questions:

- What is your insurance company, and what plan are you in? (Companies often offer different plans for different monthly payments.)
- Does your plan cover mental health services?
- If so, which mental health professionals are on its approved list of providers? Which hospitals or clinics are on the approved list?
- Do you need to have a prior approval (even if the benefit is covered) from the insurance company (or its managed care service) in order to see a mental health care professional or clinic? Do you need prior approval if hospital inpatient treatment is needed?
- What is the number of approved visits and services the plan allows? What are the copayments and deductibles?

Many patients and families have discovered that making an appointment with a mental health professional on an insurance (or managed care) company's approved list can prove next to impossible. If you must use your health insurance or managed care plan, *insist that your insurer help you arrange an appointment* with one of their approved professionals. They are responsible for enabling you to access care, not endlessly pursue names on a list that are more fictional than real.

If Medicaid is your insurer, you will almost certainly see a professional at a mental health clinic or hospital in your community. Virtually no psychiatrist in private practice (and very few other mental health professionals) will accept Medicaid because the fee Medicaid pays doctors is so low. The fees Medicaid pays to clinics and hospitals are often far greater, which allows these settings to hire professionals who would not accept Medicaid payment in private practice. Because more mental health professionals accept Medicare, patients covered by Medicare have a better chance of seeing a private psychiatric professional.

Picking an Insurance Plan

When considering which insurance plan to choose, most employees usually look at the difference in monthly premiums and pick the least expensive. But the monthly premium may not be the only cost you incur if you or someone in your family becomes ill. Before anyone, individual or family, selects an insurance plan, check out its available benefits, covered services, and procedures needed for approval. Talk with your company's benefit counselor if you need more information. You will thank yourself later. Careful research when choosing your plan can save you a lot of time, money, and headaches down the road.

Estate Planning

Some families with children (including adult children) look ahead and wonder what supports their loved one will have after they are aged or gone. Families who anticipate leaving assets to their children, however limited or considerable they may be, should consider consulting an attorney about how to leave those assets in ways that will enable the ill family member to use them over time while also qualifying for government programs like Medicaid and Medicare.

Health Insurance: An American Policy Challenge

The United States is one of the only countries in the developed world with a sizeable number of citizens without health insurance coverage. President Obama's Affordable Care Act, which created a health insurance mandate for all citizens, was challenged but sustained by the Supreme

Court. However, the ruling allows for states to make important decisions about Medicaid. You will need to understand your state's Medicaid rules and benefits; again, counselors at clinical settings are very good people to turn to for this information.

At this point the outcome for uninsured Americans remains uncertain. In the meantime, all Americans need to become knowledgeable consumers in the insurance market. And perhaps most important, families need to be vocal advocates for their loved ones when illness strikes and payment must be made.

"Out of Pocket" Payment

Seeing a psychotherapist to work through situational crises or losses, to assist with interpersonal problems at home or at work, or for wise counseling is a long-standing and valuable endeavor. Unfortunately, it can be difficult to get insurance companies to pay for psychotherapy, or to meet the fees of experienced clinicians. Further, many insurance and managed care companies require the therapy to meet conditions of what is called "medical necessity," which means there is a diagnosable illness and treatment is needed. Further, these companies often ask for proof (evidence) that the treatment you wish to pursue has a scientific basis. Even when therapy meets these stipulations, insurance companies often limit coverage to a specific number of visits. Some insurance plans will allow a limited number of visits for one diagnosis (say, mild to moderate depression) but permit more for another diagnosis (such as schizophrenia).

A few insurers will pay fully for therapy, but many require a copayment, deductible, or both. Thus, most patients are paying the bill for at least a portion of their own therapy costs. This financial situation makes you a consumer, not just a patient. In spite of the costs, some families seek private consultation and therapy—paying out of pocket—for a number of reasons:

- The ability to choose whom you want to see, independent of third-party influence or interference

- To avoid a mental health diagnosis becoming a part of your medical insurance record
- Because a growing number of clinicians are refusing to be part of insurance company clinical panels (network clinicians)
- Because the services you want (e.g., long-term psychotherapy or psychoanalysis) are not covered by any insurance

In fact, a growing number of clinicians offer discounted fees to patients and families who pay out of pocket. Direct payments enable the therapist to avoid administrative paperwork and the burden of calling care managers at the insurance company (and they often face discounted payments from insurance companies anyway). Explain your financial situation to your therapist, and see if he or she might be willing to adjust the fee.

A Closing Comment

Mental health care is a good investment—when the treatment is done well and for the proper duration. Although privately funding therapy may be possible for some families, it is beyond the means of all but the very wealthy to pay privately for hospital-level services, or for weeks or months of residential services that mental illness (or addiction) can sometimes require.

For serious and persistent mental illnesses, third-party payment is essential to cover the financial burdens of necessary and ongoing care. The more you understand the services your loved one needs, and the more you advocate for what is properly covered by your policy, the more successful you will be in getting coverage that pays for the care of your loved one. Figuring out what your insurance covers and demanding that your insurance or managed care company live up to its commitments is a vital, if difficult, part of the struggle of families who battle for the best of services for serious mental illnesses.

Mental Health and the Law

T hankfully for patients and their families, the days of *One Flew Over the Cuckoo's Nest* are long gone. Today, people with mental illness have the right to decide when, where, how, and—sometimes even with unfortunate results—*if* they'll receive care. As crucial as it is for people with mental illness to have the right to determine their course of treatment, the nature of some mental illnesses, particularly acute and chronic psychotic states, can make it difficult for some patients to assess the reality of their experiences or need for treatment. When the mental illness interferes with judgment, self-interest, and self-preservation, families and clinicians are profoundly challenged. Colleagues of mine have remarked that when patient rights exceed necessary protections, individuals with mental illness can "die with their rights on."

Most laws, and especially mental health laws, are prohibitive in nature: They describe what *cannot* be done in a certain situation. Mental health laws often protect the patient's civil rights. Although this is an important "good," it sometimes comes at a cost. For example, although we know that in a best-case scenario, doctors and families should work together, there are laws that regulate what a doctor can and cannot say to a patient's family (with the exception of unemancipated minors). Other examples include when state mental health laws prohibit certain effective treatments, or severely limit the use of hospitalization, or require extensive procedures to be done before treatment, or even urgent care, is undertaken against a patient's will.

These laws were developed decades ago when doctors and hospitals had almost unbridled control over patients and their treatments. What began as patient protections have in some cases become the rigid rules and procedures in place today where liberty interests may seem to exceed patient care and even common sense. Despite the good intentions that spawned these laws, in practice they can sometimes interfere with or delay the delivery of needed care or even important communication between caregivers and families.

Questions abound about the legal constraints on patient families. What can families do to impel needed treatment that a loved one refuses? Can the parents of a minor with a mental illness force their child to undergo treatment? Is there anything that parents of a minor with mental illness can do if their child refuses to take medication or attend therapy? Can someone having a psychotic episode be committed to an inpatient facility against his or her will? Under what circumstances can that person, now a patient at the facility, discharge him- or herself?

Jim, a college student in New York City, became acutely psychotic and was found wandering around Manhattan in freezing weather in a T-shirt, khakis, and flip-flops. When Jim's father brought him to the ER, a doctor told him that unless Jim was "an imminent danger to himself or others," she could not admit him against his will. She added, "I cannot hospitalize or treat him unless he voluntarily agrees."

These types of situations happen all the time to families with a loved one who suffers from a serious mental illness. Family members and friends must learn how to make the case that their loved one must be hospitalized (even involuntarily) when they believe the risk of a dangerous or deadly outcome has become too great. If your efforts are not working with emergency room or hospital staff, if you are not being heard, I urge you to insist on speaking with a clinical supervisor or a senior administrator. In Chapter 5 I offered specific statements you may want to use. Going to emergency or acute-care settings with a psychiatric professional, an attorney, or an experienced friend or relative will help bolster your effort if you think that your loved one will be allowed to leave without proper treatment.

The law plays a prominent role in psychiatry, perhaps more so than in any other field of medicine. Issues of personal and public safety, civil rights, accountability, privacy, confidentiality, and competency are woven throughout the practice of psychiatry. Although the law may have been written to protect the rights and wellbeing of individuals and communities, it sometimes can appear to have the opposite effect.

In this chapter, I review what confidentiality and privacy mean—as well as what their limits are. I'll discuss when someone can be declared mentally incompetent (for example, unable to handle finances or make other basic life decisions) as well as how to navigate issues of guardianship and what are known as "advance directives." My goal is to give you a better understanding of how to manage the moments when clinical needs and the laws governing medical care don't seem to make common sense—and your loved one's safety, and perhaps that of others, is at stake.

Let's first look at aspects of the legal code and consider its mandates and prohibitions. This can help you figure out how to work within the legal system to achieve the best outcome for your loved one.

Confidentiality

Patients have the right to expect that what they say in confidence to a doctor will stay within the confines of the doctor-patient relationship. That is the essence of confidentiality, and it goes back a long time—even the Greek physician Hippocrates held that doctors should not disclose information obtained from their patients.

Confidentiality is essential to establishing trust in the doctor-patient or other clinical relationship. This is particularly important in the mental health field. Unless a person can feel certain that what he or she says will remain confidential, that person will not disclose certain problems, concerns, or symptoms. We all are apt to be more willing to speak freely when we have confidence that no one else will know.

The law allows doctors to share confidential information with other parties *at a patient's request*: This is called *consent to release information*. If I want my primary-care doctor to know what medications my psychiatrist is prescribing, or I want my insurance company to pay for my appointment (though I don't want them to know too much about what I say in the appointment), I must provide written consent. Parents sign consents for their children so that the child can receive medical and other services; that consent also gives them access to medical information.

Consent to release information is usually given by a patient signing a form that permits the release of confidential medical information. Sometimes, consent to release information can be verbal, in which case it should be documented in the medical record by the doctor, a nurse, or a witness. (Consent for *treatment* is different from consent to release information and is discussed a little later.)

Seeking and obtaining consent should be a thoughtful, informed process during which the patient feels respected. Patients should be given essential information and made partners in all decisions that pertain to them. Consequently, the clinician requesting consent needs to explain why he or she is asking for it, and why this consent is in the patient's interest. Clear, simple, non-medical language is best.

In releasing information, it is often best for clinicians to provide information to others on a *"need to know"* basis. It's rare for a patient to ask the clinician to release all written records; however, when this is the case, the request should be honored. But detailed personal histories, a patient's dreams and fantasies, or speculations by a mental health clinician are seldom helpful to others and should be excluded when information is released outside of the doctor-patient relationship. Usually, the necessary information consists of facts about the patient, including current and previous diagnoses, all medical and psychiatric medications (and their risks), and any other treatments or interventions that have been provided.

Wise clinicians recognize that *families* can be the greatest support a patient has. Clinicians may want a parent or sibling to know about a change in the current treatment, possible crises or safety issues, or the onset of a serious medical problem. But according to strict legal code, families cannot obtain this confidential information about an adult patient without consent from that person. As a result, clinicians and healthcare administrators are required to have consent from their patients in order to speak with family members.

As some families discover, people with serious mental illness can and do object to their families knowing anything or being involved in their treatment, even though involving families could be a great help. The best solution to this paradox is usually clinical—*not* legal. When clinicians focus on building (or rebuilding) trust between a patient and his or her family (or selected members of the family), that patient can come to see that the family is working to achieve the same goal he or she is—namely, recovery. This can take time, and there is no guarantee. But if trust can be reestablished, a person will allow the family to help—sometimes in limited ways, sometimes more completely.

SMART TREATMENT WITHIN THE CONFINES OF THE LAW

David was 20 when the police brought him to the ER. He had harassed a bus driver, and he continued to act aggressively until the police arrived. David had never been to this particular ER, so there was no record of any previous treatment he may have received or any existing conditions he may have had—medical or mental. In the presence of the police and hospital security, David was docile; he said that he was fine and that he regretted losing his temper. But his disheveled and fearful look prompted the triage nurse to call for a psychiatric consult.

The psychiatrist learned from David that he lived with his parents, but he told her that he didn't want them contacted. David said he'd never had any such outbursts before, and that he had never received mental health care. The psychiatrist's efforts to obtain his permission to call his parents failed, but she called anyway.

David's parents were relieved to receive the call and to know that David was safe. The doctor simply identified herself as a doctor from the emergency room who was examining their son. She then stated that she had no further information to provide, but that she would be happy to listen *to them. David's parents immediately volunteered that this was David's third ER visit in 4 weeks, and that he had been involuntarily hospitalized 6 months earlier after hitting a stranger in the supermarket.*

After the call, the psychiatrist again offered David help. When he refused, she had him involuntarily admitted to the hospital.

David's doctor trusted her instincts, and although she pushed the limits of the confidentiality law (by calling his parents without permission), she was able to get the critical information she needed to get him care. As I have said elsewhere, before consent is obtained, clinicians can (and should) listen carefully to family members and impart what information the law permits, even if it is limited. But there is *no* law that prohibits clinicians from *listening to* family members about what they know and have experienced with their loved one. This can be very helpful in diagnosis and determining which treatment options might be effective or necessary.

EXCEPTIONS TO CONFIDENTIALITY

There are a few exceptions to confidentiality.

Administrative Exceptions. State and federal governmental authorities impose a variety of *reporting requirements* on clinicians for specific events. When these situations arise, clinicians are obligated to break confidentiality. Examples include: certain infectious diseases (like tuberculosis), child and elder abuse, and sexual exploitation by a professional of a patient.

When a patient's situation mandates that I (for example), as a doctor, must report it, first I urge my patient to inform the proper authorities before I do. I want to give the patient a chance to take more control (and responsibility) for whatever the situation is. However, whatever my patient does, I state that I am obligated to report the information, and I will.

In clinical settings where there are supervisors and other members of a treatment team, it is essential that the clinician share this mandated reporting information with those involved in the same patient's care. These are not discretionary situations: The law is clear and the clinician cannot violate it.

Danger to Others. There are situations when a clinician learns from a patient (or a reliable informant) that the patient is planning a specific dangerous act against another person or people. The "Tarasoff decision" (a well-known legal precedent) comes into play at these moments. Although Tarasoff can sometimes be construed as the duty to tell the intended victim (the so-called *duty to warn*), generally what Tarasoff actually mandates is that clinicians be held to a *duty to protect*. When in possession of credible information about potential danger to a specific individual, a doctor or other mental health professional must take "certain actions" meant to protect the potential victim. These "certain actions" can include contacting the potential victim, administering a specific treatment thought to reduce the danger, or hospitalizing the patient. Whatever is done to avert the danger, the doctor has broken confidentiality (because of a legal requirement) to protect the potential victim.

Patient Incompetence. When a patient is clinically "incompetent," that means he or she can no longer make sound judgments about finances, living situation, or other vital daily functions. In an ideal situation, there is a legally appointed guardian or a relative who can provide consent. In cases where there is no guardian and no relative can be found, the physician must use his or her best judgment and do what he or she believes is in the best interest of her patient. (I'll talk more about competency a little later.)

Emergency Situations. Safety for a life comes before standing on ceremony—even if the ceremony may appear legally mandated. For me, contacting another clinician, family member, or other key informant trumps everything else if I believe that a patient's life (or someone else's) is at stake and I cannot obtain consent.

For example, in an ER, a patient who is semiconscious from an overdose cannot give permission to call another doctor or a family member to find out any information that may help with the emergency treatment— you don't hear about doctors standing on ceremony at those moments.

In emergencies involving a person who is acutely psychotic and refusing to cooperate with the clinician, the doctor may decide that the need for critical medical information comes before confidentiality. Throughout my career, I have said I would rather be sued for calling a family member than see a terrible clinical outcome that might have been averted with more information.

HIPAA

No discussion of confidentiality in the U.S. is complete without mention of HIPAA, the Health Insurance Portability and Accountability Act. Since 2003, this federal law has governed the exchange of information among parties providing health care. HIPAA was enacted to address concerns that the computer age would erase any vestige of confidentiality because digital information can be so readily streamed, unimpeded, across the World Wide Web.

HIPAA has a specific provision, known as the Notice of Privacy Practices, that states that all patients 18 and over need to name the people with whom their medical information can be shared. HIPAA can make helping a loved one *more difficult*, because it means that families and friends of the mentally ill are not automatically privy to information about a loved one's progress or problems in treatment.

In order to be kept in the loop about your loved one's care, you must be designated by the patient on a HIPAA form. You will want to urge your family member or friend to sign the HIPAA consent form. This is best done when there is no emergency, if possible. The person's signature will allow you to receive information, monitor your loved one's condition, and actively participate in his or her care.

The New York State Office of Mental Health has published an advisory explaining HIPAA (www.omh.state.ny.us/omhweb/hipaa/phi_protection.html). However, it is important to check the law in your state. In New York, clinicians working in a licensed mental health setting can talk to *other clinicians in another such setting* without permission. And, as I have already said, *clinicians can listen to families* without violating HIPAA requirements. Of course, after all is said and done, common sense and clinical necessity should prevail.

Informed Consent for Treatment

A doctor is required to obtain informed consent from an adult patient for a diagnostic procedure or treatment (I'll discuss minors in a moment). This happens all the time—sometimes it's written (the patient signs a consent form) and sometimes it's verbal (after a discussion, the patient is asked if he or she consents to the procedure, and the doctor notes it in the medical record).

The first word in the term is important—*informed* means that a patient needs to know how the procedure works, what the benefits are, and what the risks are. The doctor needs to explain the diagnostic test or treatment in clear, simple, and understandable terms; why he or she is recommending it (what benefit may result); what risks come with the intervention—and the risks of not doing it; and what alternative diagnostic approaches or treatments exist. The doctor should ask the patient if he or she has any questions before the consent process is concluded. The informed consent process is also an opportunity to build trust between the doctor and the patient. This discussion can be part of an ongoing effort to reinforce that treatment is a *shared* decision-making process that requires careful communication and ongoing work.

A parent or legal guardian must give consent for diagnostic or treatment procedures for minors (anyone under 18). Exceptions include minors "emancipated" by a court, those who are married or divorced, and minors serving in the armed forces. Both the actual age and the developmental age of the child (how mature the child's thinking and judgment are) should inform the clinician about how much that child needs to be a part of the consent. Clearly a 17-year-old who's about to go to college would be considered differently from a 7-year-old with problems in thinking. Each minor and situation is different, but good clinicians can find a way to help child patients understand that the treatment is meant to help them with problems they have.

The Right to Treatment and the Right to Refuse Treatment

All patients have both a right to treatment *and* a right to refuse treatment. These rights are especially important for people who are hospitalized.

There is a long legal history leading to the right to treatment. Much of the law derives from old court cases involving people who were admitted to state psychiatric hospitals where they languished without proper treatment, sometimes for many years. The right-to-treatment law was instrumental to the development of the quality-oriented public psychiatric hospitals that exist today. In fact, in order for these public hospitals to receive Medicare and Medicaid (and other third-party) payment, they must obtain the same national certification that academic medical centers and local community hospitals have. This means that a person who is admitted to a public psychiatric hospital has a right to receive—and should receive—the best treatment available.

It may seem odd that a person can be involuntarily admitted, or "committed," to a hospital and then refuse treatment. But the right to *refuse* treatment is fundamental to the legal constraints upon psychiatric treatment. You can drag a horse to water but you cannot make him drink.

Someone who enters a hospital voluntarily and shows no imminent risk of danger to self or others is apt to express the right to refuse treatment by stating that he or she wants to leave the hospital. But a person admitted involuntarily, due to danger to self or others, cannot leave, at least not right away. However, despite having the authority to keep the patient in the hospital, the professional staff cannot treat the person against his or her will, except by court order. The right to refuse treatment was built on basic rights to privacy, equal protection under the law, and due process: In other words, involuntarily hospitalized patients still have the right to decide what happens to their bodies.

Unfortunately, the right to refuse treatment can result in a patient being locked up in a hospital where doctors cannot proceed with treatment. What's worse, and deeply ironic, is that insurance companies may step in and refuse to pay, stating there is "no active treatment." However, this cannot happen in state hospitals, which represent the true safety net of services for people with serious and persistent mental illnesses, because they are not wholly dependent on insurance payment.

As with confidentiality, there are exceptions to a patient's right to refuse treatment. In an emergency, all bets are off. A doctor may provide involuntary treatment, usually a medication given by injection or pill, but only to control the emergency—which is defined as "an imminent danger to self or others." Whatever treatment is provided in an emergency cannot be continued after the immediate danger has passed, unless the patient gives informed consent. Clinicians cannot continue the medication—even if it could prevent another emergent situation. Such is the power of patient rights.

For involuntary treatment to be delivered outside of an acute emergency, the doctor and hospital must petition a court to permit it. Laws vary from state to state, and, of course, no two judges are alike. Generally, judges rule in favor of well-prepared doctors and hospitals who show that the treatment is necessary for safety and recovery; all efforts at voluntary treatment have been exhausted; family and others were engaged to help persuade the patient to accept care (and were not successful); and the benefits of treatment are likely to outweigh its risks. Inpatient stays often last several weeks (or months) longer if court-ordered treatment is required. Once a court order is obtained, almost all patients comply with treatment within a day or so, and then, hopefully, proceed to respond to treatment.

Competency (and Treatment Over Objection)

Competency draws its importance from the values placed on individual rights, especially in the United States. A citizen's right to choose what he or she wants to say or do (within the law), how to spend his or her money, or what risks to take (such as smoking, motorcycle riding without a helmet, or sky diving), is a highly prized value in America—and is reflected in its laws.

Therefore, when it comes to medical decisions, individuals have great personal authority. One critical limiting factor, however, is competency, which is the capacity to be the reasonably responsible agent of one's personal affairs. Competency can best be understood in its two forms: *general* competence and *specific* competence.

General competence refers to an individual's capacity to handle all of his or her affairs in a reasonable manner that is consistent with that person's self-interest. There are legal standards to assess if a person has general competence. Some considerations include:

- An awareness of the circumstances of that person's life, including where the person lives, how the person supports him- or herself, relationships, and the like
- An understanding of the facts surrounding those circumstances
- An appreciation that the person's actions may result in consequences
- Logical reasoning or judgment, particularly the ability to arrive at a sound judgment that takes the person's situation into account
- Memory functioning, understanding of reality, feeling of hopelessness that is the result of a mood disorder, and capacity to reason

Specific competence is far more focused in nature. The legal questions and standards for specific competence ask:

- Does the patient have the ability to make a choice (often as simple as "yes" or "no")?
- Can the patient appreciate the facts related to a specific decision? (For treatment decisions this means a basic understanding of a proposed treatment, with risks, benefits, and alternatives.)

- Does the patient understand his or her circumstances? In mental health settings, this means that a patient acknowledges that he or she is ill, in a hospital, and being offered treatment.
- Can the patient use reasoning or judgment specific to the decision at hand? (A patient may be able to make a yes or no choice, but still not be able to make a decision regarding a will or trust, for example.)

Specific competence is particularly important when it comes to decisions about consenting to medical treatment. All treatment, except emergency interventions, requires either consent or court order. Voluntary decision making, particularly shared decision making, is far preferable to involuntary treatment. There are times, however, when the gravity of a person's illness calls for a temporary, involuntary treatment to help ensure safety, to keep someone alive, and to restore that person's capacity to resume competent and self-directed decision making.

If the patient won't consent to treatment, the doctor must go to court and obtain a judge's order to proceed with *treatment over objection*. Treatment over objection (TOO) is not uncommon in hospital settings where a person is admitted for dangerousness and refuses treatment. TOO requires the medical staff to prepare a careful and persuasive case for the court regarding the likelihood of benefit from the treatment as well as how that benefit outweighs the risks. As I mentioned earlier, judges usually support medical recommendations when they are sound and shown to be in the patient's interest. But TOO often means that treatment is delayed and that a hospital stay is protracted in order for a court order to be obtained and treatment begun. Continued involuntary hospital stays resulting from a TOO case are specific to the detailed treatment plan and duration of stay that the judge approves.

An alternative to TOO for people who lack specific (or general) competency to decide on medically beneficial treatment is *guardianship*. Courts have the power to appoint a legal guardian when needed; that guardian has the legal authority to oversee the personal and property interests of the person under guardianship, sometimes called the ward. Guardian status may be awarded over an individual who cannot care for himself, usually due to incapacity or youth. Most states regard the parents of a minor child to be the legal guardians. The court can appoint a guardian after formal hearings. Guardianship is seldom done in the heat of a clinical moment, and is best discussed with a family's attorney or public legal advocate.

Advance Directives

Advance directives are statements by individuals about their healthcare choices written *before* any decision is needed. Advance directives are often completed by individuals as they age, or when they develop serious and chronic illnesses. I have one, and I urge my family members and friends to have one as well.

Advance directives in mental health care are a critical tool in advancing patient-centered treatment plans. An advance directive should be developed with a patient when the person is in a stable mental state and can consider and express how he or she wants to be treated if a future acute mental illness were to diminish judgment, or in the event of becoming incompetent (as defined earlier). For example, a person who has been diagnosed with schizophrenia but is currently on medication and mentally stable may prepare an advance directive, indicating that if he or she falls acutely ill again, he or she would prefer to receive a particular medication (named, with explanation for why it has been chosen) and to be placed in the hospital only after efforts at outpatient treatment are not successful.

These directives are a way of respecting a person's wishes if acute illness occurs and the person requires involuntary commitment or treatment. Having a person's expressed wishes can shape treatment in ways that are attentive to what that person would have chosen for him- or herself, were he or she able to do so.

There is a national website that provides templates for advance directives around the U.S. (www.nrc-pad.org/content/view/344/80/). It can be reassuring for family members with an illness to know that although these documents can be very useful, they are not binding; someone who has written one can reject it during a time of acute illness, and some do. But many do not. Even when a patient *does* reject the advance directive during a time of acute illness, clinicians can still use the directive to see patient preferences (for types of medication or therapy) and guide their planning accordingly.

I strongly urge you and your family to have advance directives, for both health and mental health needs. In the same way that families develop wills or plan ahead for caring for one another, they can talk about advance directives. Families who have been able to write these are usually thankful they did when the need arises.

Inpatient and Outpatient Commitment

Commitment, or involuntary hospitalization, should only be used as a last resort. Thankfully, most patients receive care and can participate in decision making before it ever gets to the point of commitment. But in some cases, where lack of insight plays a large role in the illness (particularly with psychotic illnesses or eating disorders), involuntary commitment may be necessary to help your loved one.

INPATIENT COMMITMENT

Commitment for psychiatric care exists in every state in the United States and is widespread internationally. People with mental illness have been involuntarily admitted to psychiatric hospitals, once called asylums, for centuries; the same applies to psychiatric units in general hospitals today. Broad changes in commitment laws and the advent of community mental health, dating back to the 1960s, radically changed the use of and standards for commitment. You can no longer commit a patient just because he or she refuses to follow the rules of his or her parental home (by staying out late, for example), drops out of school, or neglects to take prescribed medications (without representing a danger to him- or herself or others). Clear evidence of imminent danger to self or others, or the likelihood of deteriorating to a dangerous state without treatment, now guides any clinician considering commitment. One consequence of this paradigm shift, however, is the reduction in the use of inpatient psychiatric care that might have benefited some patients in need.

Commitment laws vary from state to state, but all require that a person have a mental illness and be "dangerous to self or others" as a result of that mental illness. Dangerousness generally means that a person is at imminent risk to harm him- or herself or someone else; at times, it can also mean that the mental illness has such a debilitating effect that the person's health and welfare will deteriorate substantially if the illness isn't treated, putting the person at risk of a serious health or safety hazard, or even death.

Generally, commitment, especially for inpatient admission, is carried out by one or two physicians or other "designated" individuals (including other mental health professionals or the police). Occasionally a judge will order commitment to a psychiatric hospital of someone brought before the court by police, family, or a guardian. Mental health professional commitments are typically very brief in duration; often they are for 3 days, sometimes for a couple of weeks. They are very infrequently longer.

For inpatient stays to continue beyond doctor-ordered commitment, the hospital and its doctors must to go to court and convince a judge that continued involuntary stay is needed. Most cases brought to court for continued stays are given more time. At times, however, doctors and hospitals—facing the rigor and demands of the courts, the strong advocacy of mental health lawyers representing patients, and uncertainty about the effectiveness of continued stay—will discharge a patient after a brief hospital stay rather than fighting for a court-ordered continuation of hospital care. The media is full of examples of situations where premature discharge has been associated with tragic outcomes.

OUTPATIENT COMMITMENT

Outpatient commitment, sometimes referred to as "assisted outpatient commitment" (AOT), exists as law in most states. Yet how the law is written, how it is financed, and the clinical resources it can deliver vary substantially from state to state.

The criteria for AOT eligibility in the state of New York are as follows:

The individual must:
- be at least 18 years old
- suffer from a mental illness
- be unlikely to survive safely in the community without supervision, based on a clinical determination
- have a history of lack of compliance with treatment for mental illness;

- o Prior to the filing of the petition, at least twice within the last 36 months, this lack of compliance must have been a significant factor in necessitating hospitalization or receipt of services in a forensic or other mental health unit of a correctional facility. The 36-month period does not include any current period, or period ending within the last 6 months, during which the person was or is hospitalized or incarcerated.
- o Or, prior to the filing of the petition, this lack of compliance resulted in one or more acts of serious violent behavior toward self or others or threats of, or attempts at, serious physical harm to self or others within the last 48 months, not including any current period, or period ending within the last 6 months, in which the person was or is hospitalized or incarcerated.
- be unlikely, as a result of this lack of compliance, to voluntarily participate in the outpatient treatment that would enable him or her to live safely in the community.
- be in need of assisted outpatient treatment in view of his or her treatment history and current behavior, in order to prevent a relapse or deterioration that would be likely to result in serious harm to self or others.
- be likely to benefit from assisted outpatient treatment.

These criteria are similar to those of other states and thus serve as a good template. However, to determine the criteria for your state, you will need to go online or call your state agency.

Outpatient commitment in the state of New York was legislated and then instituted in 1999 after a man with an untreated mental illness pushed Kendra Webdale to her death in a New York City subway station. Evidence of the effectiveness of outpatient commitment has been marshaled by careful and independent studies, which demonstrate reductions in re-hospitalization, imprisonment, and violence, as well as improved functioning for the individuals under outpatient commitment. As a result, Kendra's Law has been renewed twice by legislative action in the state, each time for 5 years.

Yet a debate continues about why outpatient commitment is so successful. Is it the threat of being picked up by police officers or a sheriff and transported to an ER if the person under AOT does not comply with treatment? Is it the powerful shadow cast by a judge who firmly informs a person that he or she is under court order? Or is it that people under court order are first in line when it comes to receiving community services, and thus have the most robust and continuous effective treatment for their conditions?

Efforts to distinguish why Kendra's Law works (what elements actually produce the desired benefits) have not been conclusive. In fact, the use of the law in upstate New York is markedly different from its use in New York City. Upstate, AOT is largely "voluntary" commitment by individuals who agree to comprehensive services when faced with the alternative of involuntary services, whereas in New York City it is involuntary, with AOT teams carefully monitoring if prescribed treatments are being delivered.

Although we may not be certain about what elements of AOT are actually the "therapeutic" elements, it does keep people out of hospitals and in the community. These benefits, as well as the risk of not retaining AOT in the state of New York, have prompted elected officials to sustain the law. Other states, and countries, struggle with whether to implement or continue outpatient commitment, as well as how best to modify it and fund it.

But, like inpatient commitment, outpatient commitment should be a last resort. What we should be funding is more readily accessible community-based outpatient care that delivers continuous, comprehensive, and evidence-based treatments. Which brings me back to a basic theme in this book: namely, that mental health services in this country don't work very well, despite the dedicated people who work to better them.

What this means for you, as a family member or friend, is that you will see how far the mental health system has to go before it reliably and ably serves your loved one. Lack of good community care for mental and addictive disorders—sometimes coupled with the lack of safe and supportive housing—is the principal driver of the clinical deterioration, chronic homelessness, incarceration, and suicidal and violent behaviors among those who are mentally ill. As I have said, you will have to advocate persistently to help ensure that your loved one receives the best care that community services can offer. It is not right, or fair, but it is the reality of what exists today. When you advocate, you can make a difference for your loved one and your family.

Recovery: Why Believe?

T hroughout this book, I have said that recovery from mental illness is possible. Recovery takes hard work, quality treatment, the ceaseless help of family and friends, and sustained hope, but when those come together, recovery can happen for your loved one.

Perhaps one of the most important things about recovery is how your loved one defines it. Just as patients need to clearly define their goals at the start of a treatment, they also should establish their *goals for recovery*. What's the difference? *Recovery* is a patient's unique and ongoing endeavor to make his or her life one of full relationships, purpose, and contribution—*with illness*. For example, a patient may identify competitive employment as a recovery goal, and training in computer science as a treatment goal.

Recovery may be best understood as a *process* rather than an end state. A person in recovery remains in recovery—he or she does not become "cured," nor is he or she ever "recovered." The realities of persistent illness—in mental health, physical health, and addictions—requires that patients, clinicians, families, and friends be ever-vigilant about risks of relapse while continuously working on recovery in an active, daily way.

Recovery is rooted in *hope*. Patients must have hope—a belief that recovery can be a reality for them. Hope is the source of motivation and the antidote for discouragement; it is what people with mental illness and their families and friends need to share and support in one another. When there is hope, there is reason to participate in treatment, to learn to manage disease, and to reach for life when faced with setbacks. Patients who are in recovery take greater responsibility for themselves and insist on dignity and opportunity. Recovery, thus, is as welcome a concept for people with mental illness as it is for their families and friends, as well as those who provide them with the services they use to rebuild their lives.

One Woman's Recovery Story

Dr. Carol North sits in her office at the University of Texas's Southwestern Medical Center in Dallas when she is not traveling to New York City, Washington, New Orleans, Oklahoma City, or Nairobi. She holds a named professorship in crisis psychiatry, and she has advised the White House and various federal agencies on disaster mental health, posttraumatic stress disorder, and terrorism. I met Dr. North in New York City following the September 11th terrorist attacks, and she became one of my most important teachers and advisors during the years I directed the mental health crisis and recovery services for the city.

I later learned that Dr. North had published a book titled *Welcome, Silence: My Triumph Over Schizophrenia*. I was surprised to discover that my close colleague and mentor was living—no, *thriving*—with illness. In her book, with bravery and candor, Dr. North spoke of her journey through the emergence of symptoms of mental illness during adolescence, a full-blown psychotic break in college, and receiving the diagnosis of schizophrenia. Although she took antipsychotic medications, which reduced some symptoms, she had considerable problems with their side effects.

Dr. North completed college and began medical school while living with schizophrenia. Her illness did not abate, and after another episode of acute psychosis in medical school she was again hospitalized. Hearing voices telling her to kill herself, and thinking others could read her mind, she became mute. She described in her book how, after discussion with her family and doctor, she started a now-defunct experimental treatment that involved filtering her blood (similar to dialysis). After 2 weeks, Dr. North had stopped hearing voices, and she continued the treatment for 20 weeks. Since then, she has been free of psychotic symptoms.

What happened to help her cannot be known. It may have been the blood treatment, but it could have been a delayed effect from the conventional treatments she received.

Shaken by her illness but not cowed by it, Dr. North decided to return to medical school, but at a different school in a different state. When it came time to pick a specialty, her research in epidemiology and her own experience with mental illness led her to a career in psychiatry. Dr. North believes that her illness actually gives her an advantage when treating psychiatric patients, as she also has experienced their specific form of human suffering.

Dr. North now says: "It's important that when patients get better they have the opportunity to pursue their dreams." Her story is a wonderful example of recovery and how the pursuit of personal goals can give people purpose throughout the recovery process.

Defining Recovery

The vision statement of the President's New Freedom Commission on Mental Health (2003) reads:

> We envision a future when everyone with a mental illness will recover, a future when mental illnesses can be prevented or cured, a future when mental illnesses are detected early, and a future when everyone with a mental illness at any stage of life has access to effective treatment and supports—essentials for living, working, learning, and participating fully in the community.

Fundamental to this vision is the belief that people with mental disorders can *achieve a life among family and friends,* as full and active members of their communities.

When the report's vision statement was published, the federal agency responsible for mental health services, the Substance Abuse and Mental Health Services Administration (SAMHSA), released a consensus statement, developed by consumers, families, clinicians, advocates, public officials, and service-delivery organizations, that identified the essential components of recovery. Their updated "working definition" (2012) of recovery is as follows:

> **Recovery emerges from hope:** The belief that recovery is real provides the essential and motivating message of a better future—that people

can and do overcome the internal and external challenges, barriers, and obstacles that confront them.

Recovery is person-driven: Self-determination and self-direction are the foundations for recovery as individuals define their own life goals and design their unique path(s).

Recovery occurs via many pathways: Individuals are unique with distinct needs, strengths, preferences, goals, culture, and backgrounds including trauma experiences that affect and determine their pathway(s) to recovery. Abstinence is the safest approach for those with substance use disorders.

Recovery is holistic: Recovery encompasses an individual's whole life, including mind, body, spirit, and community. The array of services and supports available should be integrated and coordinated.

Recovery is supported by peers and allies: Mutual support and mutual aid groups, including the sharing of experiential knowledge and skills, as well as social learning, play an invaluable role in recovery.

Recovery is supported through relationship and social networks: An important factor in the recovery process is the presence and involvement of people who believe in the person's ability to recover; who offer hope, support, and encouragement; and who also suggest strategies and resources for change.

Recovery is culturally-based and influenced: Culture and cultural background in all of its diverse representations—including values, traditions, and beliefs—are keys in determining a person's journey and unique pathway to recovery.

Recovery is supported by addressing trauma: Services and supports should be trauma-informed to foster safety (physical and emotional) and trust, as well as promote choice, empowerment, and collaboration.

Recovery involves individual, family, and community strengths and responsibility: Individuals, families, and communities have strengths and resources that serve as a foundation for recovery.

Recovery is based on respect: Community, systems, and societal acceptance and appreciation for people affected by mental health and substance use problems—including protecting their rights and eliminating discrimination—are crucial in achieving recovery.

Many articles, government policy papers, and books have since been written to elaborate on these components of recovery. The SAMHSA website (see Appendix B) has many of the latest materials, but the core principles and values are unchanged from what was first issued and is noted here.

Why Does Recovery Matter?

The goals of recovery are twofold: (1) for your loved one to return to a healthy and functional life, and (2) to reduce the risk of relapse. Mental illness relapses not only are deeply disturbing and disruptive but also can be dangerous (for the patient, and for those around him or her). Preventing relapses also helps to reduce the risk of becoming disabled from a serious and persistent mental illness.

People can respond to trauma and loss, including illness, in a variety of ways: They can succumb to the impact, or they can recover—even thrive. We all are at risk for an event that suddenly (or slowly and progressively) upends our lives. If you are reading this book, your family has not been spared. But there are actions that individuals and families can take to optimize health and minimize illness.

Resilience and Risk

Resilience refers to the qualities that enable a person (or community) to rebound from adversity, trauma, tragedy, threats, or other stresses. Resilience is the ability to restore a life—to build on our capacities to master our environment with new or greater competencies, and with hope.

But how does a person become resilient, and how can we foster resilience among our families, friends, and communities? Research tells us that resilience often derives from a positive childhood. Temperamentally, people with positive individual traits (for instance, optimism and good problem-solving skills) are more likely to be resilient. Beyond the good fortune of a healthy childhood or temperament, faith also can help build or grow resilience. Close-knit communities are often resilient because of the supports they provide for their members.

With resilience comes its nemesis: *risk*. Risk factors are what increase a person's likelihood of becoming (or remaining) ill. Studies show that untreated depression is associated with a fourfold increase in death after a heart attack. Poverty is associated with a greater risk of mental illness, and growing up in foster care carries with it a far greater risk of becoming homeless. Risk may seem predetermined, but it can be reduced. Clinicians, families, and friends can help to build resilience and reduce risk in those affected by a mental illness.

Defining and Managing Wellness Is Crucial to Recovery

Recovery from a serious mental illness calls for "sweat and tears" from everyone involved—patients, families, friends, clinicians, and policymakers. Nothing less will do to achieve real progress in the mental health field. Crucial to recovery is the concept of *wellness*.

What is wellness? Traditionally, medical texts have defined *wellness* as the absence of disease. But as the human lifespan has increased, the concept of a good life has changed along with it. Wellness no longer means merely being free of disease; it also means living *well*—that is, relatively free of pain and suffering. Wellness also means having a life worth living. Medical definitions of *wellness* have expanded to encompass both the quality and the functioning of a person's life.

The World Health Organization (WHO) now defines health as: "a state of complete physical, *mental*, and social wellbeing and not merely the absence of disease or infirmity" (italics are mine). It is noteworthy that *mental* wellbeing has found its way into the global definition of health—as it should, given the great prevalence of mental disorders and their impact on human suffering and social burden.

To achieve wellness, patients must work on recovery. There are many guides and templates (both for patients and families) that can help make wellness a realistic goal.

WELLNESS SELF-MANAGEMENT

One of my colleagues, Dr. Tony Salerno, is an expert on wellness. He has taught many patients, families, and clinicians about wellness management in ways that educate and excite.

Dr. Salerno's approach to wellness self-management (WSM) provides individuals with the knowledge and skills to manage everyday events as well as the challenges that come with their illness. Daily functioning skills are essential in overcoming the limitations posed by a disease.

Wellness self-management involves three primary activities:

Education. Education focuses on the symptoms of a person's mental disorder, the medications that treat it (as well as their side effects), principles of recovery, how to manage stress, and how to recognize the early warning signs of relapse.

Skills Training. This involves improving skills in relating to other people, taking care of oneself, coping with illness, and dealing with everyday stress, anxiety, and disappointment.

Cognitive-Behavioral Therapy. I have already discussed how this treatment is used for depression, anxiety disorders, and symptoms of psychosis. The WSM program incorporates CBT according to a person's particular needs.

WELLNESS SELF-MANAGEMENT PROGRAMS

Many clinics and rehabilitation (recovery) programs include some form of wellness management; there are programs online for those who prefer this medium or cannot easily access programs in their community. Wellness programs generally are a mixture of group therapy, individual therapy, and skill-building sessions. If your loved one is in a wellness program, ask him or her how you can assist with the program's work.

These programs can have a tremendous impact on a person's life. Listen to what one patient with a serious mental illness wrote when asked for program feedback:

> My name is Barbara. I am in the Community Wellness Program. I am 43 years old . . . I have been told that my diagnoses are Major Depression (without psychosis), Anxiety Disorder, and Personality Disorder.
>
> The Wellness Program I have attended has been a tremendous part of my life. Before I started the program, I basically did nothing but sit with my headphones on at a community mental health "Social Club." I now attend WSM several days a week. The WSM program not only helps me to take responsibility for my health,

it has supported me in building a better and more active life. After I joined, I joined the Advisory Board at the Social Club (we plan trips and activities for ourselves and other club members) and am now very active there. I now do more activities and have become a more outspoken person.

The Wellness Program started me on a road where I have more courage to face some of the fears that have bothered me, to be an active partner in my mental health treatment, to care for my nutrition and health, to stop smoking and to gain the day-to-day skills I need to rebuild my life. With the WSM program, I have also successfully obtained a part-time job, which I thought would never happen. We have very good instructors who have all been a huge part of helping me "get well."

People with a serious mental illness need to learn how to cope with their illness and optimize their functioning and health. Good wellness self-management programs work in partnership with the patient (often called a consumer) *and* the family; at their best, they also coordinate work with the treating psychiatrist and others involved in a person's treatment, including a therapist or case manager.

A key activity in self-management is the *relapse prevention plan*, which assigns roles and responsibilities to people in a person's life to help prevent the recurrence of illness. I'll talk more about the relapse prevention plan later in the chapter.

WSM offers a workbook for patients to use during group sessions. The workbook helps patients understand what is going on in their lives and with their illness, and what they can do to improve their functioning and health. The workbook takes participants through a series of lessons. Group leaders use the workbook to facilitate discussion on topics as diverse as setting goals, developing strategies to overcome barriers, identifying personal strengths, using social supports and community resources, meeting new people, coping with stigma, choosing medications, and working with a doctor.

Following are some excerpts from the workbook. For more, go to: vet2vetusa.org/LinkClick.aspx?fileticket=aY9UPl%2BL6uY%3D&t abid=67.

From the lesson "Understanding Positive and Negative Thinking":

The way we **think** affects the way we **feel** and **act** (you can recognize its basis in CBT). Our thoughts come from our life experiences and how we make sense of these experiences. There is usually more than one way to understand the things we experience. Some ways of thinking may move us forward in life. We refer to these as **positive thoughts**.

Negative thoughts, however, may get in the way. These negative thoughts make us feel bad, bring us down, and stop us from taking steps to improve our lives. The big problem with negative thoughts is that we often accept them as true even when they're not.

The workbook continues:

This lesson gives us an **opportunity to figure out**:
- What kinds of negative thoughts might be getting in the way of moving forward.
- How to replace negative thoughts with thoughts that are positive and real and that move us forward in life.

The workbook then asks the person to develop an "action step."
Here's an excerpt:

Action Step: Choose a negative thought that you most want to change.

Negative thought that I want to change is: _____

_____

What feelings go along with this thought? _____

_____

Take some time to examine this thought very closely with a friend, family member, counselor, or your WSM group.

Put your thought to the 3 Question Test:

Question 1: Is this thought really true?

Question 2: Is this thought moving me forward or holding me back?

Question 3: What other things could I say to myself (positive thoughts) that would be closer to the truth and helpful?

The workbook also includes a worksheet on "symptoms of mental illness" that helps patients understand symptoms and identify their everyday consequences. This becomes a foundation for learning how to cope with and master these problems:

Recognizing Your Symptoms

What symptoms have bothered you the most? Identifying these symptoms may be the first step in gaining control over them. The next few pages are designed to help you recognize symptoms you're having now or those you may have had in the past. Not all of these symptoms will apply to you, or you may have other symptoms not listed here.

Check the box if you've ever had the symptom described.

Symptoms that Mostly Affect a Person's Feelings and Mood

Symptoms of Mania (extremely high moods)

❏ Feelings of extreme happiness or excitement

❏ Feeling irritable

❏ Feeling unrealistically self-confident

❏ Sleeping less

❏ Talking a lot

❏ Having racing thoughts

❏ Being easily distracted

❏ Being extremely active

❏ Having bad judgment

❏ Other:_____

Symptoms of Depression (extremely low moods)

❑ Sad mood

❑ Eating too little or too much

❑ Sleeping too little or too much

❑ Feeling tired and low energy

❑ Feeling helpless, hopeless, worthless

❑ Feeling guilty for things that aren't your fault

❑ Suicidal thoughts or actions

❑ Trouble concentrating and making decisions

❑ Other:_____

Symptoms of Anxiety

❑ Feeling anxious much of the time

❑ Having fears about being harmed or killed

❑ Believing someone is watching me

❑ Being frightened that I'm losing my mind

❑ Other:_____

Symptoms That Mostly Affect a Person's Thinking
Having Trouble Concentrating

❑ It's hard to pay attention for long periods of time.

❑ At times, I have too many thoughts.

❑ My thoughts are sometimes jumbled or confused.

❑ At times, I have trouble reading books or following movie plots.

❑ It's sometimes hard to focus on what people are saying to me.

❑ At times, it's hard getting my thoughts together.

❑ I can't hear well over background noises.

❑ Sometimes I lose my train of thought.

❑ Other:_____

Recording Your Symptoms

Look at the boxes you've marked. Which symptoms have bothered you the most over the past month? List them.

1._____

2._____

3._____

How do your symptoms affect the quality of your life?

_____

_____

_____

_____

Which symptoms have gotten better within the past month?

1._____

2._____

3._____

Another section of the workbook is the "daily hassles checklist," which helps people understand the link between a stressor and their symptoms, thus serving as a basis for symptom management and relapse prevention:

Daily Hassles Checklist

Please check each event (HASSLE) you have experienced in the past week.

❏ Taking medication

❏ Taking part in a treatment program

❏ Not enough money to take care of necessities

❏ Not enough money to spend on leisure

❏ Crowded living situation

❏ Crowded public transportation

❏ Mental health stigma

❏ Long drives or traffic back-ups

❏ Feeling rushed at home

❏ Feeling rushed at work

❏ Arguments at home

❏ Arguments at work

❏ Doing business with unpleasant people (sales clerks, waiters/waitresses, transit clerks, toll booth workers)

❏ Noisy situation at home

❏ Mental health housing

❏ Noisy situation at work

❏ Not enough privacy at home

❏ Minor medical problems

❏ Lack of order or cleanliness at home

❏ Lack of order or cleanliness at work

❏ Unpleasant chores at home

❏ Mental health treatment

❏ Unpleasant chores at work

❏ Living in a dangerous neighborhood

❏ Dealing with your treatment team

❏ Dealing with children

❏ Other:_____

Now that you have checked off a number of daily hassles, have any of these experiences **triggered** a relapse or an increase in symptoms?
If yes, please write them down:

_____

_____

We can see here how a person with a serious mental illness can learn to link a stress with symptoms, which encourages attention to relapse prevention.

FAMILIES AND WELLNESS SELF-MANAGEMENT

Families and friends want nothing more than to see a loved one regain confidence and better cope with and manage illness. When that happens, the patient and those close to him or her all benefit. But families have to understand that recovery from a serious mental illness is a slow process, and even small steps are reasons to celebrate and to stress hopefulness. There are no shortcuts to recovery, and patience may be one of the greatest gifts you provide your loved one. Over time, remarkable steps can be achieved.

That said, no family can—or should—tolerate behaviors that endanger their loved one or themselves, whether that behavior is self-destructive or threatens the welfare of other family members or the community.

In addition, other behaviors that involve taking responsibility for family life, like household chores or keeping a schedule that respects others, need to be negotiated thoughtfully and over time, depending where the family member is in the course of recovery.

Families also may learn that some of the ways that *they* behave may not contribute to recovery. This can happen when families are overprotective or impede self-reliance out of worry that their loved one may fail or become discouraged. But everyone who tries something new encounters both some success and some failure. People with mental illness are no different. What's important during recovery is to turn "failures" into learning opportunities (as we all might aspire to do).

WELLNESS RECOVERY ACTION PLAN (WRAP)

Mary Ellen Copeland is another leader in wellness and recovery; she is also a person in recovery herself. Copeland is perhaps best known for developing a specific program called the *Wellness Recovery Action Plan*, or WRAP. The following is from her website (www.mentalhealthrecovery.com):

> WRAP is a self-management and recovery system developed by a group of people who had mental health difficulties and who were struggling to incorporate wellness tools and strategies into their lives. WRAP is designed to:
> • Decrease and prevent intrusive or troubling feelings and behaviors
> • Increase personal empowerment

- Improve quality of life
- Assist people in achieving their own life goals and dreams

WRAP teaches people with mental illness alternatives to poor coping strategies. Instead of taking more medication or smoking cigarettes to relax, patients can learn relaxation techniques. Instead of avoiding other people because of anxiety, individuals can learn better ways to manage their feelings and spend time with other (supportive) people. The WRAP toolkit even has a scheduling tool to help people organize their days and avert problems that can lead to relapse. A WRAP plan may prove very valuable for your family member in the recovery process. As the website states:

> People who experience mental health difficulties no longer feel that they are sentenced to a life of chronic disability that interferes with their ability to work toward and reach their goals. Instead, by using self-help skills and strategies that complement other treatment scenarios, they are achieving levels of wellness, stability, and recovery they always hoped were possible.

In addition to relaxation techniques and cognitive (CBT) skill development, WRAP tools include journals, music, peer counseling, diet modification, and facilitating adequate and normal sleep patterns. For families and friends, WRAP strategies explicitly speak to how people with mental illness need to turn to people who believe in them and can contribute as part of their support system.

WRAP also helps people see the signs when they are not doing well. A WRAP plan actually lists things a person can do *every day* to stay well. It also identifies triggers—events that stimulate anxiety and symptoms. Finally, specific signs that herald real trouble—like resuming the use of alcohol or drugs, staying up at night, or becoming paranoid or highly irritable—are identified so that people can learn to listen and respond to these early warning signs of relapse.

Recovery and Wellness Require Patient-Focused Care

My colleague John Allen, who directs the consumer affairs office at the

New York State Office of Mental Health, has been a national leader in recovery and patient-oriented mental health. John points out that people with mental illness want what we all want: a home, a job, and a date. Sometimes he adds a car in order to get to the date or the job.

John's point is that few people come for mental health treatment to rid themselves of hallucinations, or because they have delusional ideas, or because they think they need more sleep. Those are the kinds of symptoms that clinicians have traditionally focused upon. But they are not what *patients* are principally interested in. Thus, focusing on symptoms may not always be the best basis for a treatment alliance between doctor and patient.

When I have said to a patient, "Try this medication—it may help you think better so you can spend time with friends or focus on getting a job," it seems to work better than when I've said, "Try this medication—it will make the voices go away." Here's another example: When a person is facing eviction from her apartment because her collections are creating a fire hazard, she's going to be a lot more receptive to working with someone who shares her goal of not getting evicted than she will be to working with someone who talks only about changing her hoarding behaviors. A treatment plan that focuses on achieving shared goals is critical to the therapeutic alliance, and alliance is critical to a person staying in treatment.

When I'm asked by a patient, "What gets in my way of having a date, or friends and a social life?" I try to remember not to say, "A mental illness." Instead, I try to suggest that when a person doesn't take good care of him- or herself, or acts kind of strange and anxious around someone he or she likes, those are behaviors that ruin the person's social chances. If people with a mental illness can understand what they need to do to get what they want—such as change hoarding behaviors to keep their apartment, or take medication that helps them maintain healthy relationships with other people—they will be more open to engaging in wellness self-management.

As a family member, you can use the same approach. Ask what your loved one or friend wants, and then build a plan together about how to get that date, job, or home. That is how you can help with recovery.

No two people are the same. And no two recoveries will look the same, either. Recovery means meeting each person on his or her own terms, capitalizing on his or her specific attributes and strengths, and striving to meet his or her unique aspirations.

There is good reason for hope. Across the globe, people with mental illness are living lives in which they enrich and are enriched by other people—family members, friends, people in the community, as well as society at large. Your loved one can, too. And you can help.

Three "Walk-Throughs": An Urban Emergency Room, a Peer-Run Recovery Program, and Supportive Housing

To give you a better sense of the different kinds of treatment facilities you may encounter, I offer here three different "walk-throughs." We'll start with an urban emergency room.

An Urban Emergency Room

I'll talk in this section about the experience of arriving at an ER, proceeding to register, "triage," the clinical evaluation, and the closing part of the visit, namely the "disposition" (arrangements for where the patient will go after the ER visit). The site described here is a large, urban emergency room, though community hospitals are not so different.

As you'll see, I describe dedicated staff managing crisis situations with little time, space, or support. These emergency personnel also often have little information to go on; in fact, you may be the best source of information they have. You will see that other patients are there, psychiatric and medical, in varying degrees of clinical distress but all impatient for help or eager to leave. You will see how clerks and administrative staff have to do their job of collecting information, especially on how to get paid or get consent, even if no one else cares about this one bit (and can be offended by what seems like indifference to human sensitivities).

If you feel unnerved reading this, it's because that is a normal feeling to have in this abnormal place.

Our visit is to Bellevue Hospital—one of New York City's 11 munic-ipal (city) hospitals. Located on the east side of Midtown Manhattan, it has a lengthy and legendary reputation that has varied from hellish in the past to often remarkable today. Bellevue is now a modern general hospital with one of the busiest emergency rooms in the city, perhaps even in the nation. It also has one of the largest and most respected psychiatric departments anywhere, with over 300 psychiatric and addiction inpa-tient beds. Because of Bellevue's huge capacity to deliver specialty mental health services and its location in a population-dense area of New York City, it is busy day and night receiving people in urgent need of mental health services. Bellevue's emergency room includes a highly special-ized psychiatric emergency service (called a comprehensive psychiatric emergency program, or CPEP) with observation and overnight beds that can keep patients for up to 3 days. But as good as this ER is, it can still be difficult to navigate.

ENTERING THE HOSPITAL

As you walk through the front door of Bellevue, you'll enter an atrium the size of a football field, with enough space above you to make you think you are still outdoors. Facing you as you walk down two diverging wide ramps is the façade of the original hospital, saved by creative architects as a homage to the hospital's many years of contri-bution to New York City. To your left is the emergency room, which you gain access to after you show proper identification to a city secu-rity officer who controls entry. You will walk straight ahead down a wide corridor to a large sign above a double door that reads "Adult Emergency Department."

You then enter a large room with about 50 uncomfortable waiting-room chairs fastened to one another in rows of 8 to 10. Three registra-tion windows are on your left. You approach a registration window, get the clerk's attention, and say you "want to see a psychiatrist." You will be told to take a seat.

Then you sit and wait, like taking a number at the motor vehicle bureau, until you are called to provide more detailed information to the registration clerk, like why you are there and paperwork details that include name, social security number, insurance information, emergency contacts, language spoken, religion, and other things about who you are and how to reach you. Because the waiting room is usually full, day and night, there is no "good" time to go, although there are worse times (like Friday and Saturday nights). The people in the waiting room will have various problems—medical, surgical, and mental health—because this is the general adult ER entrance, which is where you start. What you *won't* see are people in severe distress who have arrived by ambulance or police cruiser; they bypass this room and enter through the ambulance bay.

TRIAGE

At the far end of the waiting room is a small, enclosed room where the triage nurse sits. He or she is both briefly meeting with people as well as keeping an eye on the waiting room, lest someone become too unstable to wait. There also is a security desk by the triage nurse to help if needed as well as to control access to the narrow corridor that leads from the inner waiting room to the ER itself. The average wait at Bellevue today, due to their ongoing efforts to be more responsive to emergency situations, is an hour to see the triage nurse (1 hour is an average, so it can be less or more). If you are clearly in crisis the nurse will see you sooner and move you along to the ER. Many ERs have wait times of several hours, depending on the volume of patients, the gravity of their conditions, and the staff available to cover the shift.

The triage nurse first makes one fundamental decision regarding "psych cases," as they are often called: Does this person need to go to the medical department of the ER *before* psychiatric assessment? This is because sometimes a person with a psychiatric illness arrives with a physical problem (like chest pain or fever), or is intoxicated, or confused. This very brief level of triage can actually provide a great deal of valuable information to a trained, experienced clinician.

If there is no acute medical need, the nurse will gather some limited information and call for a psychiatric "tech," a mental health worker, to bring you and your loved one down the corridor through several sets of doors, passing the ambulance bay, the trauma ward, the intensive care unit, radiology, and other parts of the complex world of an ER, to where a sign reads "CPEP." The tech will be talking along the way, explaining what to expect. You then enter an area that is "open" (not locked), where you will be seen by a nurse and searched for sharp objects or a weapon (for safety reasons). Some of your loved one's possessions may be held (by you or in a locked box) while he or she is being evaluated.

Many people who come reluctantly to the ER have a very hard time at this point. The delays and the demands for information add to their anxiety and they want to leave. Many a large ER in an urban area will have police who brought people in, which can add to your loved one's worries or paranoia. You will have to work extra hard to reassure your family member that entering further into the ER does not mean the person will have to stay; at Bellevue, only about 40% of those who enter the CPEP remain overnight (or are transferred to another hospital for admission). The rest leave the ER with plans to receive follow-up care.

Once through the CPEP door, you enter another waiting room where the tech introduces you to another tech who is a staff member of the CPEP. This is still a "non-detainable area," which means that a person is still there voluntarily and can leave if he or she wants. The CPEP waiting area is a bit like the ER waiting area, except that it's far smaller and everyone there has a mental health problem. You can remain with your loved one in this area. In the Bellevue CPEP there is a security desk where you log in; a registration window where you will do much of what you did at the ER registration and where you will be informed of your rights; a bank of chairs against a wall; a bathroom at the end of the room; and a Plexiglas-enclosed triage room where another nurse will conduct a psychiatric assessment.

EVALUATION

Once you are registered in the Bellevue CPEP you will be seen quickly by a "psychiatric attending" (a staff psychiatrist) or a psychiatric resident, typically within 30 minutes! (At most hospitals, however, the total wait time for an evaluation is much longer, often several hours.) If your loved one is able to tolerate being in the waiting area, you will be able to stay with him or her. If, however, your loved one's needs are emergent, a tech will bring him or her into the actual CPEP, a complex of rooms with a nursing station, and you will not be able to enter and stay, though you can "visit" periodically depending on a lot of factors, including how busy the area is. (This CPEP can be very active and crowded, with 5 to 15 people in acute distress, some in observation rooms, some seated on banks of chairs separated for men and women, and some being interviewed or examined medically.)

As a family member, you will want to look for opportunities to provide information whenever you can, because patients often won't offer much on their own out of fear of being "locked up" or because they've had bad experiences with emergency services in the past. A good doctor or nurse will ask the patient whether it's okay to speak with you or other family members, hoping for permission. He or she will try to establish trust with the patient, and say something to the effect that it is his or her "responsibility as a clinician to have essential information, especially about a person's health, medications, and safety." (Actually, the law permits doctors and nurses, in an emergency situation, to speak with anyone even if permission is not granted—though it's always preferable for reasons of trust to obtain permission.)

If, for whatever reason, you are not asked for information, don't settle for that—especially if you have information that is important and that your loved one or friend will not provide. Get the doctor's or nurse's attention and say you have information that will make a difference in the person's evaluation and treatment. If they say the patient hasn't given them permission to speak with you, then say: "You may not be able to tell me anything, but you can listen to what I have to say. There is *no* law against listening. Besides, it could help."

The CPEP staff work as a team. There is a nurse, tech, clerk, security (as needed), and the team leader is the doctor; but this is less a hierarchy than a group of professionals who work together and rely on each other to obtain information and understand the needs of your loved one, especially if there are questions about safety. You want to see all of them as there to help your loved one and you; telling something to one of them is like telling it to all of them. Their goal as a team is to provide a complete psychiatric assessment and come to a determination about what the problem is and how best to address it. Making a decision about "disposition," or the next step for further care, comes after the assessment. There are three disposition options: discharge from the CPEP to outpatient care; admission to an inpatient unit (at Bellevue or another hospital); or remaining in the CPEP in one of the "observation beds." To stay in one of the observation beds, a patient must have signed a form agreeing to stay, or have been involuntarily committed by the doctor— either way, the patient is not free to leave the CPEP in this situation. The stay there can last up to 72 hours.

RESOLUTION

At the Bellevue CPEP the average time for a disposition to be made is several hours. Longer times occur when there is a wait to go "upstairs" to the inpatient unit; when hospital staff are trying to contact a patient's therapist or psychiatrist; or when an outpatient appointment is being established. During that time, your loved one may receive some treatment—medication may be offered and counseling or crisis intervention provided to help someone problem solve about what happened that escalated into an emergency. But treatment isn't actually the main goal of the ER. This may sound strange because you came to the ER for treatment. But consider this: In an average day, 26 people are cared for at the Bellevue psychiatric ER—that's 9500 people every year, far too many for the hospital to provide anything more than brief psychiatric care. Therefore, psychiatric ERs heavily focus on *evaluation* (what is the diagnosis and why has this person become ill now?) and what is the best *disposition*, because the ER is meant to be a way station to further care. While this is the reality of the situation, it is not necessarily bad—good care must be ongoing, not an ultra-brief emergency encounter.

The "psych ER" is not much different from a visit to the medical side of the ER. You arrive, you wait, you are "triaged," you are evaluated, you get some treatment, and a disposition is made that fits the urgency of your needs. A team of medical professionals cares for you, clerks and other bureaucrats buzz about, and security is ever-present because ERs are incendiary places. Your job as a family member is the same in medical or psychiatric settings, which is primarily to provide support and reassurance to your loved one. But in psychiatry, you seldom have a willing loved one, making the process all the more challenging. Family and friends can be essential to the ER staff as a source of information as well as partners in engaging and retaining someone so that a full and careful assessment can be made; brief, focused treatment with the goal of stabilization can be provided; and follow-up can be assured.

The visit ends with the "disposition," which, as mentioned earlier, is usually a referral to outpatient treatment, though it may involve remaining in the CPEP for up to 3 days or admission to an inpatient unit. While the visit has likely allowed for important clinical work to be done, the overall experience can feel unsettling and unsatisfactory. Remember that you have almost certainly succeeded if your goal was to ensure safety and begin an evaluation and treatment process. But of course, there is much more to do .

A Peer-Run Recovery Program

I'll now describe an uncommon but remarkable program the likes of which you may have the opportunity to visit. It's uncommon because there are few programs run by professional clinicians and administrators who themselves have a mental illness but are well along in their recovery. The program is called HALI, an acronym for Hands Across Long Island, and it's located in Suffolk County, New York. HALI opened in 1988 to provide clinic and rehabilitative services to people with mental illness; it also runs housing in buildings that they have purchased, restored, and now manage.

When I visited, no one was wearing a tie but me. I entered a single-story office building with ample space and plenty of good light. There was a palpable sense of order and I wished that government buildings were as well kept. I was greeted by the executive director, who introduced herself by her first name, and I in turn did the same. As she walked about the corridors of the office area she stopped repeatedly to say something thoughtful and warm to others, who sometimes were consumers (patients), sometimes staff, sometimes both. We stopped to speak with Hal, a man in his fifties, gaunt and weathered and wearing workman's overalls and a baseball cap; he led HALI's building construction and management work and was proud of the many buildings that housed their community of consumers. We continued down a hallway of offices, with photos and program notices on the beige-colored walls, as the director told me the story of how they had hired their psychiatrist. The program's leadership group of staff and consumers had interviewed over a dozen psychiatrist applicants until they found someone who embodied recovery and respect for the clients of HALI. He was known by his first name, but always with the Doctor title before it, because of how much he was respected in the HALI community. I wondered if they would have hired me.

The director told me about the people they served and how some were doing. Not everyone was a success but she believed they all could be, in time, with hard work on the part of the consumer, family when possible, and the people who worked in the program. She emanated realistic hope and trust in a process where people could rebuild their lives—not without illness but *with* illness. I looked at the photos of buildings, before and after their restoration. We spoke with a consumer we passed as we toured the building, a woman in her twenties who had been a member for a few years. She proudly told me that when she began at HALI she believed she would never be able to work again; now she had a full-time office job nearby but she made a point of staying close to the program and the other consumers because she considered them still essential to her functioning. We went into a large, well-lit, and pastel-colored living room, replete with comfortable chairs and small tables, which was used for meetings and meals. A man was playing the piano in an alcove off the room. The director pointed to a strip of wall where the paint was peeling from posters that had come and gone and told me it was next on the list for one of the consumers to touch up. When a man dressed in jeans and a T-shirt stood up from a table and left a paper cup on it, she immediately called over to him and asked him, smiling like a good mother, to pick up after himself. He did, smiling back at her.

I was reminded of some psychiatric rehabilitation programs I'd seen over the years where patients—consumers—learn to rebuild their social and work skills. Mental illness, especially when it strikes in adolescence, detours people from developing the social skills and work habits needed for a full life. Recovery is about getting back on the main road of life and staying there. HALI felt like those programs, but different, too. I was used to programs led by people like me, trained professionals who treated people with mental illness but themselves had been spared its toll (or, if they did have mental illness, didn't speak about it). HALI resounded with people who were saying *I can help you take control of your life, as I am doing myself.*

Not long after my visit, a father of a man in his thirties with a serious mental illness asked me about services that might be different, and maybe more helpful, than the traditional medical-model programs his family had used. I suggested that he and his son visit HALI. The father was a businessman with over a decade of experience with mental health services; his son was stuck and it seemed like his disability was worsening. The father was looking for hope. When he left HALI after his first visit, he felt hope—for the first time in a long time. HALI made it clear that disability need not be a prescription for a life of isolation and inactivity.

If you have a chance to visit a peer run program, do it. What do you have to lose? If a doctor or social worker discourages you, ask him or her to come along.

Supportive Housing

This is how the Supportive Housing Network of New York describes their services:

> Supportive housing—permanent, affordable housing linked to services—provides low-income, disabled, and formerly homeless people the help and support they need to stay housed and live more independent, healthy, and fulfilling lives. Supportive housing is the single most effective, and most cost-efficient, way to reduce homelessness. It strengthens communities and helps integrate people with disabilities and other special needs into the life of their neighborhoods.

Days after I began my job as mental health commissioner in New York City, in 2002, I met with over 400 consumers (patients), families, and advocates in the basement of a large community-based rehabilitation program in midtown Manhattan. I believed, and said to the crowd, that no one gets better from a mental illness or an addiction unless that person is safely and stably housed. No matter how hard professionals may try, they are no match for the destabilizing effects of living on the streets or the turmoil that characterizes most city shelters.

I asked a colleague what the best supportive housing program for me to visit in New York City was. He said I should visit the Times Square—a former hotel on the west side of Midtown Manhattan that houses equal numbers of formerly homeless people, most with a mental illness or addiction or both, *as well as* low-income individuals working as teachers, waiters, artists, and health care workers. It is run by an organization called Common Ground, a not-for-profit agency. (Disclosure: My spouse was the founder of this organization and its president until 2011; she no longer has any affiliation.) I set up an appointment to visit.

On the day of my appointment I made my way to its location near the busy northeast corner of 43rd Street and 8th Avenue, a block that then also housed a Ben and Jerry's ice cream shop and a Starbucks. Little did I know that some of the people working in those shops were formerly homeless people living at the Times Square Hotel, which had been instrumental in bringing these and other businesses to the neighborhood and offering competitive employment opportunities to its tenants. I turned east on 43rd Street and made my way to the building.

I walked up a few stairs leading to the entrance of the building and pivoted through the glass revolving door to enter a magnificent marble-columned, two-story-high lobby that spoke of early 20th-century American urban residential elegance. Beautifully upholstered chairs and couches were placed around the room, a piano stood in a corner, and framed art hung on the walls. I thought I must be in the wrong building. But I had little time to think, as I was immediately at a long desk where two security guards were sitting and kindly asked me about my business. They were there to protect the tenants from the uninvited, including those who might want to prey on the vulnerable by selling them drugs or propagating some form of trouble.

On a nearby wall were photos of the Times Square Hotel, circa 1990, when it was purchased by Common Ground. The place was then a dump, and dangerous too. There were pictures of squalid rooms with exposed, rotten pipes and crumbling walls, of roach-infested kitchens, and a lobby that looked like bombed-out quarters for wounded soldiers in a World War I movie. At the time of the building's acquisition, the residents were a handful of poor, elderly, or ill people overshadowed by a great many drug dealers, prostitutes, and others who were society's cast-offs. No wonder this place had been featured on *60 Minutes*—twice—to portray what had been achieved.

Another distinguishing feature of the entry to this supportive housing site, in addition to the security desk, was the mezzanine, which encircled the lobby from above, and housed a set of offices for the Center for Urban Community Services (CUCS), a not-for-profit community mental health agency that offers case management and other clinical services for building residents. No need to go farther than the lobby to get help, making it easy for case managers to keep in touch with fragile clients who live in the building. A set of small, round tables and chairs abutted the railing of the mezzanine so that tenants could sit and enjoy their common space and watch the world go by.

There are 652 single apartments in the Times Square Hotel. That makes it the largest *congregate* supportive housing building in the United States. Supportive housing buildings range from as few as 20 people to larger buildings with a hundred or more residents. Many house 40 to 80 people, including youth aging out of foster care, adults, seniors, and recently our veterans returning from wars abroad, often with a mixed population of low-income workers and formerly homeless individuals. This model is normalizing in that it combines varied groups of people; it also helps with the economics of the building. Each tenant has a lease on an apartment, so it is his or her home. The apartments at the Times Square Hotel are small, efficiency studios that include a kitchenette and bathroom. Sometimes these are called "SROs," or single-room occupancies.

An alternative to *congregate* supportive housing, where everyone lives together in one building, is *scatter-site housing*, in which a housing provider (a not-for-profit social service agency) rents apartments from landlords in a number of buildings or different sections of the city. The agency either holds the lease or arranges for the lease to be held by the client.

Congregate housing takes far longer, usually several years, to develop because it requires finding and renovating or constructing a building in a neighborhood that frequently resists its presence. ("Not in my backyard" is the objection we usually hear, despite the fact that these buildings almost invariably improve the value of the neighborhood and are no cause of trouble.) Scatter-site housing is usually available within a year of a housing organization receiving a contract from a government agency (city, county, or state) to develop it.

At the Times Square Hotel, I was scheduled to visit with Mabel, a woman nearly 70 years old who'd had an apartment in the building almost from the inception of the Common Ground program. When we knocked on her door, a booming voice said, "Come in, what are you waiting for?" The apartment was stuffed with objects that defined her life: pictures, paintings, figures of saints, ceramics from places she had visited, pillows and comforters everywhere, and a host of medical supplies for her lung and kidney problems. There was a combined medicinal and lavender scent. She told us she had been homeless on and off throughout her life—that this was the longest she had been continuously housed since she was a young woman. Her life was a tale of poverty, mental illness and drug addiction, welfare, shelters, and progressive ill health until she moved into the Times Square Hotel. She attributed her long-sought stability to the "kind people" who worked in the building, her friends in the community the housing created, and the case manager who helped her cope with everyday life. She said she would move out "in a coffin." It was plain as day how fond she was of the staff in the building, and they of her.

The Times Square Hotel is rather unique as a supportive housing building in its size, commanding architecture, and history. Not even the more than a handful of other residences that Common Ground operates in New York City can quite rival this "hotel," its firstborn building. But the principles are the same: safety, stability, services, responsible and quality building management, and a commitment to the recovery of the tenants. These principles can be found in all successful supportive housing programs and settings.

Supportive housing is remarkable in its effectiveness and value. The cost of a year in a supportive housing apartment is a third less than a city shelter; half that of a prison and a fourth of a jail; a tenth of a state hospital bed; and 4% the cost of an acute-care psychiatric bed in a general hospital. New York City and New York State have made successful financial commitments to supportive housing because it works and because it saves money.

Books and Websites

Books

PERSONAL ACCOUNTS

Cockburn, P., & Cockburn, H. (2011). *Henry's demons: Living with schizophrenia, a father and son's story*. New York: Scribner.

Earley, P. (2006). *Crazy: A father's search through America's mental health madness*. New York: Berkley.

Hinshaw, S. P. (2002). *The years of silence are past: My father's life with bipolar disorder*. Cambridge, UK: Cambridge University Press.

Jamison, K. R. (1995). *An unquiet mind*. New York: Vintage.

Kandel, E. (2006). *In search of memory: The emergence of a new science of mind*. New York; London: W. W. Norton.

Kaysen, S. (1993). *Girl, interrupted*. New York: Knopf Doubleday.

Kennedy, K. (2010). *They fought for each other: The triumph and tragedy of the hardest hit unit in Iraq*. New York: St. Martin's.

Manguso, S. (2012). *The guardians: An elegy*. New York: Farrar, Straus and Giroux.

Neugeboren, J. (2003). *Imagining Robert: My brother's madness and survival, a memoir*. New Jersey: Rutgers University Press.

North, C. (1987). *Welcome, silence: My triumph over schizophrenia*. New York: Simon and Schuster.

Raeburn, P. (2004). *Acquainted with the night: A parent's quest to understand depression and bipolar disorder in his children*. New York: Broadway Books.

Saks, E. R. (2007). *The center cannot hold: My journey through madness.* New York: Hyperion.

Smith, G. H. (2006). *Remembering Garrett: One family's battle with a child's depression.* New York: Carroll & Graf.

Solomon, A. (2001). *The noonday demon: An atlas of depression.* New York: Scribner.

Spiro, C., & Wagner, P. S. (2005). *Divided minds: Twin sisters and their journey through schizophrenia.* New York: St. Martin's.

Styron, W. (1990). *Darkness visible: A memoir of madness.* New York: Vintage.

Woodruff, L., & Woodruff B. (2007). *In an instant: A family's journey of love and healing.* New York: Random House.

PROFESSIONAL AND SELF-HELP BOOKS

Amador, X. (2007). *I am not sick. I don't need help! How to help someone with mental illness accept treatment.* New York: Vida Press.

Brown, R., Gerbarg, P., & Muskin, P. (2009). *How to use herbs, nutrients, and yoga in mental health.* New York: W. W. Norton.

Brown, R., & Gerbarg, P. (2012). *The healing power of breath: Simple techniques to reduce stress and anxiety, enhance concentration and balance your emotions.* Boston: Shambhala.

Carter, R., & Golant, S. (1998). *Helping someone with mental illness.* New York: Three Rivers Press.

Compton, M., & Broussard, B. (2009). *The first episode of psychosis: A guide for patients and their families.* New York: Oxford University Press.

Erikson, E. (1987). *A way of looking at things.* New York: W. W. Norton.

Gawande, A. (2009). *The checklist manifesto: How to get things right.* New York: Henry Holt.

Goffman, E. (1961). *Asylums: Essays on the social situation of mental patients and other inmates.* New York: Anchor Books.

Goodwin, F. K., & Jamison, K. R. (2007). *Manic-depressive illness: Bipolar disorders and recurrent depression* (2nd ed.). New York: Oxford University Press.

Groopman, J. (2008). *How doctors think.* Boston; New York: Houghton Mifflin.

Havens, L. (1989). *A safe place: Laying the groundwork of psychotherapy.* Cambridge, MA: Harvard University Press.

Koplewicz, H. (2002). *More than moody: Recognizing and treating adolescent depression*. New York: G. P. Putnam & Sons.

Lefley, H. (2009). *Family psychoeducation for serious mental illness*. New York: Oxford University Press.

Malone, P. (2009). *The life you save: Nine steps to finding the best medical care and avoiding the worst*. Boston, MA: Da Capo Long Life, Perseus Books.

Mason, M. P. (2008). *Head cases: Stories of brain injury and its aftermath*. New York: Farrar, Straus and Giroux.

Neugeboren, J. (1999). *Transforming madness: New lives for people living with mental illness*. Berkeley: University of California Press.

Nuland, S. (1997). *How we live*. New York: Vintage.

Porter, R. (1989). *A social history of madness: The world through the eyes of the insane*. New York: E. P. Dutton.

Sacks, O. (2012). *Hallucinations*. New York: Simon and Schuster.

Websites

ADVOCACY, SUPPORT, AND REFERRAL

NAMI – The National Alliance on Mental Illness
www.nami.org

MHA – Mental Health America
www.nmha.org

Network of Care
www.networkofcare.org/home.cfm

National Suicide Prevention Lifeline
1-800-273-TALK (8255)
www.suicidepreventionlifeline.org

National Suicide Prevention Resource Center
www.edc.org/projects/national_suicide_prevention_resource_center

Suicide Prevention Resource Center
www.sprc.org

LifeNet (NYC)
www.newyorkcity.ny.networkofcare.org/mh

Bring Change 2 Mind
www.bringchange2mind.org

Brain and Behavior Research Foundation
www.bbrfoundation.org

Child Mind Institute
www.childmind.org

Wellness Recovery Action Plan (WRAP)
www.mentalhealthrecovery.com

Wellness Self-Management
www.vet2vetusa.org/LinkClick.aspx?fileticket=aY9UPl%2BL6uY%3D&
tabid=67

Iraq and Afghanistan Veterans of America (IAVA)
www.iava.org

Depression and Bipolar Support Alliance
www.dbsalliance.org/site/PageServer?pagename=home

Anxiety and Depression Association of America
www.adaa.org

National Eating Disorders Association
www.nationaleatingdisorders.org

National Association of Anorexia and Associated Disorders (ANAD)
www.anad.org

International Obsessive Compulsive Foundation
www.ocfoundation.org

The National Child Traumatic Stress Network
www.nctsn.org

American Psychiatric Association (APA)
www.psych.org

> APA Practice Guidelines
> www.psych.org/practice/clinical-practice-guidelines
>
> APA DSM-5
> www.dsm5.org

New York Association of Psychiatric Rehabilitation Services
www.nyaprs.org

National Resource Center on Psychiatric Advance Directives
www.nrc-pad.org

Cochrane Reviews
http://www.cochrane.org/cochrane-reviews

GOVERNMENT

NIMH – The National Institute of Mental Health
www.nimh.nih.gov/index.shtml

> NIMH Clinical Trials
> www.clinicaltrials.gov
> NIMH Post-Traumatic Stress Disorder
> www.nimh.nih.gov/health/topics/post-traumatic-stress-disorder-
> ptsd/index.shtml

SAMHSA – The Substance Abuse and Mental Health
Services Administration
www.samhsa.gov

> SAMHSA Mental Health Services Locator
> www.store.samhsa.gov/mhlocator
>
> SAMHSA Military Families Strategic Initiative
> www.samhsa.gov/militaryfamilies
>
> SAMHSA National Center for Trauma-Informed Care
> www.samhsa.gov/nctic

President's New Freedom Commission on Mental Health (2003)
www.cartercenter.org/documents/1701.pdf

National Institute on Drug Abuse
www.drugabuse.gov

National Institute on Alcohol Abuse and Alcoholism
www.niaaa.nih.gov

NYS OMH – The New York State Office of Mental Health
www.omh.ny.gov

Patient Outcomes Research Team (PORT)
www.ahrq.gov/clinic/schzrec.htm

National Institute for Health and Clinical Excellence
(NICE) United Kingdom
www.nice.org.uk

Mental Health Measurement Scales

These scales are not diagnostic tools for readers or their loved ones. They are offered as informational material to assist you in understanding what clinicians and programs may use when working with your loved one.

In this appendix you will find commonly used measurement scales for screening and monitoring mental disorders. For each, you will find information regarding:

- Its purpose
- How it is administered
- A short summary about the scale

You can search for the actual scale and further information on each on the Internet.

Depression

PATIENT HEALTH QUESTIONNAIRES 2 AND 9 (PHQ-2 AND PHQ-9)

Purpose. This tool was designed to screen (detect), diagnose, monitor, and measure the severity of depression.

Administration. It can be either self-reported or clinician-administered, and can be used in both adult and geriatric populations. A version also exists for adolescents. The questionnaire takes about 5 minutes to complete.

Summary. The PHQ-9 is a nine-item instrument that assesses the presence and severity of depressive symptoms (on a scale of 0 to 3) over the prior 2 weeks. It has been used in many medical settings including primary care, internal medicine, with stroke patients, and in obstetrical wards. It provides information to help make the diagnosis of depression as well as information about severity (which can help with the choice of treatment), and it is sensitive to change (so a person or doctor can tell if there is improvement or not).

BECK DEPRESSION INVENTORY (BDI-II)

Purpose. This tool was designed to assess the existence and severity of depressive symptoms.

Administration. This measure can be either self-reported or clinician-administered, and can be used for both teenagers and adults. It takes about 5 to 10 minutes to complete.

Summary. The BDI-II is a 21-item multiple choice self-report that assesses symptoms over the prior 2 weeks. Each item is a list of four statements arranged in increasing severity about a particular symptom of depression. Aaron Beck, one of the founders of cognitive therapy, contributed to the creation of this instrument.

HAMILTON RATING SCALE FOR DEPRESSION (HAM–D)

Purpose. This tool assesses the severity of and change in depressive symptoms.

Administration. This is a clinician-administered scale to be used with adults.

Summary. The Ham-D is the most widely used clinician-administered (and rated) depression assessment scale. It consists of a clinician-led interview that lasts about 20 to 30 minutes. The original version consists of 17 items pertaining to the prior week. It can be used to follow the response or lack of response to treatment.

MONTGOMERY-ASBERG DEPRESSION RATING SCALE (MADRS)

Purpose. This instrument was designed to measure the degree of severity of depressive symptoms, and as a sensitive measure of change in symptom severity during the treatment of depression.

Administration. This is a clinician-administered scale for adults. It takes about 15 minutes to complete.

Summary. The MADRS is a checklist of 10 items. It has been widely used in drug-treatment trials because it is particularly good at picking up treatment effects.

MAJOR DEPRESSION INVENTORY (MDI)

Purpose. This inventory was created by the World Health Organization to assess the presence and severity of depressive symptoms.

Administration. This is a self-report scale for adults. It takes about 5 to 10 minutes to complete.

Summary. The MDI is a well-researched inventory that can be used in identifying major depression. It consists of 10 questions on different symptoms and time suffering from symptoms over the prior 2 weeks.

PTSD and ASD

DAVIDSON TRAUMA SCALE (DTS)

Purpose. This measure was developed to provide a quick measure of posttraumatic stress disorder (PTSD) symptoms.

Administration. This is a self-rating scale that can be used for adults who have an 8th-grade reading level or higher. It can be used with both individuals and groups. It takes about 10 minutes to complete.

Summary. The DTS assessment is a 17-item, self-rating scale. Each item corresponds to a symptom of PTSD, and each symptom is rated in terms of frequency and severity. The DTS assessment can be used to screen clients and assess if treatment is working. The scale covers all types of trauma: accident, combat, sexual, criminal assault, natural disaster, torture, burns, loss of property, near-death experiences, and bereavement. The SPAN (Startle, Physiological Arousal, Anxiety, and Numbness) is a 4-item questionnaire based on the Davidson Trauma Scale assessment. It screens for critical indicators of PTSD and can be used for initial screening and to assess who might need further evaluation.

CLINICIAN-ADMINISTERED PTSD SCALE (CAPS)

Purpose. The CAPS is widely considered the "gold standard" in PTSD assessment.

Administration. The CAPS was designed to be administered by clinicians and clinical researchers who have a working knowledge of PTSD, but can also be administered by appropriately trained clinical assistants. It is meant to be used with adults 18 and over. The CAPS-CA is a modified version for those aged 8 to 18 years.

Summary. The CAPS consists of a 30-item structured interview that corresponds to the *DSM-IV* criteria for PTSD. The full interview takes 45 to 60 minutes to administer, but it is not necessary to administer all parts (e.g., associated symptoms). The CAPS can be used to make a current (past month) or lifetime diagnosis of PTSD or to assess symptoms over the past week. Questions also target the impact of symptoms on social and occupational functioning and changes in symptoms. A Life Events Checklist (LEC) is used to identify traumatic stressors experienced.

PTSD CHECKLIST (PCL–M AND PCL-C: MILITARY AND CIVILIAN VERSIONS)

Purpose. The PCL has a variety of purposes, including screening individuals for PTSD, diagnosing PTSD, and monitoring symptom change during and after treatment.

Administration. This self-report scale has three versions: a military version, a civilian version, and a specific-event version. They are to be used with adults.

Summary. The PCL is a 17-item self-report checklist of PTSD symptoms based closely on the *DSM-IV* criteria for this disorder. Respondents rate each item from 1 to 5 to indicate the degree to which they have been bothered by that particular symptom over the past month. This scale takes 5 to 10 minutes to complete. The PCL-M (military) asks about symptoms in response to "stressful military experiences." It is often used with active service members and veterans. The PCL-C (civilian) asks about symptoms in relation to "stressful experiences." The PCL-C is useful because it can be used with any population and can be used for multiple events. The PCL-S (specific) asks about symptoms in relation to an identified "stressful experience," thereby linking the symptoms to a specified event.

ACUTE STRESS DISORDER SCALE (ASDS)

Purpose. The ASDS is a self-report inventory created as a self-report version of the ASDI (discussed next).
Administration. This self-report is meant to be used with adults. It takes about 5 to 10 minutes to complete.
Summary. The ASDS was developed to provide a self-report measure of acute stress reactions considered to be antecedents to PTSD. The items on the scale measure symptoms of acute stress disorder (ASD) and predict posttraumatic stress disorder (PTSD).

ACUTE STRESS DISORDER INTERVIEW (ASDI)

Purpose. The ASDI is a structured interview for clinicians to diagnose ASD.
Administration. This interview is to be done by a trained individual and is to be used with adults. It can be completed in 5 to 10 minutes.
Summary. The ASDI has 19 items, based on *DSM-IV* criteria, and is administered by a trained person.

Obsessive-Compulsive Disorder

YALE-BROWN OBSESSIVE COMPULSIVE SCALE (Y-BOCS)

Purpose. This rating scale was designed to rate the type and severity of symptoms in persons with obsessive-compulsive disorder (OCD).

Administration. It is given as an interview scale and used for adults. It takes about 20 minutes to complete. There is a modified version, the CY-BOCS, for use with children.

Summary. This is a 64-item scale that combines a person's self-report with the clinical judgment of the interviewer. Additional information supplied by others (e.g., partner or parent) may be included in determining the rating. This scale is used extensively in research and clinical practice both to determine severity of OCD and to monitor improvement during treatment. It measures obsessions separately from compulsions. There are 10 items, each rated in severity. The scale includes questions about the amount of time patients spend on obsessions (or compulsions), how much impairment or distress they experience, and how much resistance and control they have over these thoughts (or compulsions).

LEYTON OBSESSIONAL INVENTORY (LOI)

Purpose. This tool was created to assess obsessional symptoms.

Administration. This inventory is self-administered and can be used for adults. The LOI-CV (child version) can be used for teenagers aged 13 to 18.

Summary. The LOI assesses obsessional symptoms and consists of 69 yes/no items that measure symptoms and traits. It cannot be used to track changes over time very easily. It tends to focus on household and other daily tasks and therefore can miss religious, sexual, or aggressive obsessions.

OBSESSIVE-COMPULSIVE INVENTORY (OCI)

Purpose. The OCI measures the frequency of a broad range of obsessions and compulsions and their associated distress.

Administration. This is a self-administered scale that can be used with adults. Children can use the modified version Child-OCI. It takes 15 minutes to complete.

Summary. The scale can aid in diagnosis and determine the severity of OCD. It consists of 42 items with ratings for frequency and associated distress over the past month. The items are comprehensive and divided into seven sub-scales: washing (8 items), checking (9 items), doubting (3 items), ordering (5 items), obsessing (8 items), hoarding (3 items), and mental neutralizing (6 items).

Panic Disorder

PANIC DISORDER SEVERITY SCALE (PDSS)

Purpose. The PDSS was developed to provide a simple way of measuring the overall severity of a *DSM-IV*-diagnosed panic disorder.

Administration. This scale is clinician-administered and is for use with adults. It takes about 5 to 10 minutes to complete.

Summary. The PDSS is a brief, clinician-administered interview. It assesses overall panic disorder severity at baseline and provides information on the severity of the different panic disorder symptoms. It is also sensitive to change over time or following treatment. It is meant for use after diagnosis and is not meant for screening or as a diagnostic instrument. It consists of 7 items, each rated on a 5-point scale. The items include an assessment of any impairment in work or social functioning.

PANIC AND AGORAPHOBIA SCALE

Purpose. This measure was designed to assess the severity of panic disorder, with or without agoraphobia. It was also developed for monitoring the effectiveness of drug treatment and psychological therapy.

Administration. There are both self-rated and clinician-administered versions that can be used with those age 15 and older. It takes about 5 to 10 minutes to complete.

Summary. The scale contains 13 items to which responses are made on a 5-point scale. Severity is computed by adding the item scores. The total score indicates overall severity. In addition to the total score, there are scores for five item clusters like panic attacks, anxiety in anticipation of an event, avoidance, disability, and worries about health.

Generalized Anxiety Disorder

HAMILTON ANXIETY SCALE (HAM-A)

Purpose. This scale was developed to assess the severity of general symptoms of anxiety.

Administration. This scale is meant to be clinician-administered and can be used with adults, adolescents, and children. It takes about 10 to 15 minutes to complete.

Summary. The HAM-A was one of the first rating scales developed to measure the severity of anxiety symptoms, and it is still widely used. The scale consists of 14 items, each defined by a series of symptoms, and measures both psychological distress and physical complaints related to anxiety.

BECK ANXIETY INVENTORY (BAI)

Purpose. The BAI was developed to measure the severity of symptoms of anxiety.

Administration. This scale can be self-administered or administered verbally by a trained administrator for people ages 17 through 80. It takes about 5 to 10 minutes to complete.

Summary. The BAI is a 21-item scale that measures the severity of anxiety. It consists of descriptive statements about the symptoms of anxiety, which are rated on a 4-point severity scale. It was specifically designed to measure anxiety symptoms that have less overlap with symptoms of depression.

ZUNG RATING SCALE FOR ANXIETY

Purpose. This scale was developed as a measure of anxiety in general populations.

Administration. This is a self-report measure used with adults. It takes about 5 to 10 minutes to complete.

Summary. The Zung Rating Scale for Anxiety has a total of 20 questions, consisting of 5 positively worded items and 15 negatively worded items. Patients report on the frequency of symptoms over the previous week, from none of the time to most of the time. This tool has been used extensively as a screen for anxiety, and it is often used to measure the response to treatment.

GENERALIZED ANXIETY DISORDER-7 (GAD-7)

Purpose. This tool was developed as a screen to detect generalized anxiety disorder.

Administration. There are both self-report and clinician-administered versions, for use with adults. It takes about 5 minutes to complete.

Summary. This is a 7-item measure based on the generalized anxiety disorder symptoms of the *DSM-IV*. Each item is also rated for severity. This scale measures symptoms over the prior 2 weeks. There is also a 2-item screen (GAD-2).

Eating Disorders

EATING DISORDER EXAMINATION (EDE AND EDE-CH)

Purpose. The EDE is generally considered the "gold standard" of eating disorder assessment.

Administration. This is a clinician-administered scale, though a self-report version (EDE-Q) also exists. It is to be used with those 14 and older, with a modified version (EDE-CH) for children under 14.

Summary. The EDE consists of 62 items and takes 45 to 75 minutes to complete. The EDE-Q has 36 items and takes 15 minutes to complete. Both are rated on a 7-point scale. There are four sub-scales (restraint, eating concern, shape concern, and weight concern) and an overall score. The questions concern the frequency by which a person engages in behaviors indicative of an eating disorder over the prior 28 days.

EATING DISORDER DIAGNOSTIC SCALE (EDDS)

Purpose. The EDDS was developed for the purpose of diagnosing anorexia nervosa, bulimia nervosa, and binge eating disorder.

Administration. It is a self-report scale that can be used with adults and adolescents. It takes about 10 minutes to complete.

Summary. The EDDS consists of 22 items that assess *DSM-IV* symptoms across 3-month and 6-month periods. This scale also can be used to detect the effects of an eating disorder prevention program and response to such a program.

EATING DISORDER INVENTORY (EDI AND EDI-C)

Purpose. The EDI was developed to assess symptoms, patient subgroups, and to measure response to treatment in people suffering from eating disorders.

Administration. This is a self-report scale that can be used for persons ages 13 to 53. The EDI-C can be used with children. It can be completed in 20 minutes.

Summary. The EDI consists of 91 items organized into 12 primary scales that provide scores in 6 areas: eating disorder, ineffectiveness, interpersonal problems, affective problems, overcontrol, and general psychological maladjustment.

THE BULIMIA TEST-REVISED (BULIT-R)

Purpose. This scale was developed to screen and identify individuals who may meet criteria for bulimia in both clinical and non-clinical settings.

Administration. This is a self-report scale that can be used for persons 16 years and older. The scale can be completed in 10 minutes.

Summary. The BULIT-R consists of 36 multiple-choice items that measure symptoms related to bulimia. Some of these questions also measure weight-control efforts a person uses. Although developed for females, it has been shown to be useful in males as well.

EATING ATTITUDES TEST (EAT)

Purpose. The EAT is a widely used standardized measure of symptoms and concerns characteristic of eating disorders.

Administration. This is a self-report measure that can be used in a wide variety of settings, with adolescents and adults. It takes about 5 minutes.

Summary. The EAT was developed to examine sociocultural factors in the development and maintenance of eating disorders. It is ideally suited for school settings, athletic programs, fitness centers, infertility clinics, pediatric practices, general medical practice settings, and outpatient psychiatric departments. It consists of 26 questions that assess for symptoms of eating disorders, all rated for severity. This is not a tool to assess for binge eating disorder.

Personality Disorders

ZANARINI RATING SCALE FOR BORDERLINE PERSONALITY DISORDER (ZAN-BPD)

Purpose. This scale was developed to assess the severity of *DSM-IV*-based borderline personality disorder symptoms.
Administration. The ZAN-BPD is clinician-administered and meant to be used with adults.
Summary. This measures severity of symptoms over 9 areas and also measures meaningful changes over time. Symptoms over the prior week are assessed. It was created by Dr. Mary Zanarini (at McLean Hospital), a leader in research on borderline personality disorder.

MCLEAN SCREENING INSTRUMENT FOR BORDERLINE PERSONALITY DISORDER (MSI-BPD)

Purpose. This scale was created for screening in groups of people to detect borderline personality disorder.
Administration. This is a self-report screen to be used with adults and takes about 5 minutes.
Summary. The MSI-BPD consists of 10 yes/no items. It is used in a population of people who have not yet been diagnosed with borderline personality disorder but who are seeking help with mood and personality issues. It shows a very good ability to correctly identify those who have the disorder. A positive screen warrants a further evaluation.

STANDARDIZED ASSESSMENT OF PERSONALITY – ABBREVIATED SCALE (SAPAS)

Purpose. This is a general screen for personality disorders.
Administration. The SAPAS is a brief clinician interview scale to be used with adults and takes about 2 minutes.
Summary. The SAPAS is an abbreviated version of the longer SAP (standardized assessment of personality). It consists of 8 items and can be used as a tool to open up communication about personality traits. Questions include ability to make and keep relationships, trust, anger, perfectionism, and dependency on others.

IOWA PERSONALITY DISORDER SCREEN (IPDS)

Purpose. This scale was created to screen for personality disorders.
Administration. This is a clinician-administered scale to be used with an adult population and takes about 5 minutes to complete.
Summary. This screen consists of 11 items that measure *DSM-IV* criteria for personality disorders, using the most common criteria for different personality disorders. Questions include excessive shifts in mood, need to be the center of attention, social anxiety, unstable self-image, and difficulty with empathy or others' needs.

Psychotic Disorders

BRIEF PSYCHIATRIC RATING SCALE (BPRS)

Purpose. The BPRS was developed to provide a brief method of assessing patient symptoms and changes in symptoms.
Administration. This scale is completed by a clinician interview and is to be used with adults. It takes 10 to 40 minutes to complete.
Summary. The BPRS consists of 18 to 24 questions on depression, anxiety, hallucination, and behavior. Ratings for several items are based on observation; the remaining items are assessed by interview. In the past this tool was used as the standard for response to treatment, but most clinicians now use the PANSS.

POSITIVE AND NEGATIVE SYMPTOM SCALE (PANSS)

Purpose. The PANSS was developed to measure the symptoms of schizophrenia and response to treatment. It has scales for positive and negative symptoms as well as the more general symptoms of the illness.
Administration. This is a clinician interview scale used with adults. It takes 35 to 45 minutes to complete.
Summary. The PANSS measures symptoms over the last week and incorporates information from clinicians and family members. It consists of 30 items on a 7-point scale from absent to extreme. There are different sections for positive symptoms, negative symptoms, and general symptoms. Scores on the different sub-scales help to determine which symptoms are most prominent and thus aid with treatment decisions.

THE PSYCHOTIC SYMPTOM RATING SCALES (PSYRATS)

Purpose. This tool was developed in recognition of the complexity of hallucinations and delusions, and to provide a more detailed and accurate measure of them.
Administration. This scale is done by clinician interview and is used with adults. It takes 20 to 30 minutes to complete.
Summary. The PSYRATS consists of two sets of scales, one for hallucinations (11 items) and one for delusions (6 items). It also measures severity (on a 5-point scale) for both hallucinations and delusions. This scale can be used to track changes in symptoms over time. It also addresses the intensity of distress or suffering and degree of conviction of the delusion or hallucination.

ABNORMAL INVOLUNTARY MOVEMENT SCALE (AIMS)

Purpose. The AIMS measures abnormal movements resulting from medication treatment.
Administration. This is a clinician-rated scale and is used with patients on antipsychotic medications. It takes about 10 minutes to complete.
Summary. The AIMS has 12 items that assess the presence and severity of abnormal movements of the face, torso, and limbs in patients on antipsychotic medication treatment. It can also assess a patient's awareness

of these movements, and whether these movements cause distress or interfere with the ability to function normally. The scale is based on clinician questions, observations, and examination.

EXTRAPYRAMIDAL SYMPTOM RATING SCALE (ESRS)

Purpose. This scale rates the presence of Parkinson-like symptoms and other abnormal movements.

Administration. This scale is clinician-administered and is used with patients on antipsychotic medications or with brain disease. It takes 15 to 20 minutes to complete. A briefer scale, the ESRS-A, takes a little less time.

Summary. The ESRS consists of a questionnaire on Parkinson-like symptoms followed by a doctor's examination for different types of abnormal movements. It can be used to assess whether antipsychotic medications are causing side effects, but is also used to assess the treatment response in Parkinson's disease.

Bipolar Disorder (Mania)

YOUNG MANIA RATING SCALE (YMRS)

Purpose. The YMRS assesses manic symptoms.

Administration. This is a clinician-rated scale that can be used in an adult population. The clinician asks questions and also makes clinical observations. It takes about 15 to 30 minutes to complete.

Summary. The YMRS has 11 items and is based on the patient's experience over the previous 48 hours. The items in the scale represent the core symptoms of mania. Each item is also given a severity rating. The YMRS can be used to evaluate manic symptoms at baseline and over time.

MOOD DISORDERS QUESTIONNAIRE

Purpose. This questionnaire was designed as a screening tool for bipolar disorder.

Administration. It is a self-report screen to be used in general populations. It takes 5 minutes to complete.

Summary. The Mood Disorders Questionnaire was developed by psychiatrists, researchers, and consumer advocates working together. It is not used to make a diagnosis but rather as a screen that may signal the need for further evaluation. It is considered best at screening for bipolar I (depression and mania) but less precise at screening for bipolar II or bipolar not otherwise specified. It consists of a series of 13 yes/no questions that screen for the symptoms of mania, with 2 questions that address the severity of these symptoms and the time frame. A positive test is a reason to have a more comprehensive evaluation.

MAS (BECH-RAFAELSEN) MANIA SCALE

Purpose. This scale was created to assess the severity of mania symptoms in a person who already has a diagnosis of bipolar disorder.

Administration. This is a clinician-rated scale that can be used with adults and adolescents. It takes about 15 to 30 minutes to complete.

Summary. The MAS Mania Scale has 11 items rated on a 5-point severity scale. This measure can determine changes in patients who are being treated with medication. It is also commonly used in research studies looking at the outcome of medication treatment.

General Services and Outcome Scale

THE MENTAL HEALTH STATISTICS IMPROVEMENT PROGRAM (MHSIP)

Purpose. This scale was originally developed by a task force of consumers, family members, researchers, and government and agency representatives to survey consumer perspectives on and outcomes from mental health services.

Administration. This is a self-report for adults; there is a youth version as well to be completed by family. The adult version takes 7 to 15 minutes to complete.

Summary. The MHSIP is a 28-item survey designed to report on consumer (patient) experiences in several areas of mental health care. There are questions on access to care; the quality and appropriateness of care that was provided; and whether the services were beneficial. There are also questions on participation in treatment planning, general satisfaction, social connectedness, and functioning. This scale is not typically used to show changes in an individual consumer/patient. Rather, it is generally used to learn what works for whom and to use this information to improve services.

I am thankful to Marisa Derman, MD, MSc, for assembling this appendix, for which I take full responsibility.

Index

Betty Ford Center, 206
binge eating
 in bulimia nervosa, 138–39
 defined, 138
biological treatments, 91
 for acute psychotic disorder, 155–56
 for anorexia nervosa, 151–52
 for schizophrenia, 147–48
bipolar disorder, 156–62
 acute treatment for, 159–60
 case example, xiii–xiv, 10–11
 causes of, 158
 defined, 156
 depression in, 160
 described, 156–57
 diagnosis of, 157–58
 maintenance treatment for, 160–62
 mental health measurement scales
  for, 288–89
 onset of, 158
 prevalence of, 156
 rapid cycling, 160
 symptoms of, 157–58
 treatment of, 31, 158–62
blood
 medication detection in, 187
borderline personality disorder (BPD),
  121–26
 case example, 121
 causes of, 123–24
 co-occurring conditions, 123
 described, 120–22
 diagnosis of, 122–23
 suicidal thinking with, 123
 treatment of, 124–26
BPD. see borderline personality
  disorder (BPD)
brain
 in mentally ill persons, 5
 psychotic symptoms effects on, 10–11
 therapy effects on, 190
brain scans
 in mental illness diagnosis, 32
Brief Psychiatric Rating Scale (BPRS), 286
British Medical Journal, 42
bulimia nervosa, 120, 137–42
 case example, 137
 CBT for, 140

described, 138
diagnosis of, 138–39
family therapy for, 141
goals of, 139–40
group therapy for, 140–41
individual therapy for, 140
medications for, 141
non-purging type, 138
nutritional rehabilitation for, 140
psychodynamic therapy for, 140
purging type, 138
relapse prevention, 140
support groups for, 141–42
treatment of, 139–42
types of, 138
Bulimia Test-Revised (BULIT-R), 284
bupropion
 for depression, 100
Bush, G. W., Pres., 52, 89, 211, 214, 241

caregiver(s)
 hope of, 35
Carter administration, 52
Carter, R., 52
case management
 for bipolar disorder, 161
case managers
 in schizophrenia management, 148
catastrophizing, 199
CBT. see cognitive-behavioral therapy
  (CBT)
Center for Urban Community Services
  (CUCS), 267
Centers of Excellence, 214
central nervous system (CNS)
  depressants
 indications for, 170
chronic conditions
 acute conditions vs., 50–51
clergy
 for mental illness–related guidance, 13
Cleveland Clinic, 214
clinic(s)
 in finding mental health professionals,
  59
 outpatient, 72–77. see also outpatient
  clinics
clinical confidence, 41

stress
  in mental illness, 5
stress reaction
  severe, 156
stressor(s)
  schizophrenia related to, 146–47
substance abuse
  BPD and, 123
  functioning, mood, or thinking
    effects of, 31
Substance Abuse and Mental Health
    Services Administration
    (SAMHSA), 241–43
suicidal thinking
  acute psychotic disorder and, 154
  BPD and, 123
suicidality
  BPD and, 123
  depression and, 93, 96
support groups
  for anorexia nervosa, 136
  for bulimia nervosa, 141–42
  for mentally ill persons, xx–xxi
supportive housing, 209–10
  "walk-throughs" at, 265–68
Supportive Housing Network of New
    York, 265–68
symptom(s)
  of anxiety, 249
  of depression, 249
  feelings and mood effects of, 248–49
  lack of improvement of, 34
  of mania, 248
  in mental illness diagnosis, 29
  recognizing, 248
  recording, 250
  of schizophrenia, 144–45
  thinking effects of, 249
  treatment for, 33
symptom-based improvements, 43
"symptoms of mental illness," 248–50
take care of what needs to be done, now,
    35–36
"talking cure," 195–98
talking with families
  in mental illness diagnosis, 29, 31

"Tarasoff decision," 227
TARP. see Troubled Asset Relief
    Program (TARP)
teenager(s)
  anorexia nervosa among, 128–37.
  see also anorexia nervosa
tertiary prevention, 55–56
The British Journal of Psychiatry, 164
The Center Cannot Hold: My Journey
    Through Madness, 22
The Nathan Kline Institute for
    Psychiatric Research, 315
The Noonday Demon, 22
TheAtlantic.com, 28n
therapeutic alliance, 103, 193
therapist(s)
  as mental health professionals, 60
therapy. see also specific types
  building blocks associated with, 192–93
  CBT, 198–200
  DBT, 200
  DDP, 200–1
  family psychoeducation/support,
    204–5
  family therapy, 205–6
  FFEPs, 204–5
  group therapy, 203–4
  IPT, 201–2
  patient's responsibility in, 194
  PST, 202–3
  as team sport, 193–94
  therapeutic nature of, 192–93
  therapist's responsibility in, 194
  types of, 194–206
thinking
  changes in, 27–28
  delusional, 10
  disordered, 10–11
  psychotic, 123
  suicidal, 123, 154
  symptoms affecting, 249
thought(s)
  negative, 247
  positive, 247
  poverty of, 144
Times Square Hotel, 265–68

About the Author

Lloyd I. Sederer, MD, is medical director of the New York State Office of Mental Health, the nation's largest state mental health system. As New York's "chief psychiatrist," he provides medical leadership for a $3.6 billion-per-year mental health system serving more than 700,000 people annually and including 23 hospitals, two research institutes (Psychiatric Institute and Nathan Kline Institute), and community mental health services throughout New York State. Sederer is an adjunct professor at the Columbia/Mailman School of Public Health and has served as acting director of The Nathan Kline Institute for Psychiatric Research in Rockland County, New York.

Dr. Sederer is also the first medical editor for mental health for the *Huffington Post*, where his articles appear regularly. He has served in this role for over 2 years. Together with AOL, which recently purchased the *Huffington Post*, this media outlet has supplanted the *New York Times* as the most widely read online news journal in the English language. In this role, Sederer is the voice of mental health care.

From 2002 to 2007, Dr. Sederer served as mental health commissioner for New York City. In this capacity he was responsible for overseeing all public mental health services, as well as addiction and developmental disability programs.

Dr. Sederer is a former medical director and executive vice president of McLean Hospital in Belmont, Massachusetts, one of the world's foremost psychiatric hospitals and a teaching hospital of Harvard Medical School, where he also served on the faculty.

In 2000, Dr. Sederer was named Director, Division of Clinical Services, for the American Psychiatric Association, where he focused on mental health economics and oversaw the publication of the American Psychiatric Association's professional treatment guidelines and quality measures—now in standard use throughout the world.

Through his writings and leadership of hospitals and public mental health systems, Dr. Sederer has become one of the nation's leading voices on quality of care in mental health, and he has played a singular role in advancing care for people with mental illnesses and their families. In 2009, he was recognized as Psychiatric Administrator of the Year by the American Psychiatric Association and was awarded a Rockefeller Foundation Scholar-in-Residence grant. He has also received an Exemplary Psychiatrist award from the National Alliance on Mental Illness, the largest family mental health advocacy group in the country.

Dr. Sederer lectures both nationally and internationally to families of people with mental illness, as well as to mental health policymakers, government officials, and other professionals. He has published seven textbooks and more than 350 professional articles and reports.

His website, www.askdrlloyd.com, is dedicated to helping people, and their families, get the care they need to recover from mental illness and addictions.

31901051956193